Table of Contents

Author's Sources	III
Author's Introduction	VIII
My Beginnings	X

Chapter 1
The First Twelve Years in Rome — 1
- San Pietro in Vaticano — 2
- The Fontana degli Api in the Vatican Gardens — 11
- San Giovanni Battista dei Fiorentini — 12
- Sant'Andrea della Valle — 12
- The Palazzo Barberini — 14

Chapter 2
My Philosophy of Architecture — 23

Chapter 3
San Carlo alle Quattro Fontane (San Carlino) — 31
- The Chronology — 35
- The Dormitory, Refectory, Cloister — 36
- The Plan for the Main Body of the Church — 39
- The Ovals of the Dome and Lantern — 44
- The Coffering of the Dome — 52
- The Lantern — 53
- The Columns — 54
- The Balance of the Articulation — 60
- The Two Side Chapels — 63
- The Coffering and Gables of the Chapels — 64
- The Lateral Chapels — 65
- The Exterior of the Dome and Lantern — 65
- The Lower Church — 66
- The Cappelletta — 66
- The Façade — 70

Chapter 4
Santa Lucia in Selci — 79

Chapter 5
The Oratory and Monastery / Casa of San Filippo Neri — 85
- The Oratory — 90
- The Façade — 96
- The Refectory — 105
- The Lavamani — 107
- The Privies — 108
- The Staircases — 109
- The Chapels — 111
- The Sala di Recreazione — 113
- The Garden Courtyard — 115
- The Finishing Pieces — 115
- The Library — 117
- The First Courtyard — 119
- The Orologio — 120
- My Departure — 123

Chapter 6
Santa Maria dei Sette Dolori — 127

Chapter 7
Sant'Ivo alla Sapienza — 135
- The Chronology — 138
- A Personal Interlude — 140
- The Genesis and Drawing of the Ground Plan — 141
- The Interior Vault – the Main Body of the Church — 148
- The Plan for the Drum / Its Execution — 153
- The Genesis and the Making of the Lantern and Spire — 159
- The Ascent Through the Spiral — 162
- The Additions to the Drum Made Under Innocent X — 163
- The Additions to the Drum Made Under Alexander VII — 163
- The Cracks Occasioned by the Addition of the Spire — 163
- The Fraud of My Later Drawings — 165
- The Chigi Changes — 166
- Other Sides of Sant'Ivo — 167
- The Floor — 168
- The Alessandrina Library — 168

Chapter 8
San Giovanni in Laterano — 171
The Nave — 174
The Side Aisles — 181
The Door to the Lateran Palace — 184
The Overall Decoration — 185
Another Personal Digression — 189
The Tombs — 191

Chapter 9
The Piazza Navona and Palazzo Pamphilj — 203

Chapter 10
Sant'Agnese in Agone — 207
The Nave — 208
The Façade and Dome — 209

Chapter 11
Palazzo Carpegna — 213

Chapter 12
Tombs — 217
Clemente Merlini — 218
Franceso Adriano Ceva — 219

Chapter 13
The Palazzo Spagna, The Palazzo dello Spirito Santo — 221

Chapter 14
The Palazzo Spada — 225

Chapter 15
Other Places of Note — 229
The Palazzo Giustiniani — 230
The Villa Giustiniani — 230
The Casino of the Palazzo del Bufalo — 230
The Plan for the Villa Pamphilj at San Pancrazio — 231

Chapter 16
The Palazzo Falconieri — 233

Chapter 17
Sant'Andrea delle Fratte — 241

Chapter 18
The Falconieri Chapel in the Choir of San Giovanni dei Fiorentini and the Crypt — 249

Chapter 19
The Spada Chapel in San Girolamo della Carita — 255

Chapter 20
San Giovanni in Fonte; San Giovanni in Oleo — 259

Chapter 21
The Collegio Propaganda di Fide and the Chapel of Re Magi — 263
The Seminary Rooms — 265
The Façade — 267
The Chapel of Re Magi — 272

Conclusion — 276

The Events Leading Up to My Death — 280

Colophon

Gregory Pulles is a retired attorney with a love of Italian Art and Architecture, especially as found in the churches of Italy. He has written and photographed Sacred Places, Rediscovering the Churches of Rome, 1000 pages about his sixty favorite churches in Rome, fully illustrated; Sacred Places Italy, a condensed guidebook about those same churches, Due Cento Luoghi- a pocketguide to the 220 must see sites in Rome, and The Holy Pulpits of Tuscany- the beginning of the Renaissance- the sculpture of Nicola and Giovanni Pisani. In this book he covers in word and photography all the architecture in Rome of Francesco Borromini, whom he regards as the most creative architect in history.

Recognition

Graphic Design by Katie Williams of Nicollet, Minnesota

© Copyright Gregory J Pulles 2020
(no claim for public domain documents)

Authors Sources

The sources for my work are listed in full below.

My favorite of these is Paolo Portoghesi's book, a very large one. I like it the best because of the photographs. Although they are black and white, they are numerous and comprehensive. I especially like the catalog at the end where he groups his photographs by type. For example, there is a series where he captures all of Borromini's works that use "ears". The Professor's description of Borromini's works are sometimes difficult but reflect unparelled understanding of Borromini.

Next is Professor Joseph Connor's work on the Oratory, because it is so thoroughly thorough and authoritative. Unfortunately, so far as I am able to determine, the Professor's complete work on Borromini's buildings was never published.

Next is Professor Kerry Downes' English translation of Borromini's Book, The Full Relation of the Building of the Roman Oratory. It has splendid, thorough, painstaking footnote elucidation, and the Professor's own voluminous commentary. His research is extensive, his insight very deep, mostly about the Oratory but also of Borromini's work in general. My chapter on the Casa has extensive material directly from Borromini, Professor Downes' book.

Next is Anthony Blunt's work on Borromini. Professor Blunt is very authoritative and penetrating and convincing. The Professor's descriptions are the easiest to follow, the most persuasive, and they reflect his long life in the world of architecture. Blunt also produced The Baroque Guide to Rome, an unbelievably thorough work, which also has excellent insights about Borromini's works, and which I used considerably for the captions for my photos.

Jack Morrissey's work describing the competition between Borromini and Bernini was the most entertaining. I was never able to verify the attribution of the lantern at San Giovanni dei Fiorentini to Borromini, but I have credited it to him (wrongly I now believe based upon all that I have read) based on Mr. Morrissey.

Rudolf Wittkower's two works that I cite reflect his great knowledge of Borromini and his unique contribution, though they are just chapters in Professor's two tomes on the Baroque.

Professor Hibbard's small section in his book on Carlo Maderno, Borromini's "uncle," is superlative, and the best summation of the greatness of Borromini's work.

Leo Steinberg's PhD dissertation, later made into a book, on San Carlino, is a masterpiece that I used as my primary source for San Carlino. His detail is fabulous. Michael Hill's article about the geometry at Carlino is fascinating, arguing that Borromini used the biangolo (mandorla) for his plan. Professor Connor's article about the copy of Carlino in Gubbio has important information about Carlino. Angelo Mazzotti's recent book about how Borromini used the geometry of the oval at Carlino was an excellent and authoritative explanation.

For Sant'Ivo several articles were extremely informative. Julia M. Smyth-Pinney's study of Borromini's plan for Sant'Ivo is, for me, the final word on the controversy over Borromini's geometry and his use of the hexagon versus the triangle. Her article is a masterful exposition of how Borromini drew the ground plan around a hexagon with attached lobes and triangles. Professor Connor's "The First Three Minutes" is also a masterpiece. For Borromini's most original spiral at Ivo, Professor Connor's "The Spiral" is not only the definitive treatment, it is a delightful guide through every aspect. Professor Scott's article about Sant'Ivo was also a primary source for me.

At Giovanni in Laterano, Robert Ehol's article about the barrel vault Borromini wanted for the ceiling was helpful.

The Opus Architectonicum of Virgilo Spada and Borromini with the forward by Professor Connor is a must. Kerry Downes has created an English translation which I referred to above. Virgilio Spada's un dialogo del P. Virgilio Spada, in the Archivio della Societa Romana di Storia Patria, XC, 1967, 165ff should be read too, for the Casa. I have only been able to read excerpts.

Fra Juan de San Bonaventura's Relatione should be read for San Carlino.

If you are in for more depth, the treatises by O. Pollak (Diekunsttatigkeit unter Urban VIII, Vienna, 1928, 1931) Eberhard Hempel (Francesco Borromini, Vienna, 1924) and Heinrich Thelen (Francesco Borromini, Graz 1967) are essential, but the German and Italian proved too much for me.

The Albertina in Vienna, of course, if you can gain access, has the "Albertina" drawings, the collection of Borromini originals that he did not destroy shortly before his suicide. I refer to these by number at various points in the text and footnotes. My son visited there in 2018 and was able to see many of these "for me".

For the end of the story and Borromini's end, I used Martin Raspe's article about Borromini's failed publication project and his suicide.

Accademia Nazionale di San Luca (multiple authors), Studi sul Borromini, Rome 1967

Blunt, Anthony, Borromini, The Beltenap Press of Harvard University Press, Cambridge, Massachusetts and London, England, 1979 ["Blunt"]

Blunt, Anthony, The Literature of Art, Roman Baroque Architecture (A review of Professor Portoghesi's Book), 670-674 Burlington Magazine 1967

Blunt, Anthony, Guide to Baroque Rome, Harper & Row, Cambridge 1982 ["Blunt, Baroque Guide"]

Bonaventura, Fra Juan de San, Relatione del Convento di San Carlo alle Quattro Fontane (ca. 1650) ed. J.M.M. Garcia, Polifilo, Rome 1999

Connors, Joseph, Borromini and the Roman Oratory, Style and Society, the MIT Press, Cambridge, Massachusetts and London, England, 1980 ["Connors, Oratory"]

Connors, Joseph, Macmillan Encyclopedia of Architects, Borromini, Francesco, The Free Press, New York, 1982, 248-260 ["Connors, Borromini"]

Connors, Joseph, A Copy of Borromini's S. Carlo alle Quattro Fontane in Gubbio, 137 Burlington Magazine 590, 1995 ["Connors, Gubbio"]

Connors, Joseph, Review of Leo Steinberg's Borromini's San Carlo alle Quattro Fontane, a Study in Multiple Form and Architectural Symbolism, 38 Journal of the Society of Architectural Historians, No. 3, October 1979, 283-285 ["Connors, Steinberg"]

Connors, Joseph, Virgilio Spada's Defence of Borromini, 131 Burlington Magazine, 1989, 76-90 ["Connors, Defence"]

Connors, Joseph, Borromini's S. Ivo alla Sapienza: The Spiral, 138 Burlington Magazine, October 1996, 668-682 ["Connors, The Spiral"]

Connors, Joseph, S. Ivo alla Sapienza : The First Three Minutes; 55 Journal of the Society of Architectural Historians, No. 1, March 1996, 38-57 ["Connors, The First Three Minutes"]

Connors, Joseph, Borromini l' universe barocco, ed R. Bosel and C Frommel, Electa, Milan, 2000 ["Connors, Barocco"]

Connors, Joseph, Un teorama sacro. San Carlo alle Quattro Fontane 1-19, in Il giovane Borromini, Dagli esordi a San Carlo alle Quattro Fontane, ed. Kahn-Rossi, Franciolli, Skira, Milan 1999, 459-474. ["Connors, San Carlo"]

Downes, Kerry, Borromini's Book, The Full Relation of the Building of the Oratory, by Francesco Borromini and Virgilio Spada, Translated with a Commentary, Oblong Creative Ltd. Westherby, England, 2009 ["Downes, Opus"]

Echols, Robert, A Classical Barrel Vault for San Giovanni in Laterano in a Borromini Drawing, 51 Journal of the Society of Architectural Historians, No. 2, 1992, 146-160

Faglio, Maurizio, 'L'Attivita di Borromini da Paolo V a Urbano VIII, part of Studi sul Borromini, III, Rome 1967

Hauptman, William, "Luceat Lux Vestra Coram Homnibus": A New Source for the Spire of Borromini's S. Ivo; 33 Journal of the Society of Architectural Historians, No. 1, March 1974, 73-79

Hempel, Eberhard, Francesco Borromini, Anton Schroll & Co., Vienna, 1924

Hibbard, Howard, Carlo Maderno and Roman Architecture, 1580-1630, Maderno and Borromini 88-92, A. Zwemmer Ltd. 1971

Hill, Michael, Practical and Symbolic Geometry in Borromini's San Carlo alle Quattro Fontane, 4 Journal of the Society of Architectural Historians, No. 4, December 2013, 72

Huerta, Santiago, Oval Domes: History, Geometry and Mechanics, Nexus Network Journal 9, 2007, 211-248

Martinelli, Fioravante, Roma Ornata dall' Architettura, Pittura e Scultura, Biblioteca Casanatense, Rome, 1655, published in Cesare D. Onofrio, Roma nel seicento, Florence, 1969

Mazzotti, Angelo Alessandro, All Sides to an Oval; Properties, Parameters, and Borromini's Mysterious Construction, Springer, Rome, Italy, 2017

Ministero Dell Interno Ragguagli Borrominiani, Rome, 1968

Morrissey, Jake, The Genius in the Design, Bernini, Borromini, and The Rivalry That Transformed Rome, Harper Perennial, New York, London, Toronto, Sydney, 2005

Pascoli, L., Vite de' Pittori, Scultori ed Architetti Moderni, 2 vols, Roma 1730-1736, I, 303

Portoghesi, Paolo, The Rome of Borromini, Architecture as Language, Translated by Barbara Luigia La Penta; George Braziller, Inc. New York, 1968 ["Portoghesi"]

Portoghesi, Paolo, Borromini nella cultura Europea, Rome, 1964

Portoghesi, Paolo, Storia di San Carlino alle Quattro Fontane, Newton & Comptom editori, Rome, 2001

Raspe, Martin, The Final Problem. Borromini's Failed Publication Project and His Suicide, 13 Annali di Architettura, 121-136, 2001, ["Raspe, Suicide"]

Scott, John Beldon, S. Ivo alla Sapienza and Borromini's Symbolic Language; 41 Journal of the Society of Architectural Historians, No. 4, December 1982, 294-317

Smyth-Pinney, Julia M.: Borromini's Plans for Sant'Ivo alla Sapienza; 59 Journal of the Society of Architectural Historians, No. 3, September 2000, 312-337

Soprintendenza per: beni artistici e storici, Roma Sacra, Itineraries 21-22, Rome, 2001 ["Roma Sacra"]

Spada, Virgilio, Francesco Borromini, Opus Architectonicum, Joseph Connors, Polifio, Milan, 1998

Steinberg, Leo, Borromini's San Carlo alle Quattro Fontane: A Study in Multiple Form and Architectural Symbolism, New York, Garland, 1977

Thelen, Heinrich, Francesco Borromini, Graz, 1967

Wittkower, Rudolf, Art and Architecture in Italy, 1600-1750. The Pelican History of Art, the Penguin Books, 1958, First Integrated Edition, Based on the Third Revised Edition 1973, Chapter 9, Francesco Borromini 1599-1667, 197-229 ["Wittkower, Art and Architecture"]

Wittkower, Rudolf, Studies in the Italian Baroque, Thames and Hudson, London, 1975, Chapter Eight, Francesco Borromini, His Character and Life, 153-176 ["Wittkower, Studies"]

Wittkower, Rudolf, Gothic vs. Classic: Architectural Projects in Seventeenth Century Italy, New York, 1974

Diagrams/Drawings

Taylor Hemmesch, an architecture student at the University of North Dakota, did the drawings for San Carlino and Sant'Ivo. For the former, she used the explanation of Borromini's drawing of the ground plan from Professor Steinberg (86 et seq), who firmly believes Albertina 173 is the definitive drawing. For the oval, she used Geogebra, and used Sebastiano Serlio's explanation for his fourth construction in the Robert Peake 1611 edition of Serlio's Fifth Booke, and Professor Mazzotti's explanation of how Borromini modified it.

For Sant'Ivo, she used the explanation of Borromini's construction of his hexagon, and the lobes and triangles appended to it, from Professor Smyth-Pinney, and her analysis of Borromini's earliest drawings, including Albertina 501.

Author's Introduction

Francesco Borromini is, for me, the most creative architect that ever lived. He lived at the same time as Gian Lorenzo Bernini, who many would say is the most talented sculptor that ever lived, certainly the most prolific. Together with a third contemporary, Pietro da Cortona, they were the three genii of the Roman High Baroque.

Borromini was overshadowed by Bernini, whose unsurpassed ability to sculpt the human form was prized by the Popes. Coupled with his gregarious nature, Bernini easily obtained papal patronage, while Borromini's superior skill and imagination in architecture was relegated to a distant third or lower place. Borromini was as reclusive as Bernini was effusive.

Ultimately, Borromini's sense of failure was to claim his life, at his own hand. His sense of failure was not deserved by the reality of the genius in his works, which are unparalleled. Perhaps Professor Howard Hibbard in his work on Borromini's uncle Carlo Moderno, has said it the best:

> "[He] was born to the profession, trained in its meanest detail, familiar with all the problems of building, acquainted with the methods and the men of the world of construction. Borromini created an artistic masterpiece (referring to San Carlino) that remains uniquely functional and beautiful: symbolic, complex, ingenious, thoughtfully designed in every detail, overwhelming in its monumental smallness. These qualities [raise his work] out of the level of good or interesting architecture to something like the highest level of genius – typical of Borromini alone…he took each site and space as a unique challenge, for which he found more often than not, novel and happy solutions. (see Hibbard 91-92 for more glowing language about Borromini.)

All should share in the beauty and genius that Borromini gave us. I have photographed his work, and desiring that he receive his full due, I decided to write a simulated autobiography. It is meagre and even pedestrian, but I hope that by presenting Borromini's works in the first person, I can best express all that was good about him and his work.

At the beginning, I provide you a description of my sources. These are important, as none of my writing represents original research (although I have visited almost all his works, most multiple times, and tried to study them at length) – I have taken everything from those who have studied this master at so much a greater depth and with so much greater skill and knowledge and understanding than I ever could. I have provided extensive footnotes throughout that indicate the source. I have taken material and tried to put it into Borromini's words. I have taken liberty in paraphrasing/quoting by choosing words (especially verbs and adjectives) that are for me "easier" (as in Borromini's words in his Opus as translated by Professor Kerry Downes) and simpler (Professor Paolo

Portoghesi). I have noted these quotes in the footnotes but, regardless of quotation marks, all the material comes from the sources indicated and none of it represents my own work. All interpretive errors are my own.

At times, I have Borromini talk to the present, as where he criticizes "improvements and alterations." I have made decisions for Borromini where the Professors are unsure or contrarian about a point, such as the classical inspiration for a particular church or device.

My Beginnings

I was born September 25, 1599 in the Village of Bissone, in Lombardy, on Lago Lugano, in Ticino, the southernmost and entirely Italian speaking Canton of Switzerland, son of Giovanni Domenico Castelli Brumino, an architect and a master stonemason in the employ of the Visconti of Milan, and Anastasia Garovo, from the family of the architects Domenico Fontana (my cousin) and Carlo Maderno (the uncle of the wife of my uncle Leone Garovo). I was one of four children, the others being my sister, to become Lucrezia Parlascha, and brothers, Domenico and Battista.[1] I remember little about my sister. My brother Domenico was the smart one (he was to become a notary in Bison – his son Bernardo was to be my heir), my brother Battista was to become a stonemason like me. My parents were humble but cultured, our home on the southeastern shore of Lago Lugano was a simple Italian one (though the Swiss had for years dominated here) full of what all Italian homes contained: pasta, northern Italian carne, mushrooms in season, and for us in the North, barbera wine. My family was all too quickly out of my life, as I was apprenticed to the Milanese sculptor Andrea Biffi at age nine. I do remember growing up in our village, a small one wedged into a tight peninsula on 40° foothill slopes[2], the town is only two streets wide,[3] the mountains towering all about us. Our parents were diligent in our education, and we were well read at an early age. I loved to read, and fortunately and unfortunately I withdrew from the world into my books as far back as I can remember. I loved stone cutting, which suited my parents quite well. I had few friends at this point in my life; I can't remember why. I was an introvert to be sure, but my fear of relationships went deeper than that. My love of books- and my father- drew me at a very early age to the study of architecture. My father and mother also told us of course about our famous relatives, especially Signor Carlo Maderno, who was then engaged as architect of Saint Peter's in Rome. There was no more important post in the world if you were an architect. To think- we were related to this man. Our father recounted everything there was to tell about the church of Santa Susanna in Rome, and the momentous change that Signor Carlo's façade made for the development of modern architecture. And then came the expansion and conclusion of the greatest church in Christendom- the San Pietro, all under our relative, the Master Maderno. I, of course, wanted to grow up to be the next great Carlo Maderno. And so I studied, and read, and listened, and observed. I was over the years to accumulate over 1000 books, quite a library for our time- including the texts of all the classics in architecture- from the *Antichita Romane* by Andrea Fulvio and Pirro Ligorio's *Antichita di Roma* and Marcus Vitruvius Pollio's masterpiece *De Architectura* and most important of all for me, G. Battista Montano's *Varij Tempietti Antichi*. But I get ahead of myself.

---

[1] Downes, Opus 269.
[2] Downes, Opus 261.
[3] Morrissey 37.

As I said, at nine I was sent to Milan to apprentice with the architect Andrea Biffi. Signore Biffi and his family were extremely kind to me. Signor Biffi was engaged at the gargantuan Gothic Duomo and also at the reconstruction of San Lorenzo Maggiore; I was able to help him, in a small way, and also to learn all the architecture of these churches. The former is Gothic; the latter is more classically rooted and dates to the fourth century. San Lorenzo, I will say here, is octagonal and most assuredly was my inspiration for San Carlino. Signor Biffi sent me to the Duomo's school for the children of stonemasons. Cardinal Frederico Borromeo had established a *Scuola di Architettura Specolativa* under the distinguished Muzio Oddi, the Academy attached to the Ambrosian Library. I learned so much there, most of it about the Northern Gothic tradition of Lombardy versus the classical tradition of Rome, but Signor Oddi also taught me about his specialty, mathematical instruments.[4] I owe Signor Biffi a great debt- he was my first real teacher. Today we would not call him a great architect, but he knew the technical aspects very well and these he taught me very well.

I spent all my leisure time studying the churches of Milan. I drew countless diagrams of these special places. I always aimed for fantastic and imaginative details.[5] I loved to take my panini and my tazza of wine, and spend my rest periods sitting outside the Cathedral, or San Lorenzo, drawing each and every detail of the church, from façade, to window, to column, to string course, to cornice, to pediment. I learned my mouldings, the orders and their elements, and every inch of the buildings. I made visits outside Milan whenever I could- to Pavia, to the Cortosa- to see all their architecture. I once was allowed to go with my master to Florence, and to see the great Duomo and also San Lorenzo. It was there I came to appreciate and love the work of Michelangelo di Lodovico Buonarroti Simoni, the Prince of Architects. I had to be torn from the Laurentian Library. I felt, and still feel today- that that library was more revolutionary in architectural thought than any other building, excepting perhaps Michelangelo's Palazzo dei Conservatori on the Capitoline. Michelangelo's plans for the façade of San Lorenzo, and what he made for the New Sacristy and the Medici Chapel hold much of interest, but the library made for Lorenzo the Magnificent remains for me as the Prince's *tour de force*. Michelangelo was constrained by structural limitations, which required the library to be very, very light; we can see this everywhere, even the volutes of the windows seem to have no weight. The vestibule, restricted in width and expanded in height, has no precedent. The main order has columns that are in recession that fall behind the surface of the wall, contrary to the usual projection outward. The thin foundation could not have supported these columns, and so Michelangelo invented this solution. This recessed column technique was to come into popular use, but it was revolutionary for the time. And then the volutes in the vestibule are forward of the columns! And they support nothing! The pilaster frames of the tabernacle invert the traditional design- they narrow toward the base and not the top. The capitals are thinner rather than broader than the shaft. The spectacular entry stairway didn't have a weight restriction because of the strong vault below. So, Michelangelo used

---

[4] Downes, 285. Professor's words.
[5] Hibbard 89.

bodacious curves and created an irrational form. There had never been a stairway quite like this. From the Prince of Architecture, I learned that the classical rules of architecture should not be static barriers, and that it is possible, no desirable, to innovate; yes to solve the problems presented by the project, but also to create something new. And architecture is to be enjoyed.

In Milan, my love for architecture grew but my personality unfortunately I have to say, as I look back on my life today, did not. I came to believe that I was meant to be by myself, dedicated to my work. Relationships were difficult; I could not be open with anyone. Being away from home, from my parents and my family, was not good for me. Even at this young age I felt myself withdrawing. I could not approach girls; I simply didn't know what to say. I could only speak about architecture. I was very serious about my work and my reading, studying, observing, and drawing set me apart. I loved architecture and architecture alone. That made me so different from most other boys. My Catholic Faith was one aspect of my life that grew in a positive way during these years. The memory of the native son and Saint, Charles Borromeo, was still fresh in the Milanese and in their churches. The quiet and peace and stillness of the Milanese churches were calming for me. In the first place, I was at home in the architecture of these churches, of course, but the comfort went beyond that to the spiritual. As the years would go by, I lost many things and my mental health suffered greatly at times, but I never lost my Faith or left it. In many ways it sustained me through my troubles and difficulties.

I was at the head of my class at the Duomo when it came to drawing. Using the texts there, and borrowing whenever I could, I came to know most of the architecture in the world. I drew every imaginable kind of order- Doric, Ionic, Corinthian, these in never-ending variation, and also the Tuscan, Composite, Byzantine, Egyptian, Moorish, Gothic, Norman. I turned them upside down and sideways, mixed them all together, and created new ones never seen before. I added abaci and astragal to these when I wanted. Volutes, of course, became my specialty and I made those in every conceivable way. I took apart entablatures, violated all the classical rules, and adjusted the architrave, frieze, and cornice by whim, adding and subtracting coronas and dentils. At the base, I mixed plinth, bead fillet, torus, scotia, and apophygis at will. And mouldings - which I regard as so critical an element to the final feel, look, and function of a structure- for these I had incredible variations- I took cavetto, cyma, recta, ovulus, scotia, and cyma reverse logee, to what I thought, were new levels.

When I had been in Milan for ten years, now age twenty, I knew it was time. I was a grown man. I was well educated. I knew everything that my master could teach me. I had long outgrown my school. My work was excellent, I had the technical skills I needed. Milan was limiting in that although I was now an expert stonemason and decorator, it was not possible for me to find work there, and architects with whom I could work, that would permit me to go to the next level. Lombardy had a tradition and that was to send its stonecutters to Rome. This began with the Cosmati stonecutters from Como and, of course, the latest of these migrants were my distant relatives. Rome for me meant opportunity, for there resided the Holy Father, the Pope, whose functions included the adornment of Holy Places. Popes were by far the largest patrons of the arts, and architecture. And the Rome of 1619 was a city under construction. There were new churches, new Palazzos, and an endless number of old churches in need of restoration. It was an architect's dream. There was work, and very good work. Saint Peter's was the busiest place of all. Donato Bramante had begun the church a hundred years before for Pope Julius II Rovere, and none other than my relative Carlo Maderno was finishing it. I didn't know Signor Maderno, but I knew everything about him. I knew his great Santa Susanna and its beautiful, remarkable façade, and I knew his façade of San Pietro, and the great nave he made for the church. I wanted to be just like him.

I felt that I was destined to go to Rome, to grow in my profession, and to learn from the Master and became an architect just like him. I was filled with boundless optimism and hope. And in Rome I could learn so much more. In Milan there is very little that is ancient. In Rome it is everywhere- and I wanted to see and draw the Pantheon, Santa Costanza, the Colosseo, the Theatre of Marcellus, the tomb of Cecilia Metella, the Septizodium. And Rome also had the treasures of Michelangelo: the Palazzo Farnese, Saint Peter's dome and exterior, the Palazzo dei Conservatori, the Sfroza Chapel. Rome was calling me, very loudly, and so in 1619 I set off to the city. I knew my mother's brother Leone Garovo who lived in Rome, and who worked for Master Maderno as a decorative sculptor, an *intagliatore* who would take me in until I could establish myself. I was hoping he would let me work with his group of stonemasons at San Pietro, though I couldn't be sure.

I was strong in body, even athletic, and I felt I had equal strengths in integrity and self-discipline. I did not drink intemperately, certainly was not a carouser or womanizer. I had what I felt was strong self control. I lived simply, and frugally. I had few clothes and fewer possessions. Yes, I was an introvert. I did brood. I did keep to myself. But I felt I was ready, ready for Rome, for more things, bigger things.

CHAPTER ONE

The First Twelve Years in Rome

San Pietro, Sant'Andrea della Valle,
the Palazzo Barberini

San Pietro in Vaticano

I came to Rome from Milan in 1619, aged 20, a humble decorative stonemason, an *intagliatore* and *scalpellino*,[1] with the vision to someday become a great architect. I had applied myself with great vigor in Milan and spent every minute of leisure in the study of architecture.

Perhaps I have been a bit too modest about my architectural training and that of my family. My father I have described as an architect to the Milanese Visconti, but he was also a water engineer and an expert on fountains.[2] And the Garavolos on my mother's side included designer-masons. And so when I arrived in Rome, I essentially had what you would think of as a diploma in marble work and a bachelor's degree in architecture.[3]

I wanted to go to the center, to Rome, to hopefully follow in the footsteps of so many Lombard stonecutters before me. My uncle, my mother's brother, Leone Garovo, who was in service of Carlo Maderno at San Pietro, had promised my mother that he would help me, and so he did. The Lombards had their own enclave in Rome, clustered around San Giovanni dei Fiorentini, the church begun for the Florentines, and there I settled with my uncle whose family had an apartment in the house at the Florentine Campagnia della Pieta, on the Vicolo dell' Agnello at San Giovanni dei Fiorentini.[4] I was to live in this neighborhood for the rest of my life, and die there. I ultimately made my home on the Via Giulia facing the Vicolo Orbitelli.[5] Although I came from the Swiss Canton of Ticino (the Swiss having annexed it in 1512), I considered myself a Milanese, Milan having ruled Lago Lugano for many centuries.

In Rome, I was an independent stonemason in my uncle's service. San Pietro was an incredibly busy place. Master Maderno had only recently finished the façade of Saint Peter's for the reigning Pope, Paul V Borghese (1605-1622). Its new travertine glistened in the morning sun, its imposing height and breadth took my breath away when I first saw it. I was so happy to have work, and to be in Rome. I had been hired, of course, primarily as a decorative sculptor, but eventually hired myself out where I could as a stone cutter for a variety of projects. I worked very hard for my uncle, and I was able to meet Signor Maderno, and during our breaks for lunch, and during the evenings and Sundays, I was able to spend hour after hour inspecting San Pietro, and the Pantheon, and the architectural works of Michelangelo. I drew and drew and drew, and Master Maderno eventually saw my work. One of my favorite subjects was the architectural order in San Pietro.[6] After seeing those drawings the Master challenged me to draw various other things, which I did with relish. I took such great pride in his comments and absorbed his every criticism.

---

[1] An *intagliatore* is a carver or engraver. A *scalpellino* is a stonecutter.
[2] Downes, Opus, 285.
[3] Id. Professor Downes' description of Borromini's de facto degrees.
[4] Downes, Opus 273, from Bernardo Castelli's Biographical Notice.
[5] Wittkower, Studies, 290, n 16. Professor Wittkower states that Thelen locates Borromini's house to the northwest, rather than to the south, of San Giovanni dei Fiorentini.
[6] See my Albertina drawing.

One of the first projects of my Master in which I could take a small part was the staircase at the Palazzo Mattei, made in the second decade of the seventeenth century. Here Master Maderno used false perspective in the entrance arch, and from this and other aspects of the design I learned much. The entrance arch was a forerunner of the window treatment in the top story of the west front of the Palazzo Barberini, for which I did the drawings and supervised the execution.[7]

Some of my first work at San Pietro was in the portico, where I contributed to the cherubim that sit atop the large entry portals, the Porta Santa and the Porte Angele.

Some of my earliest works were the cherubs above the entry portals.

I worked on the decoration above the entry portals.

This was 1618-1620. For the Jubilee year of 1625 I was involved in the internal and external decorating of the Holy Door. In 1626, I worked on the shells (conchiglia) and the cherubs in the tympanum of the inside of the Holy Door.[8] Of course, at this time I did as I was told, and my work, though technically correct and conforming to the instructions I was given, did not reflect what was flowering in my mind and my soul. However, you can see in these work some of the motifs which became my favorites: the cherubs, the elliptical, the dorso of the dolphin volutes among them.

Regrettably, my dear uncle Leone fell to his death from scaffolding at San Pietro in August of 1620. After this loss, I acquired Leone's tools and continued my work in a small company of stonecutters including Giorolamo Novi and Bernandino Daria. My humble works in these still formative years included the pedestal of Michelangelo's Pieta, the frame and the cherubim above Allesandro Algardi's relief of the Repulsion of Attila (1627-1628) and the steps and railing for the altar there, and the balustrade of the chapel of San Sebastiano. In the chapel of the Choir I worked on the base ring of the lantern.

---

[7] Downes, Opus 393.
[8] Roma Sacra 119, Faglio 60.

Here I was allowed some freedom, and I made the base ring elliptical rather than the more customary round, and alternated the acanthus leaf with the lily. For this same chapel in the wrought iron gate I made a heraldic coat of arms for Pope Urban VIII Barberini (who had become Pope in 1624) and cherubim heads surrounded by four small wings.[9]

In 1621, Master Maderno let me draw for him a water cascade at the Villa Ludovisi in Frascati and a number of aspects of the façade and the interior at Sant'Andrea (of which I shall write in a following chapter). I was his draughtsman for the campanile of the Monte di Pieta (1624) and I made for him a plan for the church of Sant'Ignazio (1625). For this drawing I experimented with the side chapels, giving them more columns than would have been used for their size according to the current convention.

In 1626 I had formed a new stonecutters' company with Agostino Radi, Battisa Castelli, and Carlo Fancelli.[10] With them in 1629 – 1630 I did the marble frames in the windows and the pair of white and pale gray marble doorcases in the chapel of the Blessed Sacrament at San Pietro.[11] Here I carried a little further what I was learning about Master Michelangelo from the Porta Pia, using triglyphs and other parts of doric entablature.[12] You can see that the mouldings I used describe rectangles which are "distorted" by re-entrant right angles and by corners. I also used mouldings that are duplicated one inside another. And then I used one set of elements to frame another set of elements.[13] Please pay special attention to the Barberini bees at the end of the frieze, and how I mixed scrolls and leaves in the tympanum, and the papal tiara which projects forward like a wall lamp.[14] For the corbels on the sides of the door lintel, notice the open pomegrante (a symbol of the resurrection) and the curly haired putto, whose head I pointed downward.[15]

I made the frame and cherubim above the altar of Leo the Great left of the tribune, also the steps and railing.

---

[9] Roma Sacra 119, The Roma Sacra for San Pietro states at 118 that Borromini's gate was replaced 1758-1760. But see Blunt Baroque Guide 136 who cites Hempel, Borromini at 11. Also the Roma Sacra at caption 119 seems to be contrary.
[10] Id.
[11] Downes, Opus 283. One of these doors led to the north end of the Sistine Chapel, the other is a sham with a closet.
[12] Id. Quote from Professor, see his fn 83.
[13] Id. The Professor's description here. This was a particular criticism of Borromini by Bernini: he could never stop complicating by placing things inside of other things.
[14] Id. Professor describes the scrolls and leaves as "at once flat and fleshy", his comparison to a wall lamp.
[15] Id. figure 18.

I made the portals in the Chapel of the Blessed Sacrament. The cherub springs from the capital and begins the volute.

In these same years, I designed the grills for the door to the Chapel of the Sacrament, and please note the bees, the shells, the buds, and also the rosary on the corner of the pedestal supporting the grill, and a necklace with a little oval metal, both in bronze. Here I was able to show my ability to show things in a natural state.[16]

I made the metal screens for the Chapel of the Sacrament and the Choir. Notice the volutes—four surround the Barberini impresa of the sun, two more the Barberini bee.

---

[16] Blunt, Baroque Guide, 134, citing Hempel, Borromini 11.

In 1628, I did the design for the floor grilles that give light to the chapels in the four pillars of Michelangelo's Crossing (these were cast by Orazio Albrizi). With my company, we continued work on the steps of the high altar, the decoration of the little chapels in the pillars, and the marble coverings for the niches of Popes Urban VIII and Paul III in the Tribune (1630).

All this while I was working with Master Maderno, my mentor, teacher, and inspiration. He respected my technical skills, and the time I spent studying all the ancient models in the city, and my endless drawings of the works of the great Michelangelo. I learned to use the graphite pencil in the form of a toccalapis or port-crayon,[17] which enabled me to be both accurate when I wanted to, or blunt and heavy when I needed to. I visited the Porta Pia, the Palazzo dei Conservatori, the Palazzo Farnese and the Cappella Sforza at Santa Maria Maggiore at least 50 times each! I drew the monumental orders of the Conservatori, the cornice and windows of the Farnese, and the side chapels of the Sforza, over and over. I walked the perimeter of San Pietro so many times I wore my own path, and inspected every minutiae of Michelangelo's work for the exterior of the dome, the attic, and the walls. Master Maderno helped me grow, and now he made me into a first rate draughtsman. Master increasingly suffered from the gout, especially in his hands, and also from kidney stones. Eventually, it became physically impossible for him to do his drawings. I was to replace Filippo Breceioli as his principal draughtsman, and Filippo was demoted to *misure* or measurer.

I adored my Master, he forever took interest in me, he appreciated my skills, my desire to be an architect, my admiration for Michelangelo, and he so well tolerated my idiosyncratic and stoic nature, my driven and lonely personality. I think he also sensed what was burning within me, that passion to create something new and spectacular in everything I did. In 1624, the first year of Pope Urban (Barberini) VIII's pontificate, my Master suffered a great disappointment when the commission for the Baldacchino over Peter's tomb in Michelangelo's crossing was awarded to Cavalier Gian Lorenzo Bernini (Pope Gregory XV had knighted him in 1623), many years his younger, but the Pope's favorite, as Paul V had entrusted then Cardinal Barberini with the training of Bernini when he was still a boy. It is a truth that I never forgave Cavalier Bernini for this great indignity. Master Maderno was architect of San Pietro; he had conceived the Baldacchino and even created a design for Paul V, his was the idea of colossal bronze spiral columns with a tasseled baldachin.[18] The Baldacchino should have been his to design. I cannot help but think that if Master Maderno had been given the commission, I would have been given the opportunity to work with him, and that my career would have taken so much easier a path than the one I was destined to follow.

---

[17] Downes, Opus 265.
[18] Connors, Borromini, 249.

The Maderno-Ticino group of superintendents and assistants was over time replaced by Bernini's men.[19] Bernini had criticized the San Pietro facade, and he regarded Master Maderno as a country bumpkin, who came to Rome as a simple *garzone*,[20] not a gentleman.[21] Despite my feelings, I did do work for Signor Bernini on the Baldacchino, from 1624-1626 and again from 1631-1633. For both engagements I did working drawings and saw to the proper execution of the work. I had become an accomplished draughtsman under Master Maderno; Signor Bernini had no architectural background, the great sculptor that he was. I also worked on details on the vine leaves, tassels, and composite columns.[22] With others in my workshop, we executed the four marble bases that have the eight Barberini shields- for these I must say that the Signor Bernini was responsible for the design, although you will notice that there is one coat of arms that does not have a female head but rather the head of a cherubim. That was my work. I do not know if it is true that Signor Bernini intended the other female heads to be the figure of the Pope's alleged mistress (it is perhaps unfair to repeat this slur), who was at that time in pregnancy.

I made the pedestal for Michelangelo's Pieta.

While I assisted the Cavalier, I continued my other work for Master Maderno and also became one of the leading stonecutters in Rome. I did much stone cutting, for example, at the Monte di Pieta, the Palazzo Borghese, and the Palazzo Mattei.[23] Between 1626 and 1632, my company worked intermittently on the Pantheon and the Chigi-Odescalchi, Vatican, Quirinal and Barberini Palaces.[24]

I should point out here that in 1628 I changed my last name from Castello to Borromini. I had long admired Saint Charles Borromeo, my kinsman from Lombardy. In my spirituality, he was my inspiration. By changing my name, I was also able to distinguish myself from the other Castelli stonecutters. I had used "Boromino" on occasion as early as 1619, a distant relative of Leone Garovo was named Johannes Borminus.[25]

---

[19] Hibbard 91. Professor notes that Florentines like Agostino Radi were taking over.
[20] Hibbard 94.
[21] Hibbard 92.
[22] Connors, Borromini 249. In 1625-1626, Borromini drew the plans for the two towers (the infamous "donkeyears") that Urban VIII added to the Pantheon; these were executed by Cavalier Bernini (taken down in 1883). Blunt, Baroque Guide 94.
[23] Hibbard 219.
[24] Downes, Opus 269.
[25] Faglio 59, fn 1

In January of 1629 Master Maderno died. As the Master's principal assistant, I had been making all his drawings for some time. This was, of course, a great loss for me, and greatly reduced my work. I drew the design for the Master's tomb at San Giovanni dei Fiorentini, the coat of arms of which are in the second chapel on the right.[26] Oh if only the Master could have lived a few more years. For my formation as an architect was not yet complete, though I had through self instruction and the power of observation learned so much under my master. At the time of his death, the Master was architect for the Palazzo Barberini, and I worked under him there and at San Pietro as his Assistant, in addition to my work as independent stonemason. After his death, the Cavalier Bernini was appointed Architect of both San Pietro and the Palazzo Barberini. This appointment, to a man who was not an architect at all, and the loss of my master, made my life very difficult. It is the truth that I could never hope to be the sculptor or painter that Cavalier Bernini was. But I was an architect, schooled in the fundamentals, and self taught in every aspect of building, whereas Cavalier Bernini had no training in these areas of which to speak.

I tried to make the most of the situation, although I was not capable of working for a contemporary from either a constitutional or artistic standpoint.[27] I became the *Assistente del Architetto* at the Palazzo Barberini. At San Pietro's I had already worked on the screens of the chapels (prior to 1629), which I now finished. These screens are based for their structure on Master Maderno's design for the façade of San Pietro.[28] But in their decoration, especially the part up above, I introduced some of my preferences. I was always in a search for the new, and I never wanted to repeat simply what had been done before. If you look at the Barberini coat of arms, the bees and the sun, you notice the volutes. The sun is enclosed in four of these; two more crown the Barberini bee. I also worked on the stemma, or coat of arms, for the niche of Santa Veronica before the Master's death. Note that I turned the keys of Saint Peter upside down and see how I have placed the cherub's innocent young face inside serpentine ringlets and a hollow conch, and his wings have become volutes!

I did the arms about the niche of Sant'Andrea in 1631 (rightfully described as a capricious transformation of the cherubim's wings into volutes) and finished the portals for the chapel of Santissimo Sacramento 1629-1630.[29] In all of these, while I was permitted some latitude, I still worked under instruction, now that of Cavalier Bernini.

Work on the Baldacchino continued, and from the late 1620's Cavalier Bernini used me increasingly as architectural draughtsman and not as stonemason. My function was to prepare in full scale the designs furnished by the sculptor and to oversee the execution of the details in the bronze. I also helped with the design problems the Cavalier encountered for the crossing and the apse, creating a spatial rapport between church and Baldacchino.[30] From April 1631- January 1633, I made large drawings of all the details of the crown of the Baldacchino.[31] I remember one of the payment receipts I received in 1633 spoke of

---

[26] Hibbard 97.
[27] Hibbard 91.
[28] Portoghesi 29.
[29] Id. 28.
[30] Hibbard 91, Portoghesi 30.
[31] Wittkower, Studies 159.

my drawing for "curvatures", "plants", "mouldings", "foliage", "ribs and cornices".[32] The Cavalier knew that I was gifted in design and that I was expert in all the technical aspects of architecture whereas he was not. He paid me, of course, only a small amount of the large salary that he was drawing, and he took full credit for all the work. For the canopy of the Baldacchino, the Cavalier had designed crossed arches surmounted by a large statue of Jesus the Redeemer. I convinced him, based on my calculations, that the structure would not support the weight of this statue. In my studies and observations I had become enamored with the figure of the dolphin. Up until the time of Constantine Christians used the dolphin, regarded as the King of the fish, and not the Cross, to represent Christ. The dolphin had great affection for men, was the emblem of absolute strength, and Christians saw themselves as gathered confidently around the dolphin in the midst of storms. I loved the movement of the dolphin, and the gentle curve of its back. It so reminded me of the gentle curves of the volute. In my drawings I would create so many variations of these volutes and dolphins. I inserted these in the frieze in the cornice.[33] The four ribs that look like dolphins replaced Bernini's crossed arches. This upside down "S" has no Roman or Tuscan precedent, but can be found in Lombardy- Benedetto Briosco's arch in Santi Pietro e Marcellino in Milan, in the crypt of the Duomo in Cremona, in Amadeo's tomb of San Lanfranco in Pavia (which has an actual image of a dolphin – an upside down volute), and other places. I so loved this upside down "S" that I used it not only here in the Baldacchino, but later at the side altars at San Carlino, the Landi altar at Santa Lucia in Selci, Santa Maria dei Sette Dolori, the façade at the Propaganda Fide, and in the Orologio at the Casa of San Filippo.

The baldacchino of Gian Lorenzo Bernini, my dolphin ribs. I loved the gentle curves of the dolphin's back, for me so much like the gentle curves of the volute. Here I created triple membered volutes—an upside down "S". Bernini had designed crossed arches with Jesus the Redeemer above. I convinced Bernini that the statue was too heavy and to use these graceful volutes. I used the upside down "S" at San Carlino in the side altars and also in the Orologio at the Casa.

---

[32] Portoghesi 31.
[33] Portoghesi 31.

FIRST TWELVE YEARS IN ROME

Detail of my dolphin volutes, the reverse "S".

    The top cornice of the Baldacchino has convex curvatures in the form of segments of a circle. These effect a diagonal dispersion of the compositional forces operating in the Baldachchino. The dolphin, symbol of the resurrected Christ, reemerges very explicitly in the running frieze of the cornice. The fundamental structure of the whole image here, with the triple membered volutes I designed, which serve to dilate the top cornice on oblique directives, was beyond Bernini, who had not yet acquired the maturity of architectural means that were required for this conception, though I grant you that Cavalier Bernini's theatrical direction certainly drove the project.[34]

    Cavalier Bernini's Baldacchino as completed is magnificent. However, the canopy and crown are disturbed by changes he made to my design. I proposed the large angels supporting the canopy with festoons. I made these compactly,[35] which serves to highlight

---

[34] Portoghesi 31. Professor Portogehsi's comparison of the architectural skills of Bernini and Borromini here is convincing, best stated in his phrase: "[Bernini lacked the] maturity of architectural means."
[35] Portoghesi 31, 32, direct quotes of compactness and architectural value.

their value architecturally. Cavalier Bernini in his drawings inserted additional small angels. These detract from the vertical lines of the project. These small angels disturb the volute-ribs because they have unhelpful extemporaneous and anecdotal poses.[36] Cavalier Bernini also gave the large angels a sense of agitation, which hides the base of the volutes I designed. I intended them to be vertical weights, and in the final product they have lost this function.

I also designed the high impost blocks for the Baldacchino. I did a series of perspective studies designed to ensure that the upper parts of the Baldacchino would align with San Pietro's entablature.[37] In order to correct the height, I devised the impost blocks. The drawings of the columns and entablature of the Baldacchino, by the way, are all by my hand.[38]

I left work at San Pietro in 1633 (I received my last payment January 22 of that year),[39] after a situation in which I felt exploited by the Cavalier Bernini. He earned all the accolades for the Baldacchino and certainly most of the money paid for it. I do not mind that he has the money, but I do mind that he enjoys the honor of my labors. I regarded my designs "come i propri figli", "like my own children", and he was in effect stealing my family from me.[40] And so, in addition to grossly underpaying me, he gave me no credit in the design of the uppermost elements, especially my dolphin volute ribs, which are together with the twisting columns, the most distinguishing aspects of what I admit is a grand work of art and architecture made by the Cavalier, for which he justifiably receives great admiration.

One of the final straws was the kickback Cavalier Bernini was receiving at my expense. I had formed a partnership with the Cavalier's brother-in-law Agostino Radi to provide marble and stone for the Cavalier. I discovered that Radi had been returning part of the profits to the Cavalier![41] Enough!

The Fontana degli Api in the Vatican Gardens

This is a special work of which I must make mention before we leave San Pietro and the Vatican. It imitates an ancient Roman fountain, which is in the shape of a mountain. Above it is a tablet inscribing a distych by Pope Urban himself.[42] The water spouts from five bees, which combine with laurels and the sun to complete the Barberini *concetto*. I carved this fountain in 1626, pursuant to a design by Master Carlo Maderno. Others have attributed this fountain, in error, to Cavalier Bernini.[43] Pay special attention to the fact

---

[36] Quotation of "extemporaneous and anecdotal poses". Portoghesi 32.
[37] Connors 249.
[38] Blunt 25.
[39] Morrissey 93.
[40] Id. 92, Portoghesi 30, who gives us the Italian.
[41] Morrissey 95.
[42] Blunt, Baroque Guide 231.
[43] Blunt 17.

the surface of the fountain is continuously modulated and that there is no undercutting. The fountain was originally in the theatre area of the Belvedere Courtyard, then moved to the papal stables, then to its final resting place on the north side of the Via del Pellegrino facing the wall of Sant'Anna dei Palafrenieri.[44]

San Giovanni dei Fiorentini

After 1608, Master Carlo Maderno was designing and constructing his dome for San Giovanni dei Fiorentini. I will take some credit for designing the lantern finally placed atop the dome. It is in the form of a tall cylinder with thin windows and coiled stone buttresses. I played a small part only.

Sant'Andrea della Valle

I am so proud of my work for Master Maderno for this great Basilica that he designed. In the 1620's I did many drawings for the Master pursuant to his designs. Gradually I gained his confidence. Since I was a young boy I had been drawing buildings. I drew San Lorenzo in Milan over 20 times. And so I was quite good at it, and this the Master came to appreciate. After he took me under his wing upon the death of my uncle in 1620, his reliance on and faith in me increased year by year. Eventually, I went from drawing using the Master's plans to actually designing my own versions of architectural members. This was my dream- to take the best of what I had learned from the books of the masters, from the classical Vitruvius to the modern Palladio, and from the buildings of the ancients, the French and the Lombards, and most of all from the great Michelangelo, whom I regarded as the pioneer of revolutionary architecture, and then arrive at new and dynamic solutions to the problems and situations presented.

The first real opportunity I had to actually independently design was here at Sant'Andrea, where my Master allowed me to draw for the cupola and actually design the lantern. This was in 1622, just three years into my work with him. Probably in part because the lantern was some 50 meters above the ground Master Maderno allowed me free reign to design. I love the Ionic volutes. I love to use cherubs. Here I combined the two in the capitals- I took the volutes and led them to become the ends of the cherubim's wings. I took this capital and made it single, broad, and alive, and then paired the columns below and capped the result with what I believed was a very original capital. When I paired the Ionic columns, I left just enough room for the angel's head between the two volutes. A very special ending to my first original work, this capital foreshadowed many more in the future that many have described as "fantastic".[45]

---

[44] Downes, Opus 269, "modulation" and "undercutting", 266, fn25.
[45] Portoghesi 28. In Professor Hibbard's words: "one capital serves for two and a large cherub's head looks out from the centre." The Professor's description as "fantastic".

Early in my career my uncle Carlo Maderno allowed me to work on the lantern here. I designed the capitals here, where I have the cherubs' wings serve as volutes.

The Palazzo Barberini

The Barberini Pope Urban VIII purchased the Sfroza Palazzo on the slopes of the Quirinale Hill in 1625, and engaged my Master Carlo Maderno as architect to construct a palazzo that would house both his brother Taddeo Barberini (north side) and his other brother Cardinal Francesco Barberini (south side). I really served as his superintendent for the project, the *Soprintendente*, which was planned 1625-1627 and begun in 1628. My master engaged Pietro da Cortona and Cavalier Bernini as well. The work had not progressed far at the time of my master's death in January 1629. At my master's death, the Barberini Pope established the Cavalier Bernini as architect of both San Pietro's and the Palazzo Barberini. It is not necessary to recount to the reader my sorrow at my master's death. His loss meant so much to me, on so many levels: father figure, teacher, and companion. He was the one who would help me control my temper and emotions. He helped me avoid confrontations and to think positively. And while I worked for him, I had no failures. He was always behind me. From strictly a professional level, his death meant that I had no voice, no advocate, and my work opportunities would suffer in consequence.

The façade of the Palazzo.

At this time, I had acquired a close friend, to be sure, Fioravante Martinelli, whom I met in the artists' circles and who stood by me from beginning to end, and who later was to write a manuscript guidebook that championed my work, but he had only limited influence on the patrons of art.

I stayed on at the Palazzo Barberini and collaborated with the Cavalier Bernini. The Cavalier was only too happy to have me stay, as I had the technical skill in architecture that he knew he lacked. The site was situated between the Piazza Grimani (now the Piazza Barberini) and the Quattro Fontane (the intersection of the Via Felice [now Via Quattro Fontane] and the Via Porta Pia [now Via Venti Settembre]), on a steep hillside. The project was to be a combination palazzo and villa. It was actually Pietro da Cortona who synthesized all of the family's plans in 1628 into a new coherent design. Pietro took the river loggia of the Palazzo Farnese as his model, resulting in the open arcade so integral to the final form of the palace façade. I drew the doors and windows on the façade to Master Maderno's ideas. When construction reached the highest story, however, the Cavalier Bernini and I collaborated in the design. And so the grotesques in the entablatures, the cluster pilasters, and the small windows with diagonal volutes that serve to shape the

space around them, reflect the cooperative effort of Cavalier Bernini and myself.[46] This collaboration continued into the doorframes and fireplace of the main salone. The portals repeat the diagonal orientation of the attic windows. I worked as the *Assistente del Architetto* for Cavalier Bernini during this time and made his drawings, such as that for the central pavilion of the garden façade.

Which brings me to a very real breakout moment for my career – the attic window of the Palazzo Barberini. Work on the Palazzo had progressed to the windows of the west façade. I was tasked by Cavalier Bernini for the windows flanking the central loggia of the façade, and he gave me great liberty here, to his credit.

Michelangelo in the windows of the attic at San Pietro took the hood of the window and composed a shell/oval and on each side of it stretched an architrave supported at the ends by two consoles, which are divided into two parts, each of which has two appended guttae. Master Maderno took up Michelangelo's formula when he made the windows for the façade of San Pietro. He combined the shell and oval opening, and placed them inside a pediment, accentuating the chiaroscuro and articulating the outline of the frame at the bottom of the window. The massive consoles were abandoned in favor of more traditional curved features, and garlands of laurels were hung from these.[47]

Carlo Maderno's façade window at San Pietro, adapted from Michelangelo's attic window at San Pietro

---

[46] Connors, Borromini 249. Professor Connors goes so far as to describe this as an "active collaboration".
[47] Blunt 29-31, Portoghesi 34, quotes.

For the windows of the ground floor I took Michelangelo's model from the apse area of San Pietro followed by my Master Maderno on the façade. I kept the tympanum and the long consoles with triglyphs essentially intact, but I changed the frame so that the mouldings go round uninterrupted to the opening. Note dear reader that where the frame moulding converges with the capital, the string course comes together with it. All the members are woven together and compressed.[48]

For the windows of the second story the Ionic column is taken from San Pietro, but the cornice is different. The aedicula and twin consoles are actually taken from the Palazzo Farnese.

The Palazzo Farnese, where Michelangelo radically changed the design of Antonio da Sangallo the Younger, and created the massive cornice and redid the portal.

And now for the attic windows, my *tour-de-force*, the breakout of which I have spoken. Many have told me that this represents my "birth certificate". I started, as I say, with Michelangelo's attic windows at San Pietro and Master Maderno's windows on the attic of the San Pietro façade. Flaminio Ponzio (1560-1613) created a variation of this Michelangelesque theme in a blind window on the outer wall of the Palazzo Rospigliosi. Ponzio eliminated the console completely, shrunk the shell, which now fit comfortably with the architrave. Projections were added at the top corners, and a ledge supported by two rectangular panels with rams' heads.

---

[48] Portoghesi 33, 34, "weaving" and "compressing" the Professor's terms.

From these precedents, I took the theme of the rectangle lying lengthwise (mine is almost a square, Michelangelo's had the width greater than the height), the shell, and the link between the console and the cornice. It was the pediment that I changed most dramatically. Here I broke from the Renaissance tradition of frontality. The cornice, normally rectilinear, has been changed in two significant ways: I curved the cornice around the shell, and then rotated each side about 60 degrees. I broke away here from all previous models[49]. What I desired was continuity: by curving the architrave into a semi-circle to enclose the shell, I created a single continuous swing – an animation - and did away with the interruptions in Michelangelo's and Master Maderno's models. Some have said the 45 degree cant of the sides of the window are "revolutionary". I leave you dear reader to decide. You will note that the architrave cants, along with the sides of the window. I also turned the rectangular projections at the top of Ponzio's window into curved ears, and then I wound a neo-classical band of laurel through the ears (the laurel was a heraldic symbol of the Barberini). Then in the middle of this is a triglyph with guttae; the laurel band passing behind. The festoon of laurel appears in the concavity of the console, advances into the volute of the console, and then reappears, forcing its way up to the triglyph, creating a "U".[50] I love this hood. I thereafter repeated it a number of times, especially at the Collegio di Propaganda Fide and the Cloister at San Carlino; it is thoroughly in the baroque, bringing forward the whole concept of dynamic movement.

My signature, the famous window at the Palazzo.

---

[49] Blunt 21.
[50] Portoghesi 34, 35, description of the ears, parts and decoration of the hood; the Professor traces the path of Borromini's festoon.

18 | FIRST TWELVE YEARS IN ROME

I also designed eight windows for the garden front of the palace, four on each side of the central portal. In the outermost one I placed a shell in the tympanum and placed a triangular pediment on top of a segmental one.⁵¹ The triglyph here is similar to my window on the façade.⁵²

The rear façade of the Palazzo Barberini where my work is chiefly in the windows. Pay special attention to the window on the far left, where there is a shell in the tympanum. Here I placed a triangular pediment on a segmental pediment.

I then did the oval spiral staircase on the right side of the Palazzo Barberini, but in candor it simply repeats the one by Ottaviano Mascherino in the Palazzo del Quirinale. As designed and built it was open to the sky; this has regrettably now been roofed. Later in my career I would never have submitted to producing what is essentially a replica- I would have done a critical and thorough reworking of any work of recent tradition.⁵³

You will also see my "touch", if you will, in the atrium where through the use of the cornice I connected the niches and at the far sides of the atrium, where the framings are also linked by the cornice. I left my style as well in the perspective arcades you see in the principal staircase, the anterooms of the Gran Salone, and the top story of the main façade.⁵⁴

---

⁵¹ Id.
⁵² Id. Please read the second paragraph of page 35 where Professor Portoghesi describes Borromini's skill in linkage in difficult situations.
⁵³ Id.
⁵⁴ Id. Professor Portoghesi describes this linkage as "anomalous".

My oval staircase

    I left work at the Palazzo Barberini in 1631. It was not because of the Cavalier Bernini, as many have said, though his failure to give me credit for any of my designs there would certainly have justified my departure; rather the two main factions in the family, Taddeo Barberini and Cardinal Francesco Barberini, started to build aspects in their respective areas which destroyed, in my view, the unified skyline of the palace.[55] When viewed from the rear, this disunity was conspicuous. I wanted a unified design, and I became frustrated, and left the commission in 1631. It is true that this reflected poorly on my ability to restrain my emotions and frustrations. In truth, though, I did not have the preeminence that obtained for my Master Maderno, who would certainly have controlled these two factions and kept their individual tastes in check. It was truly not my fault that this divergence developed, and I was powerless to stop it. I had no choice but to leave. But leaving was a part of the rug of unhappiness and disagreeableness that I was weaving and that would eventually lead me to my end.

---

[55] Connors, Borromini 249.

CHAPTER TWO

My Philosophy of Architecture

Here, dear reader, I must fall back and tell you about my approach to architecture. After the Barberini, I was "on my own". What guided me? Just how would I describe my "philosophy of architecture", or my "method"? What were my purposes, my style, and my theories? How did I conceive architecture? How am I different from other architects of my time? I must speak to that now.

My overall objectives were three in number. In the first place, an architect creates buildings,[1] and these buildings are to be used and seen. And so I would say, as most architects would, that I designed structures that could be easily, efficiently[2] and joyfully used. A church that is not useful for worshipers in their worship is a failure. A refectory that is poorly designed for eating is a failure. Part of utility is practicality and economy. I am proud of the fact that my buildings are original and exceedingly complex, but they are not expensive.[3]

Second after utility comes beauty. Structures are to be admired; in their beauty they facilitate use, for beauty attracts. Thirdly, when it comes to sacred places, architecture is meant to glorify God, and both the utility and beauty of a church are to that end.

In striving for these three objectives, I bring two broad convictions. First, I operate within the architectural culture of my times, which is directly descended from the Renaissance,[4] which in turn received its nature from classical antiquity, the principal element of that classical architectural grammar being the architectonic order. Second, I seek variety and novelty- I avoid tedium ("per fuggire il tedio"), and in this aspect I am fond of quoting Michelangelo ("one who follows others never gets ahead of them"). In the *Opus Architectonicum*, I write about the Oratory, and I speak there about my need to produce "new things" and not "conventional designs". Yet novelty is not inconsistent with simplicity, and simplicity is most consistent with spirituality. I never used color, for example, and the interiors of my churches were painted white, and I used neither rich materials, nor drama (as did the Cavalier Bernini).[5]

My architecture then draws on four sources: the ancient, then Michelangelo and those who followed him in the Renaissance renewal of the classical, then the Gothic/Lombard of my homeland and Milan, and finally the use of mathematics and geometry. I should say here that historians now call the period and the architecture in which I worked the "baroque", characterized by movement, drama, tension, and exuberance. My sources may indeed have led me to this new form, but other artists whom you might regard as "baroque", like the Cavalier Bernini, or Pietro da Cortona, I do not regard as a source for my architecture.

---

[1] Borromini does not dwell on architectural integrity of the structure, it is assumed that the building is structurally sound in all respects. He does not think that Cavalier Bernini began with this assumption.
[2] See discussion later about the privies at the Casa of San Filippo Neri.
[3] Blunt 23.
[4] Portoghesi 11, 12.
[5] Blunt 24.

My critics call my inventions capricious, that I abhor the rules laid down by our ancestors, and Cavalier Bernini called my work "chimeric", but in truth, although I have a very free and open interpretation of classical grammatical laws, and although my work goes, I think, far beyond what others led me to, my interior architectural drive is spiritually bound to that of Michelangelo himself. I am a conscious innovator. Yes, I gave significance to the exceptions of a rigorous classicism, but every one of my inventions has a precedent in classical architecture, as I will show you. The link with the Prince of Architects is also clear. Many also criticize my work as "Gothic". While it is true that I incorporated Gothic aspects, my method and style is not Gothic, rather I gleaned selected aspects from the Gothic, which were susceptible to a synthesis with the Renaissance-Classical tradition. To these three sources, I overlaid mathematics and geometry, which I learned in my northern stonemason upbringing, and I evolved all of my complex designs through multiple series of geometrical manipulations.[6]

Let me discuss further each of these four sources in turn. First the ancient. The ancient authority to which I appealed was extensive. I imitated the ancients rather than the moderns.[7] I owned a copy of Pirro Ligorio's *Antichita di Roma*, which reconstructed Hadrian's Villa and the topography of ancient Rome. I copied descriptions of Nero's Golden House from Seutonius' work, and I drew the garden of Licinius, studying the work of archaeologists Andrea Fulvio, Giacomo Lauri and Vicenzo Scamozzi.[8] Cassiano dal Pozzo was a Roman collector who owned the *Codex Coner*[9] (now in the Soane Museum), which was an early sixteenth century sketchbook. This sketchbook had drawings of bases and capitals from the time of the Augustans and Flavians, when extremely elaborate detail was applied, with many beautiful variations. I found the imperial buildings, such as Hadrian's Villa at Tivoli, were full to the brim with complex and ingenious aspects. I was able, of course, to visit many of the ancient sites, such as the Canocchia tomb near Capua, which has a very complex example of Roman masonry, and a fragment of the Augustan Temple of Apollo Sosanius, lying below the Theatre of Marcellus, which has the most unusual flutings in the pilasters. Cassiano dal Pozzo was also kind enough to share with me the drawings he had made by Giovanni Battista Montano. Signor Montano drew both whole ancient monuments and also details from these monuments, including elaborately fluted columns, and a temple which by some miracle reproduces the late Imperial circular temple at Baalbek, and facades with a single concave curve or with a combination of concave and convex curves,[10] and colonnades that create false perspective. Signor Montano didn't draw the obvious- he made a catalog of exceptions,[11] and also constructions of minor importance. My architecture was not dogmatic, in large part because I sought out the unusual, the unique, the exquisite, and the exception in ancient

---

[6] Blunt 47.
[7] Blunt 34.
[8] Blunt 37.
[9] Blunt 37.
[10] Blunt 41.
[11] Portoghesi 6. Professor Portoghesi at 5-8 provides an extensive discussion of G.B. Montano, and he speaks of the "cultural relationship between the two architects". If you want a good understanding of the influences on Borromini, you must read this.

architecture. Montano, in his drawings, dealt with so many compositional problems,[12] including the centralized plan (the mausoleum at Santa Costanza), the perspective contraction of space (for example, two converging rows of columns), ternary symmetry[13] (the vestibule of Piazza d'Oro of Hadrian's Villa), the juxtaposition of concave and convex surfaces[14] (which I took up over and over again over the years) (the Temple of the Divine Romulus in the Roman Forum), the use of diagonal axes (Michelangelo focused on these in his plans for San Giovanni dei Fiorentini). All these found their way into my works.

Porta Pia.

---

[12] Id.
[13] Id.
[14] Id.

26 | MY PHILOSOPHY OF ARCHITECTURE

The Sfroza Chapel at Santa Maria Maggiore in the left aisle. Now the Chapel for the Holy Sacrament.

The Palazzo Conservatori.

The second great influence for my architecture was Michelangelo. A century before me the Prince of Architects broke vast new ground for architecture. Michelangelo in his letter to Cardinal Rodolfo Pio expressed his conception of a building as a body in movement and in action, and not a static object. He moved from the two dimensional linear and planar architecture, then dominant in the Renaissance, to the fully three-dimensional concept of building. Michelangelo did not consider himself bound by any rigid rules of classicism. One has only to look even casually at the Sfroza Chapel at Santa Maria Maggiore to see his willingness to challenge the dominant rules by his placing of the column- buttress directed diagonally toward the interior. The sloping corona and curved frieze at the Palazzo dei Conservatori, the interrupted architrave in the attic windows at San Pietro, the giant pilasters in the Capital palaces, the volute of an Ionic capital supporting a ball on the Porta Pia,[15] all were themes that challenged the existing order, which I took up, and hopefully advanced, in my buildings. I borrowed freely from those few who followed Michelangelo and took up his themes- Giacomo del Duca in his façade at Santa Maria in Triviso (which I drew after visiting and measuring its height with my ladder!), Pellegrino Pellegrini, called Tibaldi, in S. Fedele in Milan and the Collegio Borromeo in Pavia and his work in Milan's Duomo, Francesco Maria Ricchino in his church of San Giuseppe and his curved façade at the Collegio Elvetico in Milan, Jacopo Barozzi called Vignola, in his niche- window on the façade of Sant'Andrea on the Via Flaminia, and his use of the rhythmic bay at Palazzo Farnese in Piacenza, and the ellipses of Francesco da Volterra's church of San Giacomo degli Incurabili.

The third influence on my philosophy/method of architecture is the Gothic. My work is clearly not Gothic. But coming from Lombardy, I saw all that Lombardy has to offer. I brought the trilobal arches, the vertical scheme of proportioning, the diagonal compositional systems- as part of a synthesis with the classical, a perfectly sensible conciliation of Gothic and Renaissance/Classical.[16]

A final, perhaps the most significant influence on my program, is the application of mathematics and geometry. As you will see, much if not most of my work was based upon painstaking application of geometric manipulations. Even when I was doodling, I drew geometric doodles.[17] Ultimately I was not engaged for the Villa Pamphilj near San Pancrazio, but in my proposal to Cardinal Camillo I laid out an exquisite mathematically grounded design for a palazzo with 32 windows corresponding to the 32 points of the

---

[15] Blunt 29.
[16] Portoghesi 14. The Professor calls this "a rational conciliation of two proportional systems."
[17] Blunt 49, figure 40. The best elucidations of how Borromini used geometry are, in my view, Professor Smyth-Pinney and Professor Connor's articles on Sant'Ivo, Professor Steinberg on Carlino, and Professor Mazzotti on the oval at Carlino. They explain Borromini's use of geometry at great length and detail. You must read these if you want to understand this influence on Borromini.

compass, and two rooms with hemispherical domes. As I told him: "in fact the whole building would be a study in applied mathematics."[18] The use of geometry, and especially the triangulation I used so often, is medieval, and it was handed down from generation to generation in the stonemason yards in which I was reared. The churches of Sant' Ivo and San Carlino are certainly the clearest examples of my use of geometric forms to shape the structure. I believe that geometry is at the heart of all good architecture. You will see this when I describe the conception of these structures in turn.

---

[18] Portoghesi 179,180.

The sinusoidal—double S curve—façade of San Carlino. The façade was designed early in my career but made much later, and the upper section was executed by my nephew, and not in keeping with my style. The founders of the Order, Jean de Matha (with his theology book) and Felix de Valois (with the royal crown of France) flanking San Carlo.

CHAPTER THREE

*San Carlo alle Quattro Fontane
(San Carlino)*

As you enter the Carlino, I know that you are struck by the unusual form of this small church—an octagonal plan with a giant order of engaged columns, and a brilliant coffered oval dome, all bathed in white, all unified by an unbroken, circling cornice.

I left San Pietro because of the Cavalier Bernini and I left Palazzo Barberini because I could not control the design over the whims of the families. I was growing in freedom of expression, increasingly I was able to take the genius of Michelangelo and the ancient and hopefully take it a step further in creative solutions. Now it was time to control my own destiny versus working for others and executing their plans and not my own. I let it be known that I was available for architectural projects, without charge, so long as I was given my freedom, within bounds. In 1633 I offered my services without charge to the Soldati of the Picini for the renovation of Santa Casa di Loreto. Unfortunately, the Soldati were not able to proceed with their project for lack of funds. In 1634 I made the same offer to the Spanish community of the Discalced Trinitarians, the *Trinitarii Scalzi*. These holy and simple men, an outgrowth of the order whose mission (1198) was the reclamation of slaves from the wicked Saracens, had been given some houses they acquired 1611-1614 near the Quattro Fontane. The Trinitarii were a reforming part of the order (Scalzi or "discalced" meaning barefoot, a symbol of their reforming nature [they actually wore sandals]), and they insisted on primitive austerity.[1]

Pope Sixtus V Peretti at the end of the sixteenth century had straightened the Via Porta Pia and the Via Felice and placed four fountains on the corners of the intersection. The Palazzo Barberini was down the Via Felice half of a block toward the Spanish Steps. The Trinitarian Brothers had already converted the first house they acquired near here into a small church for Carlo Borromeo, who had just been canonized by Paul V, and who was my patron saint, a fellow Lombard. My fervor for San Carlo greatly motivated me to reach an agreement with the Brothers. The Brothers wanted to begin the complex on the Southwest corner of the Quattro with the dormitory quarter, which is the part of the building that is at a right angle to the Via Felice (which I should point out to the reader became the Via Quattro Fontane). The actual church was to be at the front of this section.

I began drawings at once and construction began in the summer of 1634. This was, as you can imagine, one of the happiest moments of my life. I was finally an architect, at age 35. Up to this point I had not had the opportunity to fully utilize what I had learned about architecture since a boy. The limitations of my new commission were significant. The Spanish order was a poor body of modest monks and so cost and moderation were constraints. I tell you, with modesty, that I worked for very little money, as was my practice (I did this in part to avoid direction from the patron).[2] In the end the church was built on debt financing. Although Cardinal Francesco Barberini donated land, he was lavishing money on Santi Luca e Martina for Pietro da Cortona and dodging the poor Trinitarians. In 1638, there was a crisis when the Padres actually rejected my plan for the church, thinking it over elaborate. Cardinal Barberini did come to my rescue here (persuaded I think by the Brothers' dedication to him of the principal chapel at Carlino), and with his support, the Brothers finally approved the plan, although it was to cost five times as much as they wanted to spend.[3]

---

[1] Connors, Borromini 250. Connors, San Carlo 1.
[2] Blunt 21.
[3] Connors, Steinberg 284.

The site was a very great challenge, as the southwest corner of the Quattro Fontane property was very small, with just 80 feet of frontage on the Strada Pia. The property was not rectangular since the two streets ran at an obtuse angle and the corner of the property was appropriated to the fountain. On this property I had to place a dormitory, a refectory, a library, a cloister, and a church.

The Chronology

A short chronology. The dormitory and related rooms were begun July 6, 1634, completed in August 1635. Then construction began on the cloister, February 6, 1635, finished June 4, 1636 (my illustrious balustrade was not completed until 1644).[4] The church itself was begun February 23, 1638, and was consecrated on May 26, 1641.[5]

The lower section of the façade was made 1665-1667. My nephew Bernardo Castelli made the upper level 1665-1677, though in large part, due to the poverty of the Trinitarians, work on it ceased for many years after 1667.[6]

The sacristy-originally the refectory. No corners here—the cherubs forming the junctions of the walls.

---

[4] Steinberg, quoting Pollak (79), 123, fn1.
[5] Hill, 580, note 1.
[6] Id.

The beautiful vault of the sacristy. Four volutes held together by festoons and luxurious foliate. I eliminated all corners here. Eight deeply recessed arches with lunettes.

I used cherubims at the junctions to assist in taking out the corners. Beautiful foliage in the cornice with the eight pointed Barberini star.

The Dormitory, Refectory, Cloister

Construction began with the dormitory quarter in the summer of 1634, including a refectory (now the sacristy), fourteen dormitory cells, and a library, all of which were finished in the early autumn of 1635. The refectory, located behind the tribune, has a beautifully designed vault, made with eight arches that are deeply recessed, accompanied with lunettes. You see here four volutes which are held together by both festoons and a foliate full of luxury. Here at the junction I placed cherubs- a favorite theme I would use repeatedly. These are not the mature emotionless variety, but have a smile faintly ambiguous and adolescent, the wings light and resistant.[7] I eliminated the corners here, corners being the bane of all good architects- by using more cherubims. I used curves generously- again a favorite technique for me. The cornice links the walls with a curve. The niche is shallow and filled with coffers- this too became a recurrent feature in my work.

---

[7] Portoghesi 25. Professor Portoghesi gives us the apt phrases "ambiguous and adolescent" and "light and resistant," for Borromini's cherubs which he individually modeled.

The Cloister.

The Cloister—a rectangle from which I took away the corners. There is no break around the octagonal perimeter. The balusters completely unique- triangular- three slightly concave sides, the bulge alternating between top and bottom.

From the refectory I went to the cloister of the monastery, (to the right of the nave of the church) begun in February 1635, mostly finished by June of 1636. I made good use of the small space available to create what others have called an exceptionally revolutionary work.[8] I had in my mind Tibaldi's cloister at Collegio Borromeo in Pavia, which I had visited from Milan. Tibaldi used the Serlian arch with alternating flat and round-headed openings,[9] and also an angular triplication of the column.[10] I began with a rectangle, then I took off the corners; in the lower story the corner bays are slightly convex, above the architrave is straight. The rhythmic bays are connected; there is no break around the octagonal perimeter. I made the flat openings in the lower level with wider openings, gave the columns simple capitals (resembling the Tuscan), and unified the abacus of the close-

---

[8] Id. 39.
[9] Blunt 55.
[10] Portoghesi 40, the Professor's description of Tibaldi's use the Serlian arch and columns.

standing capitals,[11] and had an uninterrupted cornice around the entire area. In the upper order, I again used the Semi-tuscan, but turned to octagonal capitals that will remind you of late Gothic,[12] and the entablature traces the circuit of the octagon. The octagonal capital permitted one face to be parallel with the plane of the colonnade on the long side, and at the corners it was possible to have a corner of the capital be on a line which bisected the angle formed by the two sides of the cloister.[13] In the flattened mouldings you will see a similarity to Donato Bramante's bases in San Pietro- I had drawn them so many times during my rest times there. I covered the walls with smoothed stucco covered with tempera. Here I was aiming for a soft chiaroscuro, trying to move from a lighter to a darker gray hoping that the columns and convex surfaces of the vault would alternately emerge from the shadows and then be absorbed in the darkness of the shadows. I was learning how to transfigure a material by the light.[14]

In the balustrade I made my most significant invention, though it may seem to be a small part to you. Renaissance architects used circular balusters. Bramante made them symmetrical at their middle. Michelangelo broke away from this symmetry, and put the bulge on the lower half. I made two further changes to the classical norm. First, I made the baluster out of triangles; three slightly concave sides/circles. Second, I alternated these with the bulge at the top, then the bottom. What this did was permit far better viewing from behind the balusters to the floor below. I used these balusters at the Neri Oratory (where they were very helpful for the audience in the balconies) and the Filomarino altar in Naples. These at Carlino Cloister were actually not installed until 1644, after my first experiments at the Oratory and the Filomarino. I got the idea for the form of these balusters from Michelangelo's plans for military fortifications in Florence, where he was concerned with lines of vision for the defenders.

The famous "Borromini baluster" which is designed with its "bulge" to alternate with each baluster top to bottom to permit better viewing of what is below. I used these at the Oratory, on the balcony of the Oratory façade, and on the façade of Carlino, also in Naples in the Filomarino altar, and in the chapels of the side aisles at the Lateran.

---

[11] Id. 39, the Professor's description of Borromini's articulation of the remarkable cloister.
[12] Blunt 55.
[13] Blunt 57, description of use of octagonal capital to achieve parallelism with the sides and to bisect the angles at the corners.
[14] Portoghesi 40, direct quotes of the chiaroscuro Borromini sought to work here.

The well of the cloister- an oval surrounded by an octagon.

We added a well in the center of the cloister - an oval surrounded by an octagon (the octagon/oval being the form I used for both the cloister and the Church), surrounded by iron work (for which I drew 10 plans until I achieved what was desired).

The Plan for the Main Body of the Church

It took me some time to settle on the final form of the plan for the church itself. The symbol of the Trinitarians was the cross, and so I wanted to use a cruciform if I could. But I also very much loved the octagon and the oval, and I had in mind Michelangelo's plan for a church body in the form of an octagon with four semi-circular lobes attached.[15] I felt the oval best lent itself to a post-Trent congregation, permitting the congregation to focus on the Eucharist.[16] There is an "ovalized" cruciform in the lower room of the tower of Roccaburna that came to my mind, as well as Vignola's oval at Sant'Anna di Palafrenieri (made in 1565),[17] and finally Francesco da Volterra's oval plan at San Giacomo degli Incurabili (made in 1590).[18]

At first I thought I would place a circular dome over the central space as at San Pietro. But I was to settle on an oval dome. I wanted an undulating church body, and so this required me in my plan to accommodate the oval dome with pendentives, which I then had to support with piers. In the final plan, I placed these crossing piers at a 45 degree angle to the longitudinal axis of the church, again reminiscent of San Pietro.

I am now going to describe for you the steps I took to draw my plan. I actually drew the plan I am about to lay out for you many years after the church was constructed, part of my late-in-life project to set forth my plans in an *Omnia Opera*.

In the working out of my plans for Carlino in the 1634-1635 timeframe, I was far less precise and visually pleasing. Nonetheless, I did proceed mathematically from the beginning. The shape of the oval and its genesis and drawing do not, however, conform to my working plans, although the plans do present the kind of integration I had in mind.[19]

---

[15] Steinberg 75 (also see Professor Steinberg's figure 21).
[16] Blunt 67.
[17] Portoghesi 42, 43, the Professor uses the term "ovalized cruciform."
[18] Blunt 68.
[19] There are those who are perhaps too insistent in the view that all these mathematics are latter day imaginations intended by Borromini to enhance the idea that he always proceeded mathematically – and to increase the attraction of his forthcoming *Omnia Opera*. Connors, Barocco 110.

And so after two drawings – with many *pentimenti*[20] (drawn largely freehand) which show my transition from rotunda to cross to the ovalized cruciform, I settled on the final form, which I set forth for you here. I began by drawing two equilateral triangles with a common base, which as you can see created a diamond. Then I drew perpendiculars over the sides of these triangles. This creates the long axis of the diamond. The intersections of the perpendiculars then give us the centers of two circles which I inscribed within the triangles. Next I drew a four segment (four arc) oval, following Serlio's Book I, folios 13V and 14 (but see the discussion below which provides the detail about how I drew the oval – the process for that oval was in fact more particular and intricate). I then created a double-line rectangle where the inner sides were tangent to the oval, the outer sides falling at a point midway between the minor axes of the oval and the diamond.

From there I inserted the main altar apse and entrance chapel. For this I used a semicircle. Here I drew the radius having a length equal to the distance from the intersection point of the major axis and the outer side of the rectangle on its short end to the apex of the diamond. That semicircle I then doubled, but the width here I made somewhat less than the width I had in the rectangle. This semicircle at each minor side of the rectangle gives the plan of the entrance chapel and the apse.[21]

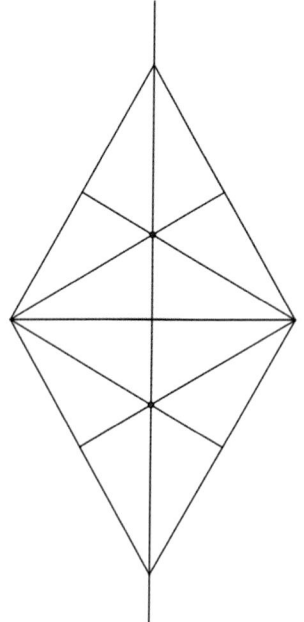
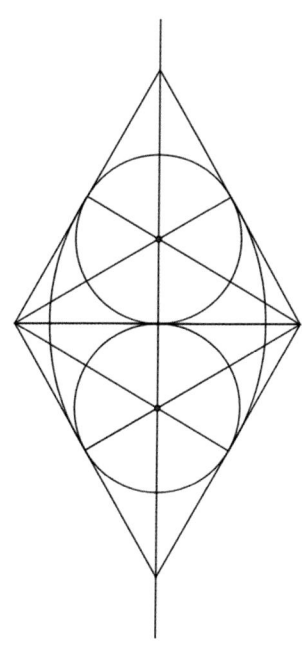

I first drew two equilateral triangles, then perpendiculars over the sides of the triangles. Steinberg 85-93.

The intersections of the perpendiculars gave me the centers of two circles inscribed within the triangles. I drew a four segment oval following Serlio's Fourth. Steinberg 85-93

---

[20] Albertina drawing 171, 172.
[21] Steinberg 85-93. The step by step geometric process described in the text comes directly from Professor Steinberg. The Professor concludes that the Albertina drawing 173 gives us "the elusive plan of S. Carlo". Professor Steinberg confirmed the geometry of the quandrantal (pie shape} sector by measurements in the entrance chapel. Id, 88, fn 26. This is a "quandrantal sector within a perfect semicircle".

40 | SAN CARLO ALLE QUATTRO FONTANE

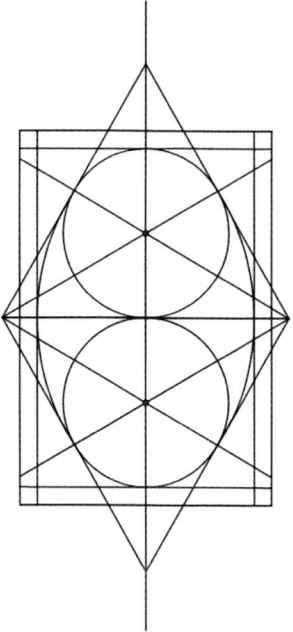

I drew a double-line rectangle-inner sides tangent to the oval, outer sides midway between the minor axes of the oval and the diamond. Steinberg 85-93

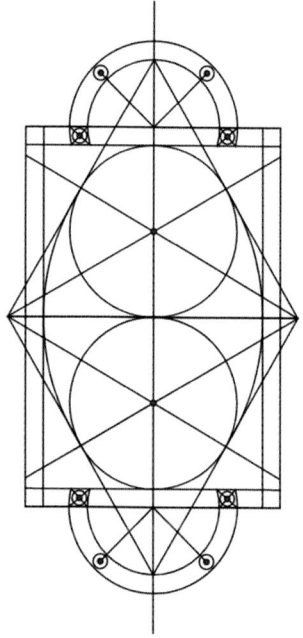

I inserted the main altar and the entrance.

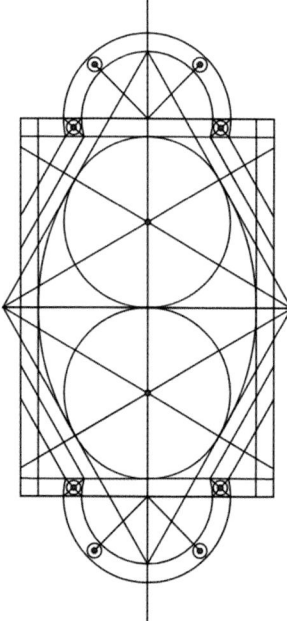

I chamfered the rectangle's corners with straight double lines parallel to the sides of the interior diamond. This located the columns for the lateral arches. Steinberg 85-93

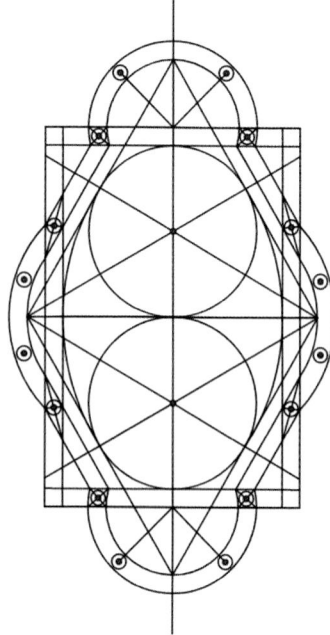

I made the perimeter of the side chapels free hand.

You can see that the apsidal semicircles are now horseshoes, with overlaps where the double line of the semicircle intersects with the short side of the doubled rectangle. The columns which were to carry arches at right angles across the longitudinal axis are in the "square" of these intersections.

Then inside the apse, I placed columns by bisecting the right angle formed by the major axis and the exterior rectangle. These bisectors, as you can see, are the radii of the semi-circular apse. The arc that they contain gives a guandrantal sector, or pie shape.

Next I chamfered the rectangle's corners with straight double lines that are parallel to the sides of the interior diamond. By this method, I converted what was a rectangle into an "elongated irregular octagon". I also by this device located the columns that would carry the lateral arches.

Finally, I traced out the double perimeter of the side chapels. The internal lines do in fact touch the poles of the diamond's short axis, but the curvature really takes a path all its own.

And so, to summarize (again with the caveat about the drawing of the oval dome):

1. Draw two triangles with a shared base which gives us a diamond
2. Place perpendiculars over the sides of the two triangles
3. Inscribe two tangent circles. These give us the foci and the short segments of an oval we inscribe within the diamond
4. Create a double-rail rectangle which is tangent to the oval
5. Draw two semicircular chapels in the long axis articulated with four columns each
6. Chamfer the corners of the rectangle creating an octagon
7. Creation of the side chapels with a free hand curve

I have a need to speak to you somewhat further about what I created in this plan. You note that there are seven geometric forms that I have described above:

equilateral triangle
lozenge (diamond)
circle
oval
rectangle
quarterfoil
lobed octagon

Some of these forms helped me in drawing the plan but did not become part of the building. The triangles are not part of my building, for instance, but the intersections of the perpendiculars of the triangle gave me the centers of the circles which were essential. The lozenge formed by the triangles create the lateral poles that provide the furthest point of the curves of the two side chapels. The sides of the lozenge serve to guide the chamfering of the rectangle. But if you examine the physical church, you will see that there is no wall on any part of the track of the lozenge. There is not a bit of masonry in the church on the track of this lozenge. Likewise for the tangent circles and the rectangle. The purpose of the plan and the geometric forms in it was to help me resolve the reciprocal correlations that were in my mind. My plan was of no use to the masons on site, and if you study my working drawings[22] you will not see any of the lines in the drawing I am discussing.

I must also point out to you that I refused requests to reveal the underpinnings of the design of the Carlino, even from my good friend, the Fra Juan de Bonaventura, who was writing his *Relazione*.[23] I must also repeat: the plan I have been describing was instrumental for me but it was subsequent to my idea for the church and certainly not coincidental with my idea – my ideas existed before recourse to drawing the plan. The plan helped me conceive the dome (though, as I will explain below, the drawing of the dome does not derive from the plan), fix the shape of the octagon for purposes of supporting the pendentives and the arches, and to layout the four chapels. The plan helped me bring to fruition the oval, the octagon, and the cross, all of which I wanted to include in Carlino.[24]

---

[22] Professor Steinberg fully describes Borromini's use of these geometric forms at 89-91, and sets forth in detail the distinction between use in drawing/designing the plan for the nave and actual physical embodiments in the church. The description set forth here comes directly from the Professor's description. Albertina drawing 170, 179r.

[23] Borromini's Plan, Albertina drawing 173, was to be kept a secret for over 300 years, until 1958 when 70 Borromini drawings from Vienna were exhibited in Rome. Steinberg 19, fn28; 85, fn23. It was this drawing that confirmed Professor Portoghesi's belief that St. Peter's was Borromini's inspiration for Carlino, not Vignola's Santa Anna.

[24] Professor Steinberg identifies the threefold purpose of Albertina 173 for Borromini at 93. This part of Borromini's story is difficult. All of the material about Borromini's plan and the geometry comes from Professor Steinberg, who wrote his master's thesis about the Carlino, and there are many quotes from his subsequent book, from pages 85-94 especially. It is an exquisite work that definitely settles how Borromini made his plan for the Carlino. But Joseph Connors, perhaps the Professor with the most comprehensive understanding of Borromini, believes that Albertina drawing 173 is an after the fact drawing made as part of Borromini's project of the 1660's to create a compendium of plans designed to enhance Borromini's reputation and that they perhaps overstate the architect's geometrical formulation of his ideas. When it comes to the dome, this is certainly the case, as demonstrated by Professor Mazzotti's book on Borromini's oval dome, and how Borromini masterfully drew a four-segment dome based on Serlio's fourth oval, and not what we see in Albertina drawing 173. And so I ask you to keep in mind here: the description of 173 is almost completely from Professor Steinberg, but I have added the caveat that it may not have been so early drawn as Professor Steinberg believes, but could have been drawn much later, as Professor Connors believes, and the added caveat that the dome oval was drawn separately.

The Ovals of the Dome and Lantern

In making the shape of the impost of the dome, I was driven by the intrados I intended for the dome. The four levels of coffers of crosses, octagons, and hexagons I planned required an oval with properties that would accommodate a grid for these coffers.[25] I needed an oval where the perimeter could be divided into equal parts.[26] I had knowledge of just such an oval, from the design books of Sebastiano Serlio: it was his so-called fourth construction, which oval has the properties of easy division into "equal" wedges that I could use to place the four levels of coffers. Serlio's oval has a perimeter which can be divided into eight arcs of equal length by the intersections of the arcs with the horizontal and vertical axes of the oval, and with the four "connection points" of the oval where the four separate arcs in the oval meet.[27]

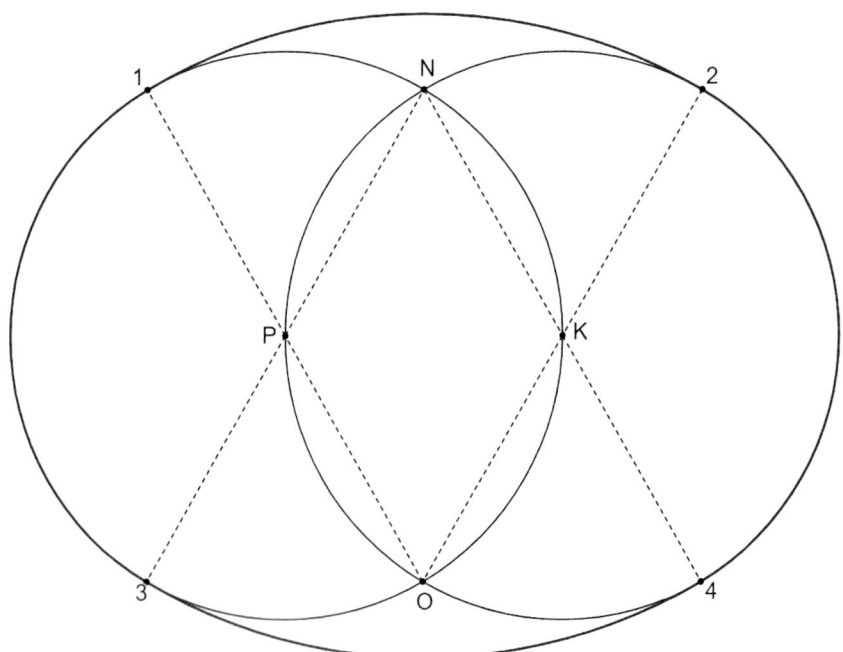

Sebastiano Serlio's explanation of how he drew his fourth construction: "make two circles that may cut through each other's center, the other two circles for closing the circle be N.O., after that, whether you obtain the right lines or not from the points O.N. you shall by the lines from 1. and 2., and from 3. to 4."

---

[25] Mazzotti 125. Professor Mazzotti's Chapter 7 is specifically about San Carlino. It is masterful.
[26] Id. direct quote.
[27] Id. 126. Professor Mazzotti more fully describes Serlio's fourth at Figure 63 in Chapter 6 of his book.

An oval, of course, is, in my world, polycentric (having two centers) made up of convex arcs of circles, with two symmetrical axes, connected in such a way that the arcs have a common tangent at their connection points. In Serlio's oval, two circles are drawn such that they divide the horizontal axis into three equal lengths; that is the two circles intersect such that the distance between their two centers is their common radius. The perimeter of Serlio's fourth construction oval can be divided into eight equal parts, as I have described, then into sixteen using the bisectors of the angles corresponding to the eight arcs. Through this method I created "wedges" into which I could slot my coffer decoration. The radii of the wedges, by the way, do not converge to the center, they actually converge to points on the major axis with a distance of 1, 2, and 3 palmi from it.[28]

There was one problem in using Serlio's fourth construction oval: the length of the vertical axis. For any oval, the ground plan of the building determines the rectangle into which the oval is inscribed, establishing the horizontal and the vertical axes. And so the horizontal axis for my oval, using Serlio's fourth, would be 52 ¾ palmi long and the vertical axis would be 36 1/20 palmi long. If I were to replicate the Serlio oval, the vertical axis would exceed the vertical axis allowed by the dimensions of San Carlino by about 4 palmi.[29] Fortunately, I could still use Serlio's oval: I would just have to alter the "top" and "bottom" arcs by choosing different centers for these arcs, "flattening" the impost of the oval at its top and bottom. And so for the two centers on the minor axis, I selected a distance from center equal to half the major axis (Vignola's golden oval used this formulae).[30] This achieved the flattening I needed to fit the oval into the impost rectangle dictated by the dimensions of the church.

---

[28] Id. 126.
[29] Id. 125. Also see Professor Mazzotti's fn17.
[30] Id. 128. Professor Mazzotti here discusses the mechanics of Borromini's flattening.

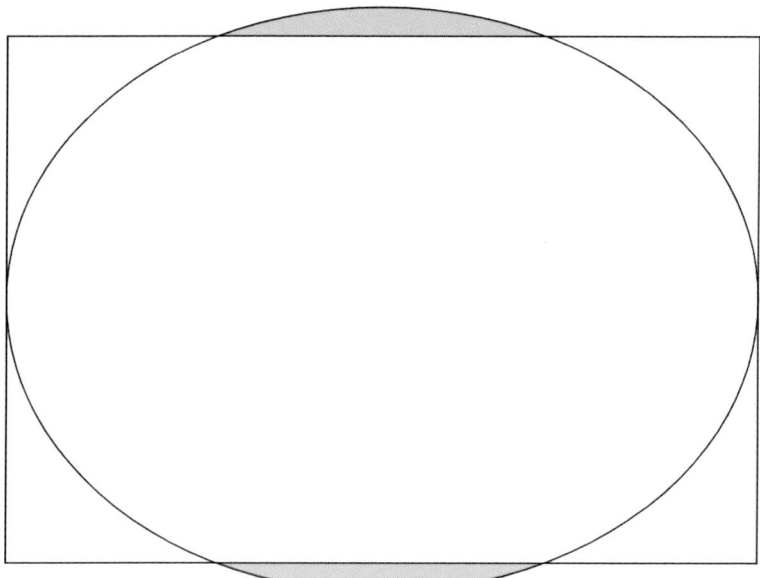

Serlio's fourth construction would not fit into the rectangle allowed by the Church's dimensions.

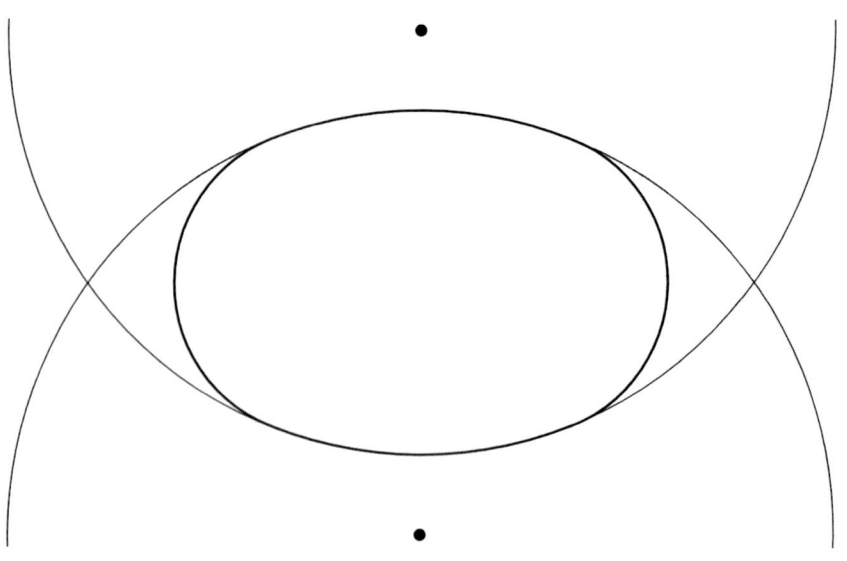

The four circles I used to create the arc's, modifying Serlio's fourth to fit his oval into the rectangle given by the church's dimensions. The four points of intersection are shown here.

The oval dome and the continuous cornice supporting the three conches and the area above the entry.

As with the construction of any oval, its drawing is "automatic" once the lengths of the two axes are known and the centers for the four arcs are established. I knew the lengths of the two axes – 11.7871m for the main axis CA (52.7623 palmi) and 8.0535m for the minor axis BD (36.0497 palmi). Now for the centers of the arcs. I decided to establish a center on the minor axis line (J) (this yielded a radius for the circle creating the upper arc equal to half the major axis such that OA = OJ). Next I established the connection locus (where the "upper" and "side arc" will connect - where the two arcs are tangent to each other) and connected the arcs, repeating the process for the other three quadrants.[31]

For the impost for the lantern oval I selected a length for the major axis equal to the difference of the impost axes values (52 ½ palmi - 35 ¾ palmi = 16 ¾ palmi). I then chose two centers on the horizontal or major axis four palmi away from the center of symmetry. I used the endpoints of the minor axis on the oval impost for the two centers on the vertical axis.[32] I followed the same connection locus methodology to determine the connection locus. It is interesting to note that the triangle I created in the half oval using this methodology is almost equilateral; i.e. I used the angles from the canonical oval.[33]

Detail from the lantern with its octagonal cornice, resting on an oval impost. The rays of the Holy Spirit in gold.

---

[31] Id. 24, 25, 26 figure 3.6. This method of drawing the oval uses the "Connection Locus" or "CL"; Professor Mazzotti cites F. Ragazzo for "first conjector[ing]" this. 128, fn 21. See also Id. at 11, figure 2.6. Any errors in my description above are all my own. Id. 131, figure 7.10.
[32] Id.130, 132, figure 7.11.
[33] Id. 130.

Detail of the lantern and its oval impost and octagonal cornice.

I should point out the human fallibility involved in executing architectural plans: the final impost of the dome is actually slightly egg-shaped, compressed along the longitudinal axis on the side of the altar; moreover, the longitudinal axis of the lantern is slightly rotated, and finally the four levels of the coffer decoration do not belong to perfectly horizontal planes.[34]

Castanza and the barrel vault at Santa Costanza. The pattern I borrowed.

Detail of the coffers of the domes: the cross, the octagon with inscribed circle and the hexagons, above the cornice palmettes, the small globes of universality, the Cross of the Trinitarians.

---

[34] Id. 123. Professor Mazzotti calls this out from the stereoscopic photogrammetric survey of the Carlino conducted by many and supervised by the architects Margherita Caputo and Elena Ippoliti. Id. 122.

The coffered dome, the lantern with the Holy Spirit.

The Coffering of the Dome

I made the dome of San Carlo as a "semi-ellipsoid shell", if you will, over which I placed a stucco coffering of octagons, crosses, and hexagons, all interlocking. Although my product is indeed stunning to the viewer, the pattern I used was hardly unique, being found in the ancient drum mosaic at Santa Costanza, the aisle vaults of San Pietro, made by my uncle Carlo Maderno, and the ceiling at the Cancelleria. I used directly Serlio's Terzo Libro which contains a woodcut of the pattern from Santa Costanza the "*Tempio di Bacco.*"[35] I was, however, the first to use the pattern on an ellipsoidal surface. I brought together a honeycomb pattern with a radial system with ribs.[36] I also expanded on what had been done before by placing circles inside the octagons. Moreover, I rejected the use of any ornamentation, like gilt studs or rosettes, which usually populate such a pattern. I gave the partitions in the pattern high relief, and I kept the fields within the partitions free of any ornament so that the contours would be clear and clean.[37]

The Paraclete in the lantern.

Detail of the cornice.

---

[35] Steinberg 219-224, quote.
[36] Id. 225, quotes.
[37] Id. 227, 228, 229 quotes.

The Lantern

I placed at the top of the lantern the Dove of the Holy Spirit, within an equilateral triangle, symbol of the Paraclete. My dove is not hovering, and I did not use clouds here, so as to put the focus on the Spirit. A circle envelopes the triangle, golden rays then project to the surrounding octagonal cornice of the lantern. The octagon then rests on an oval base.[38]

Left Photo: Here the continuous cornice, supported by the sixteen engaged composite columns, then above are the conches and pendentives supporting the impost of the oval dome.

Bottom Photo: The small beautiful church of San Carlino. Eight of its sixteen columns. The conch above the main altar. The enveloping continuous cornice.

---

[38] Id. 257-259. Professor Steinberg notes that the lantern is one of the zones of the church, all the zones are "shaped to the same forms." The lantern is seen as a "procession", the dome a "juxtaposition", the church proper as a "reciprocal penetration". From German idealist metaphysics, the three zones can reflect respectively, the "properties" of "time, "space", and "matter". Id 259-261.

The Columns of the Main Body of the Church

When you enter the Carlino, I think you experience five things all at once: the brilliant and dominating oval white dome above with its magnificent coffering of cross and octagon and hexagon, the small form of the central space in the shape of an ovalized cross which is brilliantly white, the uninterrupted cornice that ties the small space into one, almost as the ribbon on a package, the pendentives below the dome (these have de Matha's vision at Mass and the wind that blew the Trinitarians safely back to Italy) and the arches between them, and finally, but not least, the sixteen wall socketed composite columns that draw the elements together vertically.

As you enter the church, look up and back to see above the hidden window above the portal the sign of the Trinitarians.

My columns serve three functions: they provide support for the entablature, they carry the burden of the pediments and they support the arches, and finally through the pendentives they provide the support for the dome.[39]

You can read these columns in three separate rhythms. In the first count, there are four groups of four, which corresponds to Carlino as a "quarterfoil".[40] There are four chapels, each of the arches of the chapels rests on a pair of the columns. Then I have two additional "aedicular" columns behind these first two. I made it clear for you that the first two columns which bear the arches were twins by creating like bases and capitals for

---

[39] Id. 173, quotes.
[40] Id. 173. The three rhythms – counts – are brilliantly described in perfect detail by Professor Steinberg in his Chapter IV: The Articulation.

them. As you see, the volutes of the capitals of the arch-bearing columns curl inward, not outward. The outer two in each group of four chapel columns are like this.

The second rhythm can be deciphered from a view downward from the pendentives. The pairs of columns can once again be twinned by their special capitals. These pairs hold the straight entablature sections of the chamfered diagonal. In the drawing of the plan for the main body of the church I explained to you above, you can see that these columns function as the end terms for the chamfers which make up the octagon of the nave.[41] The eight columns that are inside the chapels are twinned as well, serving as aedicular posts. These, as you can see, all have "normal unfurled volutes".[42]

The third rhythm is based upon the separation between the three altars and the entrance.[43] The four groups of four columns collect three adjacent "travees" into "coherent" wall units - I would tell you that you can look at this as the three exposed sides of a crossing pier.[44] The substructure for Carlino was put up in four connected quadrants which support the entire structure, and each of these corresponds to this described grouping of four columns. Please note that the shells of the chapels are not bearing walls.[45]

---

[41] Id. quotes 173. See Albertina 173.
[42] Id. 172-174 quotes, figures 80, 81, 82.
[43] Id. figure 82.
[44] Id. quote from 175, also fn 5.
[45] Id. 177-178.

Four of the composite columns, the conches supported by the piers, in turn supporting the pendentives which in turn carry the dome.

As I have told you, I had the cross, the octagon and the oval all in mind when I planned Carlino. The first rhythm of columns corresponds to the cruciform, where the members are the paired columns beneath the arches, opening on aediculae and perspectives at the four cardinal points.[46] For the octagon, the second rhythm has two columns from each group of four which follows or creates the octagon.[47] And for the oval, the third rhythm envelopes the oval form of the church.[48]

Looking back towards the entrance.

The columns of the Carlino are an impressive part of the creation. They are large and powerful and they serve to bring the eye back to the walls, which curve their way around the octagonal nave. Their bulk in such a small church gives them extraordinary importance and that bulk helps to unify the admittedly complex shape I gave the church.[49]

---

[46] Id. figure 85a. See the Professor's drawing which corresponds to the description set forth in the text.
[47] Id. figure 85b. See the Professor's drawing which corresponds to the description set forth in the text.
[48] Id. figure 85c. See the Professor's drawing which corresponds to the description set forth in the text.
[49] Wittkower 201. Professor Wittkower in discussing the "overlapping triads" says they may be likened to the "warp and the woof of the wall texture. In musical terms, the arrangement may be compared to the structure of a fugue".

Columns, cornice, conch, arch, pendentive—magnificent I am sure you agree.

Before I leave the columns, I must speak to the bases and capitals. These bases may well be the only ones of their kind, for half of them are trapezoid, and the other half pentagonal.⁵⁰ The ones that are five sides support the paired columns at the straight bays.

These have "faces" with two fronts – one accommodates its column "neighbor" to the left, and the other accommodates its column "neighbor" to the right, which enables continuity from base to base. Then where the walls bend, as in the chapels, I made the bases trapezoidal. The sides of these move to the point from which I had the chapel set out from the plan. At those points where I had a wall moving to the rear at an angle (for example, where the chapel meets a straight diagonal bay), the base of the capital follows the same direction as the wall. Please note how I kept the various elements in synchronized fashion. Note that the arris on the "bi-frontal face" of a pentagonal base matches the break in the entablature and also the spring of the arch.⁵¹

A capital. See the Pomegranate with its gem-like seeds.

---

⁵⁰ Steinberg 194, fn 14. The Round Temple at Baalbek has three column bases which are five-sided. Borromini also used Pentagonal bases for the wooden balustrade at the library at the Casa. Professor Steinberg notes that Baalbek was known in France by 1650, and thus Borromini's knowledge of it is "probable but not certain".
⁵¹ Id. quote, 194-198, figures 0v at 195, 91, 92, 93 at 197-198. Sadly, eight of these column bases were mutilated (1778) when confessionals were installed. Steinberg 198, figure 93, 199, fn 15.

I used Corinthian capitals at the Carlino, some with volutes curling inward, some outward. These were most decidedly not a "capriccio" as some have suggested.[52] Hadrian's Villa in fact employs this device. Four pairs of the Carlino capitals have an inward furl, the rest furl outward. The aedicular columns in the chapels have normally everted scrolls (they stand on trapezoid bases). Columns on pentagonal bases (those that flank the pendentive bays) have inverted volutes. As you can see, all the columns are twinned. A final note: Each pair also has distinguishing elements within the capital. Capitals with turned-out volutes have pomegranates in place of the egg-and-dart, while capitals with turned-in volutes have continuous laurel festoons.[53]

Looking back at the façade wall, above the entry portal. Here the symbol of the Trinitarians, and I must say exquisite stucco decoration.

---

[52] Id. 201.
[53] Id. 202, fn 18, 204, figure 97.

The Balance of the Articulation

When you enter San Carlino, I feel it safe to say that you are impressed with the beauty contained in such a small space, and with the undulation of the walls, the height and bulk of the columns, the oval dome atop the pendentives, carried by the arches, the niched chapels. Yet for many the powerful entablature brings it all together. Michelangelo used recurrent horizontal accents-string courses or bandings (as at the Julius II monument at San Pietro in Vincoli and in the apse at San Pietro) and I followed him here at Carlino.[54] The entablature is amazingly unbroken as it follows the undulating perimeter of the church.[55] I believe that certainly I created a very powerful architecture, which literally snakes around the church, remaining straight under the pendentives, then bending to make four substantial nicchioni (small niches). Please see that the straight architecture under the pendentives follows the sides of the invisible triangles of my plan. The nicchioni are "deep" on the long axis and "shallow" on the short axis.[56] I placed oval roundels in the pendentives. Then I have arconi jump from "pier to pier".[57] You will see, I am sure, in the piers, angled as they are, and with their pendentives and arconi, a great similarity to the crossing at San Pietro. But you will also see a similarity to Raphael's end wall in the garden loggia at the Villa Madama (my niches ended up not in isocephalous form as are Raphael's).[58]

One of the pendentives, held by the cherubim.

In my articulation, I was fond of the "elegant superimposition of orders", as used by Raphael who in turn took it from the antique. Here at Carlino I opened up the wall more than Raphael did, and I made the structure more skeletal, more in keeping with my Northern traditions and gothic subconscious. In doing this, you will see I used very little marble here - the door in each pier has a marble architrave – and that is it.[59]

I carried the entablature over each of the doors in the piers. I then carried it over apertures to the left and right. At this point the entablature is stucco over brick, polished to look like marble.[60]

---

[54] Blunt 29.
[55] Wittkower 199.
[56] Connors, Gubbio 594, quotes.
[57] Id. quote.
[58] Id. 595, and figure 14, 596. Albertina drawing 205 (figure 12) shows these still isocephalous. Villa Madama is in Borromini's Albertina drawings 416r and 920.
[59] Id. 595, some direct quotes.
[60] Id. Professor Connors tells us that when John Evelyn saw San Carlino in 1644 he thought it was "built all of new white stone".

Please note, once again, that I did not use color in the Carlino, or at least very little – the painted altar pieces with gilt frames and stucco panels above and below the large niche, and the dark of the wrought iron grills of the chapels are the exceptions.[61] I aimed for a church sleek and streamlined. And so only in the deep cavetto of the cornicione will you find decoration. In keeping with the simplicity, I gave the church many cherubs, but no angels and no statutes.[62]

Seven cherubs, above the symbol of the Trinitarians.

---

[61] Blunt 68.

[62] Connors Gubbio 595. See Borromini's drawing of the cornice at Albertina drawing 1409. Also see fn 33. The two stucco figures of Jean de Matha and Felix de Valois (members of the Order) in the niches near the high altar were made 1900-1909 by Isidora Uribesalgo. Professor Connors: "many small cherubs…peek out of corners with lively attention."

More of my trademark cherubs, all with different expressions and hair.

One of the many cherubs at Carlino. Each one has a different expression, all have flowing hair.

Detail of my cherub.

The Two Side Chapels

The larger chapel on the left was dedicated by the Trinitarians to their benefactor Cardinal Francesco Barberini, really in thanks to his uncle who was responsible for the grant in 1636 of complete independence of the Scalzi from the unreformed Trinitarians.[63] I took as my model here the imperial columnar sarcophagi and also the closeby Barberini gardens.[64] Some have said that this chapel is "an essay in allegorical botany" of the sort found in Giovanni Battista Ferrari's *Flora*.[65] I placed the altar on the main axis of the chapel so that it could face into the central nave of the church.[66]

The side chapel dedicated to Cardinal Barberini, patron of the Trinitarians.

The smaller chapel on the right is dedicated to the Crucifixion. Here I gave the chapel trim and noble mouldings (I did not use any figurative decoration except the altar piece) and a central oval that is recessed from the cornice thus seeming to be "suspended by invisible forces".[67] Unfortunately, the area available for this chapel, also hexagonal, was so restricted that I had to put the altar on the left, against the wall backing on to the cloister, and the door on one of the smaller sides.[68]

A look from below at the columns, cornice, and conch, with the half hidden pediment that creates an illusion of greater depth. Note the alternating volutes in the capitals, half inverted. The oval above supported by the pendentives supported by the piers below.

---

[63] Id. 595, also figure 10.
[64] Id.
[65] Id.
[66] Blunt 68, quote.
[67] Connors Gubbio 595, quotes, figure 11. Professor Connors says this is more like "an essay on magnetism".
[68] Blunt 68.

The Coffering and Gables of the Chapels

I must call these out for you as they are important for the formation of the cruciform in the church (the symbol of the Trinitarians). I was working with a very small space which precluded, of course, extensions of the arms of the Crucifix. And so I resorted to illusion. The altars in the chapels can be seen to "emerge from, or recede into, a depth that is indeterminate".[69] I lavished much energy on the gilded frames for the paintings over the altars. Here I allowed some color, in a church interior that is my customary white. Note that the altar paintings themselves are of the illusionist style of the day, perhaps best executed by my contemporary Pietro da Cortona at the Palazzo Barberini.

And now for my coffers. I made the graduated coffers in the conches of the half domes diminish downward instead of the standard upward. I was fond of the conch, it being the symbol of eternity. The device I used make them seem to recede, and facilitate a cruciform by "deepening the lobes of the quarterfoil," as some have said.[70] The cross, if you will, extends itself beyond the actual limits of my plan. Some have described it as "optically adjusting" the coffering to make the nicchioni "seem deeper than they are".[72]

And now for the gables, the pediments in the chapels. With these, I was able to remove from your view the bottom of the shell. This was no longer an apse. This now seems like a barrel vault.[73] If you visit the Villa Madama, you will see an illusionist barrel vault made of stucco.[74] I created a true conch to be sure, but one that looks like a tunnel with parallel sides.[75] I was able through the pediments placed as they were to create the illusion that you are looking at a barrel vault which has been sheltered by an aedicula of two columns.[76]

The tradition of illusionist barrel vaults, of course, goes back to Bramante. And see, if you can, the false choir at San Satiro in Milan, and the Santuario dell'Incoronata at Lodi. One of the chapels at the Santuario, the Nicchione della Cantoria, in fact, has the coffering pattern that I was to think of most when I made San Carlino's dome. I counted on this tradition to work for me "in reverse", so that you would see a barrel vault.[77]

As a final note, see that in the capitals here I used open pomegranates, like those at the Temple of Solomon (1 Kings 7:18).

---

[69] Steinberg 138, direct quotes. Professor Connors relates that "because the space on this tiny site was so constrained there was no question of having a normal Greek cross, with four equal arms." Connors, San Carlo 1.
[70] Id. 138, 139 figure 65, 140.
[71] Id. 139, direct quote.
[72] Id. 139, 140, the last comment here comes from Professor Connors. Connors, San Carlo 1.
[73] Id. 143.
[74] Id. figure 68.
[75] Id. 143, quote.
[76] Id. quote.
[77] Id. 146, quote.

The Lateral Chapels

On the south side is the altar of Sant'Agnese, which has the relics of Santi Claudio e Maxime, on the north side is the altar of Sant'Ursula, which has the relics of San Theodulo.[78]

The Exterior of the Dome and Lantern

I had special pleasure in the dome at San Carlino, for the one I chose is in the Lombard fashion where the cupola is enclosed in a cylinder of masonry.[79] This method takes the issue of the lateral thrust and disposes of it, and thus there is no need for further buttressing. This dome is like the dome of the Pantheon in that it begins to narrow only at the top where it takes three steps.

    The exterior lantern I designed is oval like the dome, and I gave it six-curved re-entrant bays,[80] which have different widths and which I separated with single Tuscan columns. The reader will appreciate the similarity to the circular temple at Baalbek and also to Montano's drawing.[81] I ended at the top with a flourish- there are further steps, and then an orb with a cross on top.

---

[78] Hill, fn 20, citing Fra Juan's Relatione del Convento 82.
[79] Blunt 80.
[80] Blunt 81, quotes.
[81] Id.

The lower simpler church articulated with simple flat pilaster bands. The vault is depressed just a few centimeters. I created the feeling of a depressed sail.

The Lower Church

In the lower church, I created a very simple decorated space for the monks. I designed the crypt with virtually the same size as the church above, but simpler, with very flat pilaster bands. Two of my drawings show additional features (columns in the semi-circular chancel and behind the altar) and the decoration of the vault - which through diagonal framing lines draw a rhomboid- again a scheme of two equilateral triangles with one common side. The pilasters support a low vault, which is lowered by a few centimeters in the center. I used acute arches here. Above the lunettes you can see I recessed the arches to a great extent. My intention with the vault and its central lower area was to create the impression of a depressed sail, which flows out to the walls.[82]

The Cappelletta

On the Gospel side of the crypt, I made a small chapel which is underneath the Cappella della Madonna.[83] Remarkably, it is in its original condition. I made a near regular octagon, and gave it convex diagonal sides.[84] I drew my ideas from Baiae, the Small Baths at Hadrian's Villa, and the Sepulcro Statiz Poeta on the Gianicolo hill, but none of these has the break-out articulation and vaulting that I gave the Cappelletta, which completely abandons the classical horizontal tradition.

---

[82] Albertina drawings 180, 223v, Steinberg 180; Portoghesi 46, quotes, Blunt 61, 62. Professor Portoghesi likens the "depressed sail" "flow[ing] out to the walls" to a cavern or the hold of a ship.
[83] Steinberg, figures 127, 128, 129, 130, 131, 132, 133.
[84] Steinberg, 267, quotes.

I designed this chapel, dear reader, for my tomb. I requested permission of the Padri Trinitari to be buried in the lower church at San Carlino in 1666, some twenty-five years after I built the Carlino. I did not tell the Padri of my intentions when I built the church, for fear my enemies would somehow tamper with my desire.[85]

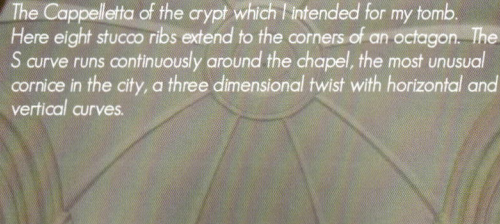

The Cappelletta of the crypt which I intended for my tomb. Here eight stucco ribs extend to the corners of an octagon. The S curve runs continuously around the chapel, the most unusual cornice in the city, a three dimensional twist with horizontal and vertical curves.

---

[85] Professor Connors believes Borromini was thinking of the main altar of the crypt for his tomb. Connors, Stienberg Review 284 ("My guess, on the other hand, is that Borromini was thinking not of this small chapel but of the high altar in the crypt, which is redesigned on Albertina 180").

The diameter of the chapel is only 223.6cm. I articulated the corners of this small space with thin pilasters and thin stucco ribs which extend into the vault. I used the ribs to create alternating plane and convex gores. The crown of the vault is barely 12 feet from the pavement. Here I had the concentric circles "bring the ascent of the ribs and the billowing motion to rest". If you were to place this on a ground plan the eight ribs would radiate from the central circle to the corners of an octagon. The diagonals of this octagon become reentrant curves, thus making a form of cross. Here, make sure you see the light shaft to the windowlet leading to the street.[86] The crossed windowlet and the shaft are angled so that the east light would have struck the forward part of the floor, towards the church altar – my intended tomb!

Bottom photo: From below you can best see the sinusoidal curve of the façade, and the wings of the herms that surround San Carlo. Note the six and eight pointed stars in a wreath under the entry lintel (the Star of David - wisdom - and the Chigi star of Alexander VII).

[86] Steinberg 268, 269, figures 132, 133, quotes.

I placed round-headed niches of differing dimensions in the walls. In the straight bays, these have high arches and flat backs, while in the diagonal bays, the arches are low and the backs are rounded. Thus the large niches "break through" the entablature right up to the cornice, while the entablature is intact over the smaller niches. I combined the convexity of the bays with the waves I created horizontally and vertically for the S curve of the cornice, which runs continuously around the chapel – a three-dimensional twist that I dare to say no other architect could have created in such a small place. I combined movement and variety to create perhaps one of the most unusual cornices in the city,[87] something that is as I have said, a complete break from the classical tradition of horizontal zoning.

[87] Blunt 62, 63, 64 quotes.

The Facade

The façade of the monastery of San Carlino was made 1662-1664 and the main façade was not made until 1665-1667. I took my inspiration for this main façade from the rock tomb of Petra – a late Imperial work – which of course was still undiscovered but which by some miracle was in the drawings of G. B. Montano, of which I have told you I had use.[88] The sculptural pieces for these were made by others in 1682 (these include San Carlo, and also Jean de Matha (with a theologian's book) and Felix de Valois (with the crown of France). The latter two founders of the Trinitarian Order. I should perhaps have saved this discussion of the making of the facade for later in this guide (since my style and work changed and I would say matured even further over time), but I feel I should cover the church in one place, since you may, if you are foolish, only visit once. I began the drawings in the mid 1630's, and they were revolutionary for those times. All my drawings utilized curves. The key concept of the baroque, of course, is movement. In the pursuit of movement, I sought to move away from facades which are all on one plane and instead to introduce the curve. Prior to this time, the architectural tradition was that a church façade should be designed in parallel planes.

The beautiful curving façade of San Carlino, with the saint framed by my angel herms, concavity and convexity in full form.

---

[88] Blunt, 39, 43.

I know that Pietro da Cortona used a curve at SS Luca e Martina, which was begun in 1635. But I had been planning San Carlino before that. And to say that I invented the curved façade would be to disregard Antonio da Sangallo's Porta di S. Spirito, and Francesco Ricchino had used a curve in 1629 for the Collegio Elvetico in Milan.[89] Work on the façade was delayed until 1665, and my final plan is substantially different from my plans of the 1630's, except that the curve is still central.

A cherub, below the cornice with small cherubs with horseshoe vine in place of the egg and dart.

The façade at San Carlino was my last major work. In 1655 I had been discharged from both the Oratory of San Filippo and the church of Sant'Agnese. Subsequently I suffered a further humiliation when- I believe through jealousy- my church of Sant'Ivo was criticized as chimeric, and even structurally unsound. Although I continued my work, and was able to achieve, I think, great successes, my mind - and then my body - were increasingly troubled. Therefore to produce the final designs in 1665 was a great effort of my mind, soul, and body.

In the final plan, I completed what I truly believe was a virtuoso in movement. It has been called "the most musical and movemented of all [my] works". I created a continuous double S-curve[90] - a sinusoidal profile.[91] These curves came primarily from the curves of Martino Bassi's reconstruction of San Lorenzo in Milano, which I had witnessed.[92] The central bay here is convex, taking its form from the semi-circular bay behind it- a very good link with the interior. The adjacent side bays are concave. I kept with my geometric plan, for the arcs of these side bays have the same radius as the semi-circular bay of the entrance vestibule!

I organized the façade structure into two registers. The major columns attach to the cornice. The minor columns that are astride make up a second register that accentuates the rising height of the major columns. The wall recedes. I derived this form of articulation for San Carlino from Michelangelo's Capitoline Palace and also the façade of San Pietro, where Master Maderno continued Michelangelo's theme round the outside of the dome and tribune.

---

[89] Id. 76.
[90] Id. 80. The "musical movemented" language is from Professor Connors. Connors, San Carlo 1, 15.
[91] Portoghesi 300.
[92] Hibbard 37, 38.

I placed the deer with the Trinitarian cross in its antlers on the facade. Jean de Matha and Felix de Valois, founders of the order, came across this deer on their way from France to Rome.

From the façade, the central bay. This convex bay with the central window I repeated at the tomb of Sergio IV at the Lateran and the façade at Sette Dolori.

I was not able to finish the second story of the façade. I had completed the four plinths of the upper story and the balustrade that is in front of the central window. My nephew Bernardo then stepped in, finishing the upper story 1674-1676. Regrettably he introduced some elements contrary to my thinking (he even had one of Cavalier Bernini's pupils, Antonio Raggi, make the statue of San Carlo).

The façade consists of three bays- the center convex and the two outside concave. In the lower tier these are tied together by my unbroken, waving entablature.[93] In the upper tier the three bays are concave. The entablature is broken into three. My plan did not call for the second tier to be as tall as the lower tier. And the angels supporting the medallion are not to my liking or style, but something the Cavalier Bernini would have ordered. The design of the oval aedicula in the middle bay is, however, my work, and very like the tombs I did at San Giovanni in Laterano for Alexander VII.

Saint Charles Borromeo (by Antonio Raggi) in the niche above the central door. The herms and their wings form the frame and the cornice, one herm looks to the outside, the other to the inside.

---

[93] Professor Connors provides the evidence that Borromini made the plinths and balustrade. Connors, San Carlo 18. Wittkower, Art and Architecture 205.

I would ask you dear reader to enjoy the herms I placed in the lower tier, around the niche for San Carlino. These herms have the ambiguous, juvenile heads of angels, and disproportionate but beautiful wings, two of which rise up to create a protecting arch for the saint. The façade, in addition to San Carlo (here because he was a reformer like the Trinitarians), de Matha and de Valois, has the snow-white deer with a cross in its antlers that de Matha and de Valois saw on their way from France to Rome. The ornament I gave the façade teams with foliage; the tendrils that I wove into the crown, the palm fronds on the oval window frames and in the consoles and the laurel leaves.[94]

I would like to bring you now to the adjoining façade of the monastery, which I made 1662-1664. I added the Travertine portal you see, and substantially modified the windows.[95] I used flat stucco bands to tie the windows together.[96] I added the large insignia up above and the portal. I placed curves at the sides of the three steps (the Strada Pia was so close I could not further curve the steps but had to leave them flat in the middle).[97]

Detail of the steps to the cloister portal.

Then I took up these curves and continued them into the jams of the door. I created deep mouldings for these jambs (deep mouldings had become one of my trademarks!). I created the best element in the hood. It is far more complex than my most famous hood in the window at Palazzo Barberini. The latter had a flat center and projected jambs at 45 degrees. Here at Carlino, I curved the whole hood- it is a three dimensional curve, uninterrupted.[98]

Right Photo: The travertine door to the cloister. The hood and cornice are very special. A three dimensional uninterrupted curve. The winged cherub holds the medallion and connects the hood to the door. The three steps make use of the scant space to the street and continue into the jambs of the door.

---

[94] Id. 205. For the ornament language, Connors, San Carlo 18.
[95] Portoghesi 298.
[96] Blunt 81.
[97] Id.
[98] Id.

Detail of the cornice over the lower level of the façade.

This curve serves to fuse the three elements you see at Barberini into one. The winged cherub heads sit atop the door, holding the medallion and connecting the door to the hood. These four winged cherubs became my signature or trademark. My inspirations were the fifteenth century lifesize full length cherubs with four wings that flank the apse windows of the Milan Cathedral.[99] I found the cherub to be ideal for linking one architectural element to another and I used them at the door to the saint's room at the Oratory Casa, all of the keystones in the Oratory, all the covers here at Carlino and in the refectory, the doorcases at Sant'Ivo and its dome, and the inner and outer aisles at the Lateran and the tombs I redid there.

Finally, before we leave San Carlino, a word about the campanile. Thirty years after its construction, I was very dissatisfied with this campanile which had gone up with the exterior of the dome, especially because I felt it was inadequate in light of the final height of the planned façade.[100] I designed a new one in the last years of my life with larger dimensions, with concave facades formed by aediculae with supporting paired columns (this is similar to what I had done for the windows at the Propaganda Fide). I could not finish this campanile and again my well meaning nephew Bernado stepped in. Again, he did not do so well, I am sorry to say. I will say that the cornice and the belfry are representative of my work.

---

[99] Downes, Opus 337.
[100] Portoghesi 299.

And permit me a final word about Carlino: to it I owed my career. I had accomplished what many thought impossible- to create a church that was ingenious (artificioso), fantastic (capriccioso), rare and extraordinary in the smallest and most inconvenient of places (all praise from my Trinitarian client). And it was done for remarkably low cost (though certainly far more than the Order wanted to spend), as the official receipts show. I developed much of my style at Carlino: the elimination of corners, the use only of white, the alternating balusters, the triangular method, the oval, the cherubs, the curve, the convex and the concave. Because of this church, the Oratorians and those who were in charge of the University of Rome now gave me commissions for their buildings. Someone has rightfully said: "[Carlino] was the one [commission] that stood closest to [my] heart for [my] whole life."[101]

---

[101] Blunt 84. The quote is from Professor Connors. Connors, San Carlo 1.

The unimposing entrance to the church.

CHAPTER FOUR

Santa Lucia in Selci

The nave. The Landi chapel on the left.

In 1637-1638, I was brought into this small church near San Martino ai Monti to finish the decoration of what Master Maderno had constructed. The second chapel on the left is the Landi chapel which is my principal work here, which has been changed, of course, in subsequent renovative work. My style is still here though, and see the cornice where I used the cherub head with wings in place of the common use of egg-and-tongue. I was to repeat this over two decades later in the cornice at Sant'Ivo. The cartouche at the top of the archivolt is special – see the emblem of the river that springs from a sacred mountain and arrives at the sea.[1] I call your attention to the two kneeling cherubs flanking the alterpiece gable who make anthropomorphic volutes – like the ones on the façade of Sant'Andrea della Valle. I made the angels here almost like dolls, in accordance with the wishes of the nuns.[2]

Detail of the Landi Chapel.

---

[1] Blunt 19, Portoghesi 61.
[2] Steinberg 361, quote (anthropomorphic), Portoghesi 61.

The Landi Chapel on the left. In the cornice I used cherub heads and wings in place of the traditional egg and dart. I also used the dolphin in the curvature above the painting. The two angels are formed as volutes.

The singing gallery above the entrance bears the Barberini sun, the anchor, an olive branch, a trumpet, and above in the oval is the Trinity painted by the Cavalier d'Arpino.[3] In this gallery, I attempted to draw back the cornice and "flatten" it out on the wall. Then I extended the screen to either side so as to create a continuity of transparency.[4]

The singing gallery above the entrance. See the Barberini emblem of the sun and the anchors at the ends of the corbels. And olive branches above.

---

[3] Portoghesi 61. In looking at the painting currently in place, it does not appear to be the Trinity.
[4] Portoghesi 61, quotes on the cornice and the screen. The Professor's terminology here.

CHAPTER FIVE

The Oratory and Monastery (Casa) of San Filippo Neri

San Filippo Romolo Neri (1515-1595) (the "Third Apostle of Rome") came to Rome in 1533 or 1534. In his first years, he was noted for his attention to the poor in the hospitals (much like my patron San Carlo Borromeo), but he was not an ordained man and really lacked direction. In 1544 he went through an experience, I would call it mystical, which manifested itself in tremors, detachment of his ribs, and an enlarged heart. After his recovery, he embarked on a life for Christ. With Padre Persiano Rosa, he established in 1548 a confraternity of laymen who cared for poor pilgrims coming to Rome. He was ordained in 1551 and went to live as a chaplain at San Girolamo della Carita. There he founded the Oratory, a confraternity of Catholic laymen. He was primarily a confessor; he drew more and more penitents to himself, and every afternoon he gave a discourse to the Oratory, and informed ragionamento sopra il libro. The word "Oratory" came to be used for the room (which you can think of as a combination of hall and chapel) in which this new devotion was held.[1] Over time, people began to call this new devotion itself "Oratory". A book would always be read aloud, and the Filippo and one or two of his close adherents would engage in a teaching dialogue. The lives of the saints and church history followed, and the meeting always ended with professional musicians singing religious motets.

San Carlo greatly admired Filippo and tried to get him to place the headquarters of the Filippini in Milan, but in 1575 Pope Gregory XIII gave official recognition to the Congregation of the Oratory and gave them the little church of Santa Maria in Vallicella in Rome.

Filippo insisted on rule by consensus (I mention this to you as the need for consensus among the Order was to become a great source of frustration for me). The confraternity decided to rebuild the church on a much larger scale in order to accommodate the growing faithful. Although work began in 1575, due to lack of funds the church was not finished until after Filippo's death, in 1606. It came to be called the Chiesa Nuova. Filippo's fellow Fathers lived in the Casa Vecchia, old homes and structures attached to the east side of the church. Filippo himself lived in the Casa Vecchia for twelve years, and died there in 1595. He indulged himself with a rooftop loggia, for he loved to pray, alone, on rooftops, hilltops, and even treetops! Closer to God!

The most important place in the Casa Vecchia was the Oratory, a dark and damp place that nonetheless served the growing congregation well. The need for a new Casa was clear, and after Filippo was canonized in 1622, the order grew even more quickly. The Romagnan nobleman Virgilio Spada (1596-1662) joined the order in 1622; he was ultimately to become the leader, the Preposito, and my great protector, advocate and one of my few very close friends. I met him in 1635 during the Padre's restoration project for the Palazzo Spada, which his family had acquired from the Capodiferro in 1632.

The properties to the West and North of the Chiesa were then acquired, including the Chiesa di Santa Cecilia, in whose name the new Casa and Oratory were dedicated.

---

[1] Connors, Oratory 6.

From 1621-1636 there was great planning for the new Casa, which would have not only an Oratory, but also a sacristy for the church, a refectory, cloisters, porters' quarters, a kitchen, a library, and a dormitory. Only the sacristy and a small group of rooms that were near the chapel of Filippo were constructed in the years before I arrived. The architect Paolo Maruscelli (1596-1649) became chief architect in 1624. He was to work on the Casa for 13 years. I was to succeed him and work on the Casa for the next 13 years. Senor Maruscelli is responsible for the overall plan of the Casa, and indeed the Oratory. As I write this at the end of my life, I regret how I treated Signor Maruscelli, which caused him to be removed. It was his plan that I was able to execute. Signor Maruscelli was responsible for the Caption Project of 1627- these drawings included the whole Casa, in great detail, marking every room with a caption number. The Oratory was placed exactly where it is today. There were to be three courtyards- one on the south of the Casa, just to the north of the Oratory, a large garden courtyard on the north, and a small service court on the northeast.[2] The project was organized around an enfilade: this was a door to the outside that allowed the passerby a clear vista several hundred feet into the interior. In fairness to Signor Maruscelli, whose work I criticized at the time (and as I was to learn to my great suffering later), he had to work with the Oratorian democracy, responding to their criticisms and their ideas. All the plans had to proceed through the consulta, a review process where the design was submitted to other architects for criticism. Counter designs were often submitted. The patrons - here the Oratorians - were free to accept any features of these that suited them- imagine!- and the architect was obliged to accept them. After Signor Maruscelli's plan was finally accepted, construction began in 1629, and by 1637 the sacristy, service rooms, corridor and the area around Filippo's chapel were finished.

In 1636, I was engaged with others to work on the interior decoration of the sacristy, specifically, in my case, on the high altar. It was through this work that I came to know the Preposito, or head of the Order, Padre Angelo Saluzzi.

Right Photo: The sacristy. I worked on the high altar with others. My first work at the Casa.

---

[2] Id. 15. All of the discussion here is from Connors, Oratory.

At the beginning of 1637 construction of the Oratory was to begin, but there was a problem with Signor Maruscelli's plan. The windows of the Oratory did not relate properly to the bays of the adjoining cloister. At the corner of the cloister, which was astride the middle of the oratory, there was already in place a thick pier. This thick pier made the spacing in the cloister irregular. Evenly spaced windows in the Oratory would not correspond to the openings in the cloister. I was asked by Padre Saluzzi to draw a solution, and I came upon the idea of inserting two loggia-porticoes, at either end of the Oratory. I then made the middle pier of the Oratory- corresponding to the corner bay of the cloister- wider than the others in the Oratory. This then matched the troublesome corner pier in the cloister. I then put a niche for a bust of the saint in this wider north wall pier of the Oratory, and a corresponding pulpit on the south wall.

After I solved the problem of fenestration, I was asked for more plans. There were other problems that needed resolution. The windows of the sacristy, which was on the north side of the cloister adjoining the Oratory, did not have proper relationship to the windows of the Oratory. I came up with the solution of double windows for the sacristy, one of each of the double windows is a sham window. Another problem lay in the fact that the level of the sacristy, and the Casa, was 4 palmi higher than the church. The portal to the vestibule of the Oratory had to be on the same level as the adjoining, and more important, Chiesa Nuova. My solution here was to put at the end of the vestibule that was inside the main entrance a flight of six steps, with round seditori, or messenger's seats, that make this ascent very elegant.

At a point in this process (the actual date being May 10, 1637), the fathers labeled my plans as "piu a proposito", and the Deputies of the Congregation appointed me as Associate Architect with Signor Maruscelli. This was unsatisfactory to Signor Maruscelli, who resigned in June. As I reflect back on my conduct, it was not free of reproach, since I did criticize Signor Maruscelli's drawings and the defects in his plan. But the overall plan for the Casa was his, and he had earned the right to be Architect. I am sorry for stepping in. I was only too happy to show my skill. It is the case that my drawing ability, and my ability to reason through and solve problems, was superior. But I should have acted with more honor. Virgilio Spada was a close associate, even friend, to the Signor, having worked with him for over ten years on the plan, and it was painful for him, even more so than for the Signor, to choose me over the man who had conceived the plan for the Casa. I am sorry now, for as Cavalier Bernini wronged me, and as the Cavalier's greater talent in sculpture overshadowed all that I did, I wronged the Signor, and my greater skill unduly humbled him.

Right Photo: From the plates of Sebastiano Giannini, the plan of the Casa, the Chiesa Nuova on the right, the Oratory lower left, the Sacristy above the court adjacent to the Oratory. The Sala di Recreazione is above the Refectory, the oval room to the left and above the Tribune of the Church. The Rooms of the Saint are left of the Tribune of the Church. The Lumaca staircase is left of the Chapel of the Saint which is lower left of the Tribune of the Church.

Bottom Photo: Regrettably the Oratory is now closed, perhaps forever. This is a view towards the street showing you some of the splendid vault – a low coved vault with applied ribs that give the impression of a cupola. On the right the performers' loggia (you can see the pipes of the organ). After I left the project, the Oratory was dramatically changed from my plan.

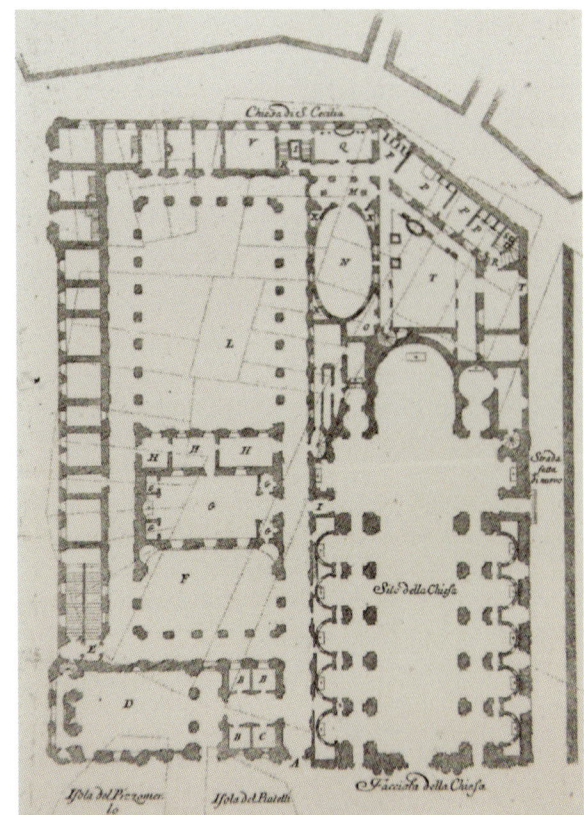

The Oratory

The Oratory was built in great haste from May of 1637 through June of 1640. The walls went up quickly[3] and the vaulting began in May 1638. Stuccoing of the interior was finished in 1639 and the ceiling fresco was finished by summer of 1640 and the inaugural performance, a simple one with no cardinals, was on the Feast of the Assumption, August 15. The formal opening was held on St. Philip's Day (also Trinity Sunday), May 26, 1941.[4]

In making the Oratory, I used Signor Maruscelli's basic plan and configuration. The Oratory, as you can see from the plan, is not, as you would expect on entering the central portal, on a parallel axis with Chiesa Nuova but at a 90 degree angle to it. It is, if you will, sideways to the facade! The visitor must then turn to the left to enter. This is a clear deception, but the plan was too far along, and it would have been impossible to secure any radical change through the deliberative, collaborative process of the Filippini.

The Oratory was conceived as a rectangle. I do not like corners as I have already told you. I was also faced with the necessity that the space be very wide to accommodate the audience. And so I placed pilasters at the corners to help carry the load.[5] I borrowed this corner pillar from the ancients and the model of Hadrian's Villa and the Baths of Diocletian. If you remember, I had previously removed the corners at the small cloister of San Carlino.

The limitations with which I was working at the Oratory included the need for a public and private door, an altar loggia, a spiral staircase to a lower overflow room, two niches on the sidewalls, and the windows which I have already discussed. I concentrated on what I felt were the two keys to creating a unified structure: the two porticoes at both ends (one for the performers, the other for cardinals and other important personages), and the giant vault.

I made the loggia for the cardinals much larger than the performers' loggia, and placed a grand billowing vault above it[6], and hidden lighting at both ends. I believe that in the loggia of the cardinals the viewer will have the best opportunity of feeling the essential character I sought to impart to the Oratory. Here dear reader, please pay special attention to the transparencies and the manner in which the bands of the vault, crisscrossing, play on the eye and the mind.[7] Here, I turned the pilaster 45 degrees (I could have given it a curve). This introduces the whole motif of diagonality, a diagonality that the ribs of the vault were then obliged to obey.[8]

---

[3] Id. 28. Unfortunately, at this writing, the Oratory is closed, restoration unknown.
[4] Downes, Opus, p. 451.
[5] Blunt 99. Borromini placed a spiral staircase in the pillar in the northwest corner. A small door opens towards the court so that the musicians can go up to the choir galleries without encountering the crowd in the Oratory. The sacristans and preacher can also use this. Paraphrasing Borromini's words, Downes, Opus 71.
[6] Connors, Oratory 29.
[7] Portoghesi 59. This is the Professor's reference to the crisscrossing bands.
[8] Id. Quote regarding diagonality and obligation.

From the Giannini plates. This shows you the Oratory below, looking to the performers' stage (the pulpit is to the right) and the library above (it was later extended to relieve stress on the wall of the Oratory - complicating the facade to the left). Unfortunately, I cannot show you the beautiful ribbed vault of the Oratory here.

I used flat architraves to carry the thrust over the cardinal's loggia to the solid bearing walls that serve also as a partition between the porters' quarters and the Oratory itself. Inside the frames of the lateral openings beneath the Cardinals' loggia, I inserted a smooth diaphragm with a window cut into it, and I quite deliberately provided no framing details. These diaphragms, of course, were essential to provide support for the small vault of the portico which lay behind them. For all the interior surfaces of the loggia, I did my best to enrich them with gentle levels of light.[9] I call your attention to the rounded projections in the angles of the jambs, where this gradation can be best seen.

From the Giannini plates. The Cardinals' loggia with my famous balusters that promote viewing to below.

---

[9] Id.

In Florence Michelangelo designed gunports for the city's defense. Their splays allow a soldier to see all across the field and everything below. These were my inspiration for using a triangle for the baluster, and alternating the bulge, from one on top, the next on the bottom. If I had placed the pedestals or base socles close together, the Cardinals' sightline would be raised by the height of the socles. With my alternating bulges, the outlines become parallel from top to bottom, and you can see the same amount all the way. Plate XLIV in my Opus Architectonicum shows you this. Some have said this was a mere caprice. Not so, the balusters which have half the bulges at the top, in fact, imitate nature where trees are larger at the foot than above and where man is the thicker above than at his feet.[10]

A few more words about the porticoes. The porticoes were designed to make the Oratory more stable, since they buttressed the walls, but also more skeletal. To do this, I used Ionic pilasters to articulate the walls and I continued these over the entablature by flat pilaster bands. To provide support for the skeleton and reduce the stress, I also tied the small hexagonal closets here with chains and imbedded a chain in the musicians' choir.[11] I believe the two porticoes I made here, reduced to a skeletal minimum, are the tallest and most slender I ever made. They are much like the porticoes of Saint Teresa in Caprarola, made by Girolamo Rainaldi in 1621.

Which brings me to the magnificent vault- the crowning feature of the Oratory.[12] This is a low, coved structure,[13] which is divided by applied ribs- this is a system of flat bands that give us the impression of a cupola. They do not run across the vault but abut on the oval panel in the middle, where Giovanni Francesco Romanello painted the Coronation of the Virgin. This creates a lofty cupola, actually a Lombard tiburio where the drum is suppressed and the rising curve of the dome is pierced by windows.[14] I meant the central painted panel to look like a real oculus, as at the Pantheon. These ribs, of course, are completely decorative and serve no structural purpose. All of this is in keeping with my desire for a skeletal structure, and I had I mind the concrete vaulting of the ancient Roman thermal halls.[15] The canted corner pilasters surely have no precedent in any of these halls, and perhaps I cite this ancient precedent in too much protest of the accusations of chimerical experiment that have been made against me. The devices I used did serve to create a more oval versus rectangular room, and a more centralized plan.

---

[10] Taken directly from Borromini's account of his balusters. Downes, Opus 73.
[11] Connors, Oratory 29.
[12] Id.
[13] Blunt 100.
[14] Connors, Oratory 30.
[15] Id. 31.

In the ornamentation for the Oratory, I used gilt-bronze grilles with stars, fleur-de-lis, and palmettes. The grilles for the loggias are richly gilded inside and out. The feet are sealed with lead into the marble cornice moulding. I deliberately kept them from touching the piers. You see here that there is no obstacle or interruption in the edges of the piers and the articulation. My Opus shows one of the side grilles – Plate XLIII – the opening above the altar.[16]

My railing in the Oratory.

---

[16] Taken from Borromini's account, Downes, Opus 73.

For the door on the north wall (for private use of the Fathers) I created richly moulded jambs, and lifted the pediment off the door, carried by a form of broken architrave.[17] The door from the vestibule is far more special – over 24 feet in height.[18] It is adorned with touchstone – pietra di paragone…senza paragone. This is a fine grained black basalt which can be polished to a mirror like image (like the cartouche on Urban VIII's tomb at San Pietro).

The entrance portal to the Oratory, twenty four feet in height, with richly appointed jambs, its black basalt polished to a mirror like image. I lifted the pediment, and broke the architrave with complicated curves. Above the bust of the Saint is the Saint's flaming heart, emblem of the Order.

Filippo Neri in the large entrance door I made of touchstone—fine grained black basalt.

I never created more richly appointed jambs than those here. I lifted the pediment. I broke the architrave with complicated curves. I inserted a bust of the Saint. Then above is the flaming heart of the Saint, emblem of the order.

The double order of windows in the lateral walls of the Oratory let in crisscrossing rays of light from both sides of the Oratory. Unfortunately, this effect was completely taken away when the arches of the loggia on the second floor level were blocked up after I left the project.[19] Then the ground floor windows of the north side were sealed in the early 1650's.[20] My plan for the west wall was never executed. I had planned an altar with a painting of the Assumption above. I intended to place diagonally positioned columns and an entablature here. Above the altar I planned urns with eight pointed Neri stars. Organ pipes would have flanked this. A festoon and crown were to be in front. I also made two low projecting corretti (little choirs), and then above, of course, was to be a spacious loggia that would serve for the oratories on feast days. We had to have an organ here for Santa Cecilia (to whose name the Oratory is dedicated).[21] To my great dismay, the west

---

[17] Blunt 100, quotes.
[18] Downes, Opus 74, fn 111.
[19] Portoghesi 59.
[20] Connors, Oratory 55.

wall with the altar and musicians' choir was transformed from my delicate perceptual base after I left the project, with a new plan of Camillo Arcucci, approved by a committee of Carlo Rainaldi, Pietro da Cortona, and Luigi Arrigucci. In the new replacement plan exotic alabaster columns and a marble revetment were installed destroying the simplicity I sought, and returned the program to what it had been before I arrived. The congregation in 1653 voted 17 to 1 in favor of this new plan (Padre Spada, who correctly noted that Arcucci's plan destroyed the symmetry on the axes and my system of diagonal bands across the vault springing from oblique corner pilasters, was the lone dissent).[22] The imposition of this altar, and the later addition of an organ in the wall whose pipes were in the way, and the screening of the windows of the musicians' loggia, has eliminated the light that was to enter from the west. And thus we now have a poorly lit hall with light from only one side whereas I designed one that would be flooded with light from three sides. And the elaborate altar destroys the diagonal concept I created!

The Façade

Fortunately, my façade has survived the changes made to the interior of the Oratory after I left, which I have described for you. The Fathers wanted a façade for their oratory, even though, as I have said, it would be a deception since it would cover the side and not the front of the Oratory, and would cover other parts of the Casa and not just the side of the Oratory. The exterior, in other words, is not tied to the interior.

Originally I planned some living space above the Oratory. In 1638 the Fathers in their deliberations decided to place the library there, and this increased the necessary height of the façade. After I left, the west wall of the library had to be extended to relieve stresses on the Oratory below, and this increase in the breadth further changed the façade in that the volutes I had flanking the façade, which should have shown themselves against the contrast of the sky, had to be imbedded in the stucco walls, destroying the brilliant silhouette I had planned.[23]

---

[21] Downes, Opus, 70, Borromini's explanation, fn 104.
[22] Id. Borromini.
[23] Blunt 91, quotes.

The Fathers insisted on a sublime façade that would not detract from the façade of the more important Chiesa Nuova to the east. The need for humility led to two decisions: first, I would use the more modest pilaster for articulation, and not columns, with a single scotia below the roof.[24] In keeping with the need for deference, I reduced the height of the second order so that it is considerably shorter than the second order at the Chiesa. Second, the façade would be made of brick, not travertine.

I used the more modest pilaster (versus the columns at the adjacent Chiesa Nuova), here bent at the angle, with the Chigi Star. See the fine thin Roman brick (placed with little mortar).

Detail of the fine brickwork of the façade on the left, contrasting with the more common brick on the right, used in nonessential areas here.

The fine brick, selected for its humility, is high quality Cortina. I saw this thin, sparsely mortared brick at the Sapolco Dorico outside the Porta del Popolo. The 1627 plan of Signor Maruscelli had no façade at all. Other Oratories were built with facades, and the Congregation agreed with me to step back from their original intentions. Padre Spada in 1637 encouraged this direction. He had been in charge of the façade of San Paolo in Bologna. I certainly was in favor of a façade, since it added edification to the just purpose of the Order. And so we proceeded with a façade that was intended to be smaller, less pretentious and ornate, and to be of a material of lesser status, than the façade of the Chiesa Nuova. We even kept the fictive podium on which the Oratory stands as low as the podium under the church.[25] If you compare the façade I made as against the façade at Santa Susanna, for example, you will say mine is lean and spare.[26] The Oratory is the son of the Church. Many come to the Oratory in order to have their Confession heard and also to receive the Eucharist. Because of this the Oratory façade had to be like a daughter to the façade of the church.[27]

---

[24] Downes, Opus 65.
[25] Connors, Oratory 33.
[26] Id.
[27] Borromini's own thoughts, Downes, Opus 77.

In the end, we arrived at a beautiful curved façade, unique in Rome. It is like a man's body, who opens his arms to embrace all who enter: his chest in the middle bay bows outward. The four lateral bays imitate the parts of the man's arms, each part divided by the several pilasters that project between them.[28] My first design, as I have said, did not anticipate the library on top of the Oratory, and consequently had only

Another view giving you a good idea of the curvature of the façade and the fine brickwork.

A view from the ground at the front door. This shows you the famous curve of the Oratory façade (the enveloping arms of a man), which is concave, and the contrast with the convex bay and balcony. Note my little cherub looking down on you.

five bays, to be made of fine brick, which were flanked by two bays of rougher brickwork. I got the idea for the finely worked façade flanked by rougher brick backdrops from the design of Francesco da Volterra and Signor Maderno at San Giacomo degli Incurabili, made 1600-1608.

Another view of the beautiful crowning pediment, from below, the cornice and the conch above the balcony.

---

[28] Downes, Opus, some of Borromini's phraseology 76-77.

The pediment for the façade was to be of three bays, and volutes connected it to the first level, again they were to create a silhouette. Michelangelo's pediment at Porta Pia and his portal at the Laurentian Library were influences here. When the façade had to be heightened in 1638, I incorporated the two flanking rougher brickwork bays into the total façade,[29] and tied them with volutes to the upper story. Inside these two bugnati I added beautiful curved window frames to give a feeling of expansiveness.[30]

The pediment of the façade.

I made here a bolder pediment, a type I had planned for San Carlino. Here I created a synthesis of the two classical models of the triangle and the segment,[31] drawing on what you see at the Pantheon aediculae and Michelangelo's portal at the reading room of the Laurentian Library in Florence. Some have said that my pediment here is taken from the old Cathedral of Milan (still standing when I was working there), others have pointed to Michelangelo's pediment at the Porta Pia where the straight pediment has a curved pediment inside it which has the two sections ending in volutes.[32] In truth, I was influenced by all of these, including the Milan Cathedral, but note that my pediment has straight and curved sections, unlike at Milan which is composed of a ogee curve.[33] I was to use this form of pediment many times in my later work.[34] The three divisions of my pediment correspond to the three central bays of the façade, and so I carried the lines of the bays below into the field of the pediment.[35]

---

[29] Id. 37.
[30] Id.
[31] Portoghesi 58. Professor Portoghesi describes how Borromini achieves a "complete synthesis" in which the two models – the "alternation" in the Pantheon (aediculae) – and the "interpretation and insertion" in the Laurentian reading room (portal) – are " no longer recognizable".
[32] Blunt 34. Professor Blunt does not believe Milan Cathedral was Borromini's inspiration because it is an ogee curve, while the Oratory pediment is "a combination of straight and curved sections". Blunt, Baroque Guide 118.
[33] Blunt, Baroque Guide 118.
[34] Id.
[35] Blunt 94. Professor Blunt likens this to "Vignola's design for the Gesù".

And now to the brick. The brick was selected for its humility. But brick comes in many types. Roman building trades of the sixteenth and seventeenth centuries made two types of walls, one rubble coated with stucco that turned brownish gray (this was the most common type of wall in the city because of its lower cost), called muro rustic, and another of brick, cortina. Brick in turn went from the more rustic cortina rustica to higher, finer quality cortina arrotata, cortina di mattoni tagliati, or pianelle tagliate.[36] Raphael had used this latter fine brick in his palaces, for he believed it was prized among the ancients. The ruins of the late second century tomb of Annia Regilla off the Via Appia are, I think, the best example of high quality cortina. I myself saw the type of thin, sparsely mortared brick I wanted to use here in an ancient tower called the Sapolcro Dorico[37] outside the Porta del Popolo. And so we were able to convince the Fathers to use brick of this type. I confess I was not entirely honest with them about its exquisite nature, for had I done so they may have rejected it as not in keeping with their humility. This brick was used only on the significant portions of the façade, and you can see that a larger brick was also used for the plainer areas.

When we designed the façade, we were ordered to be modest. But that did not exclude beauty or novelty. The Fathers wanted something of a combination between a famiglia palace and an ecclesiastical structure, since this was their casa, their family home, and it was not a church, but on the other hand it was a place of God and special worship. I thus selected what seemed to me like residential windows. I kept the façade on a single plane (though the niches add depth), and determined on a single, very slow curve. As I say, I intended the center bays to be like the chest of a man, and the curve of the bays to be like his arms. The Oratory gathers and welcomes the faithful.

Further as I have said, I desired to keep the plane dominant,[38] and so I used pilasters which were shallow, and I kept the string cornices light, and I kept the projection of the windows to a minimum. To the convex curve I gave a projecting convex bay for the door (note that the pilasters on either side of this bulge curve in two directions), and my intention here was to create part pilaster and part column-substitute,[39] and a concave niche for the balcony to the library. I kept the bays that flank the bulge fairly flat, and so the feeling of the concave curve comes mostly from the cornice of the outer bays.[40] I had these protrude far more than what was below them, and you may rightly feel that the appropriate metaphor is the wings of a great bird hovering over your head, and not the enveloping arms of a grounded man.[41]

---

[36] Connors, Oratory 34.
[37] Downes, Opus, 75-76, fn 121.
[38] Blunt 91. This is Professor Blunt's explanation of Borromini's desires for the plane of the façade.
[39] Connors, Oratory 36. Here the Professor's descriptions of Borromini's intentions.
[40] Id. Quotes.
[41] Id. The Professor's discussion of the appropriate metaphor.

The main entablature, due to the demands of the interior space, is at a height that is insufficient for the tall slender windows that were a must for the Oratory. I had to carry the windows far closer to the entablature than was usual, and they even cut into the architrave.[42] The windows of the upper story are very different. I did not give them parapets; instead I added an apron below the sill that is like the pediment at the top of the windows. I created a broken profile in order to continue what I would call the intense vibration of the adjacent architrave.[43] I was surprisingly allowed, by the way, to use travertine for the hoods of the windows and niches, and the mouldings,[44] but all the surrounds of the windows, and all the pilasters (save their capitals) are of brick.

The pediment above the central window. The Filippino star.

---

[42] Id. Quotes.
[43] Portoghesi 58, the Professor's phrase: "intense vibration".
[44] Blunt 95.

The central bay of the façade. The Fathers permitted me some extravagance in the balcony. Here I repeated the coffering in the conches at the Carlino (see the dove of the Holy Spirit). The broken pediment encloses a beautiful palmette. Note the stems and blossoms of lilies in the capitals of the pilasters.

The convex central bay. The hood here, which the Fathers allowed to be of travertine, has the same gentle curves as my breakout window at Palazzo Barberini, even gentler. The two consoles derive from Michelangelo.

In the central bay I was permitted some richness. The columns are travertine, and I was allowed to break the pediment, and give above the window a hood that will remind you of my "birthright" window at Palazzo Barberini, but with gentler curves, and which is supported by two consoles, which derive from Master Michelangelo. The balcony uses the balusters I was to employ at the cloister at San Carlino, and I also repeated the coffering from the half-domes at San Carlino in the niche above. In view of the Padres' consternation about simplicity, it is surprising that I was allowed to execute the decoration I gave the balcony door. I have two palmi supporting the jambs, and the pediment consists of two scrolls joined by a swag of laurel leaves. I added an elegant palmette (I was to use this often in my works).[45] I do enjoy, and others have commented on the "fine set of flowered capitals, where the traditional stalks, leaves, and volutes are formed by the stems and blossoms of lilies".[46]

A cherub above the façade window. No two cherubs I made are exactly alike in hair or expression.

---

[45] Id. 96, 97. Quotes. This description is all from Professor Blunt.
[46] Steinberg 361. Professor's description.

If the Oratorians had let me, I would have created a façade with an even greater curve, and there is an engraving extant of what I had in mind in my Opus Plate V. Perhaps the most striking feature of this fanciful plan was the crowning of the pediment and upper cornice, which has pedestals on which were stars, olive branches, palmi, lilies, and fleur-del-lis . Still, I am very, very proud of the façade we executed, primarily because of the gentle welcoming curve and the exquisite brickwork, and also because I was able to work within the constraints of the order, and also make the extreme adjustments required by the repositioning of the library.

This is the façade I would have made but its extravagance would have been unacceptable to the Oratorians who insisted that the facade not detract from the more important façade of the Chiesa Nuova.

---

[47] Blunt 98.

104 | THE ORATORY AND MONASTERY

The Refectory

I chose the oval to facilitate discussion, for support of the vault, and for acoustics. The pulpit was on the west side, it is now in the Chiesa Nuova. In the period 1638-1641 construction focused on the refectory wing of the Casa. In 1638 the library was eliminated from the area behind the apse of the Chiesa Nuova and then planned to be placed above the Oratory (it was built 1642-1644). This made room for a satisfactory space for the Refectory, the place for meals needing to be away from public streets. The refectory was built in 1639, the Sala di Recreazione above them in 1640.

The Refectory, now a meeting room.

Signor Maruscelli had planned a rectangular refectory, but I was ultimately able to convince the congregation that an oval plan, with its long axis running parallel with the long axis of the Chiesa, would suit them better, and, of course, I felt an oval plan was more pleasing to the eye.[48] The oval plan was not adopted until just before the foundation was laid in January 1639. I had to sink the floor level 4 palmi below the level of the garden court to the west; by this means I was able to increase the height under the vault to 34 palmi and increase the overall proportions.[49] The oval within a rectangle yielded four storage closets in the triangles of the corners, and also gave support to the vault structure, since it did not require support from the un-buttressed walls. The oval better suited

---

[48] Id. 103. The Chiesa Nuova offers a pilgrim's tour on Saturdays of the Filippo rooms and perhaps other parts of the Casa.
[49] Connors, Oratory 43, quote.

"face-to-face visibility" for the almost 60 men who would sit at the thirteen tables, which were shaped ovally to follow the curve of the room, each table sat eight Fathers.[50] The oval shape also greatly helped the acoustics. Acoustics were important. Everyday at table, two doubts are proposed, one at midday and one in the evening by one of the Fathers in turn: one of a case of conscience, the other of morals, and all the priests in order are able and accustomed to respond to one of the two doubts, and finally the proponent concludes with his opinion on the one and the other. The interior could not be too high or this conversational voice could not be heard. The interior could not be too low or it would be unbecoming to architecture. To accommodate the necessary acoustics, I kept the height of the room at 34 palmi. By making the room oval, the perceived width is reduced, and thus the height of 34 palmi, far too low for a rectangular room of 40 palmi in width, is perfectly acceptable. The oval room with this height served the acoustics well, permitted the Fathers to see each other better over their meals, and facilitated the sight lines to the speaker. The room accommodated a pulpit on the west side (which had its own little staircase of travertine), which you can now see in the Chiesa.[51]

The vault of the Refectory.

Let me tell you about another detail I attended to in the refectory, which was also made possible by my use of the oval. In one of the triangles formed from the oval shape, I made a small adjoining little room which has a door towards the kitchen court. This allows the Cardinals, when they dine here, to be served in a private way, with the servers able to avoid passing in front of the Fathers in the refectory.[52]

---

[50] Id. The Professor likens the plan to San Carlo "reduced to rudimentary form".
[51] Downes, Opus, paraphrasing Borromini words, 109.
[52] Downes, Opus, 111.

I also need to mention here the windows into the refectory. I made the outside openings high and those on the inside low, and this gave privacy while letting light enter. The walls are thick and thus it has turned out very well. I also made a flat ledge rather than a sloping one as other architects did, because when the slope gets covered with dust it makes a disgusting display, whereas the flat ledge is not seen![53]

The Lavamani

The lavamani, or the room for hand washing, was placed on the north side of the refectory. Although this room is usually planned as rectangular with two wall fountains, I created a series of vestibules, which served to combine the lavamani with a transit corridor. The smallness of this area required me to place the fountains in the center, and then to carve substantial niches into the walls. This I thought would help with both circulation and the routine of washing before the meal. I also placed windows on three sides which allowed borrowed light (lume di lume), dim though it was, to filter in.[54] I am very proud of the fountains I made for this lavamani (made from marble found in the foundation of this room) and they are regarded as among my masterpieces in decorative sculpture, for although fountains in monastic settings often used multiple basins, heraldic ornament, and spigots in the form of

One of the washing fountains for the lavamani, or washroom outside the refectory. In the form of a tulip, which had just been found and become popular in Rome. There were four petals in the middle, and four more spread out to hold the water, which came out of taps—now lost— that I made into bees, birds, and lizards. The cluster of late Gothic pillars at the base comes from the Milan Duomo.

"animalletti", mine bore my personal stamp, especially in the way they combined geometry with a sense of "exotic vegetal growth".[55] All but one of the lavamani fountains have been lost. The surviving lavamano is in the form of a huge tulip (the tulip having just become found and developed in Europe and very fashionable), with four petals standing up in the middle and four more spread out to hold the water, which comes out of taps that I shaped into birds, bees and lizards (these regrettably have now been lost from the fountain).[56] At the base I placed a cluster of late Gothic pillars, inspired by the bases of the piers in the Duomo at Milan.[57]

---

[53] Downes, Opus, Borromini's explanation, 113. The refectory was gutted sometime after 1871, and the windows were blocked and the loggia on the east side of the Casa destroyed. A victim of the new Italian nation state. Downes, Opus 113, fn 260. The refectory has now been reclaimed by the Chiesa and is used as a conference room.
[54] Connors, Oratory 43, 44. The Professor's description here.
[55] Id. Again, the Professor's description, quotes.

Please note the detail I attended to here; I even designed a cupboard into one of the walls which had sixty drawers to allow the Fathers and Brothers to put away their serviette and knife and fork. So that the wall would not appear cut out as it would if I made the front of the drawers of walnut, I had them made of ordinary deal.[58] I even affixed numbers in metal on these so that they could be read with the finger.

The Privies

Pardon me, dear reader, if I must sully your ears with a description of my work on the communal privies of the Casa.[59]

One communal privy was on the ground floor near the door. This one would be kept quite clean by water from the fountains and from rain water. Since it had only urinals, it was a small matter and not difficult for me.[60]

The other privy, to be used by the whole house, was at the highest point of the staircase that leads to the refectory and the recreation room.[61] I followed the common practice of using the closed well or anima in the staircase as a shaft for the disposal of waste.[62] The staircase turns around a newel 17 palmi long by 9 palmi wide. This was ample to receive all the waste. My objective was to ensure that the well not have to be emptied often.[63]

I was also concerned that the walls not decay, as was usual in the case of privies. I put the conduits in the void within the four walls, and I built four arches at the top of the staircase for this purpose. Within the arches next to the long walls, I put three conduits, which were only the thickness of the arch, some 2 to 3 palmi. I put two additional conduits in the two arches beside the short walls.[64] Above the conduits, I put seats such that the matter falls into the hollow space (many palmi wide and long), without touching the walls. I took great care to avoid malodours. I made the ceiling above like a chimney so that odours, which rise, would be carried above the roof. I put two wooden doors in the top flight of the stair, one at the beginning and one at the end. When the first door was opened, no bad odour would escape, because the second, after which the cubicles begin, is closed, and while opening the second the odour would not escape because the first was already closed.[65]

---

[56] Blunt 106. The lavamani fountains are not open for public view. The original lavamano, and a copy, are in a vestibule to the north of the existing conference room.
[57] Id. The Professor's description of the pillar, which he states "may be a late reminiscence of the bases of the piers in Milan Cathedral".
[58] Borromini's description, Downes, Opus 107. The drawers were "painted white to match the wall above and below". Borromini even had a little star made in the middle of each front with "a little ball of walnut so that the part touched by the hand should always keep its condition".
[59] Downes, Opus, 95. The privies are regrettably gone.
[60] Id. Also, 94, fn 197.
[61] Id. 94.
[62] Connors, Oratory 45.
[63] Downes, Opus, Borromini's description, 95
[64] Borromini's own description. Downes, Opus 95.

I also had in mind here the convenience of the Fathers. I made eight cubicles, each divided from the others by a wall, and with a door that can be closed, without a ceiling over, so as to be able to have light, and with - needing to read – an iron fixture in each to hold a lighted candle at night besides facilities for paper and suchlike.[66]

Then in the four angles between the sides of the cubicles I had marble basins placed for making water. And right at the top of the whole stair above the first cubicle I had a little hatch let into the well or newell of the stairs for emptying chamber pots in case of illness or other occasions, with a landing there for rinsing and cleansing the pots.[67]

By relating all these details for you about the privies, I wish to emphasize that it is just as important for a true architect to think about the utility of the spaces he creates as it is for him to think about the beauty of those spaces.

The Staircases in the Casa

I designed the principal staircase and began it but unfortunately, I was not retained as Architect at the Casa to see it finished. It is as generous in size and splendor as possible for the space, and in light of the Father's desire for simplicity. It is in the first court, near the main door, as it is more for visitors than the Fathers.[68] There are two flights to the first floor, then two more to the library.[69] The newell will pass further than this and end with the last steps, so that the last flights will not have a tunnel vault over them but one great barrel vault. The east side of the staircase was to have windows, but others after me omitted these.[70] I stayed long enough as architect to see the entrance to the staircase made, with four ancient columns of granite supporting a plain ceiling. The Fathers had in their possession these splendid columns which could be used despite their precious superior nature, which was not in keeping with the sought after austerity, because they were already in situ. Though the columns were too short, I used an example from antiquity in order to make them fit. From Andrea Palladio's Book IV (63). I knew of a column like this from the portico of the Lateran Baptistry which had in turn come from the Temple of Venus Genetrix.[71] I raised the columns on the bases, using some leaves about one palmo high, out of which it seems as if the columns are sprouting.[72] This is similar to the vine columns at San Pietro and the Baldacchino there, the eight ancient columns in the choir at Santa Prassede, and to a drawing in the Codex Coner.[73]

---

[65] Id.
[66] Id. Quotes.
[67] Id. Quotes.
[68] Downes, Opus 89. Most of the staircases are no longer open to view, the main staircase and the Lumaca (on the pilgrim's tour) the exception. Professor Downes notes that the main staircase at the Collegio Romano on the southside is of similar form and size. Id. 86 fn 162.
[69] Downes, Opus 87.
[70] Downes, Opus 86 fn 163.
[71] Id. fn 165-166. Professor Downes cites Thelen, figure 3.
[72] Borromini's description, by Downes 87.
[73] Blunt 99.

Cleverly I placed cavities under the staircases to store benches for the Oratory used on the evenings of feast days, and to serve as a sacristy for the Oratory. Over the Ricetto and in the upper half of the second understair space, I made rooms for the musicians to practice, accessible through the small spiral staircase off the northwest corner of the Oratory.[74] Plate XLIX of my Opus shows the window into the cloister in the room over the stairfoot. The full size plaster model that Alessandro Algardi (1595-1654) made for the Encounter of Saint Leo the Great and Attila at San Pietro was placed (after I had been replaced as architect by Camillo Arcucci) on the second half landing in 1660,[75] given to the Oratory in 1659 by the Chigi Pope, Alexander VII, via Padre Virgilio Spada.

The Lumaca oval spiral staircase (57 steps) I made that leads from the piano nobile to the Rooms of the Saint. I made these easy to climb, only six or seven inches in the rising; even close to the newell it is comfortable.

The second staircase is called the Lumaca, an oval spiral staircase (with almost three complete rotations), which leads from the piano nobile and the terrace above it to the sacristy and church.[76] I made this stair in 1638 to replace a narrow straight stair, to ease the access to the chapels in the Casa. The stairs were extended to the second floor in 1639. The Lumaca is very easy to climb, since I made the steps (57 of them in all – 20 for each rotation) not more than six or seven inches in the rising. It is therefore comfortable even close to the newell.[77]

The third staircase I made for the refectory and the recreation room, and nothing in this building has given me more satisfaction.[78] The staircase is situated towards the Via Parone, from which it receives its light. Although it stands about 100 palmi high, the order of the windows on the exterior façade is not disrupted, and all parts of the stairs are abundantly lit.[79] All of the steps are gentle and proportionate in height, none less than six inches in height, and none higher than seven inches in height, and the traditional tunnel-staircase was far better lit than most you will find in Italy.[80] Here I created comfort, easy ascent, breadth of tread, low risers with consistent height, height of the vault, light, all the while conforming with the windows of the façade.[81]

---

[74] Downes, Opus 87, also 86, 169.
[75] Downes, Opus 86 fn 170, 88 Photograph 30.
[76] Connors, Oratory 228-229, Drawing 51, Albertina 289.
[77] Again some of Borromini's description, from Downes, Opus 89 and 88 fn 171, also 76, figure 16, 17.
[78] Downes, Opus, Borromini's testimony 89.
[79] Id.
[80] Downes, Opus 88 fn 173. Borromini's self praise here. Professor Downes notes that "Borromini's was better lit than most". fn 172.
[81] Downes, Opus 89, Borromini's description.

Please note how I have shared the light from the windows of one landing with the landing below, having made a splay in the wall to the space below. With these slanting sills I combined iron balustrades that created, I must say, a quite ingenious system.[82] As you ascend this staircase, beginning at the laver, then climbing seven steps to reach the first loggia, then ascending to the piano nobile, then further up to the corridors of the second range of the Father's rooms, the terraces, then the third range of the Father's rooms, and finally to the privies, I think you will agree that I combined all of the virtues that often eluded the staircase designs of my contemporaries.[83]

There are many other staircases in the Casa: in the triangles of the recreation room; one behind the apse of the church for the services of the preacher to bring food from the kitchen to his rooms;[84] the one in the northwest corner of the Oratory to the terrace for the use of musicians to go up to the lower and upper galleries without having to pass through the Fathers' House; one for the doorkeeper to go up to his mezzanine; one from the visitor's rooms going to mezzanines; one from the first floor loggias to the rooms over the sacristy, and a spiral staircase from the kitchen to the cook's rooms.[85] If you will study my Casa staircases, I think there is much you can learn from the comfort, utility, proportion and grace I worked hard to achieve here.

The Chapels in the Father's House

San Filippo's relics are under the altar of the Cappella Esterna, or Chapel of San Filippo in the Chiesa Nuova. There were so many priests who wanted to say Mass in these chapels that the Fathers, who did not want to be disturbed in their Casa by the constant traffic, separated a section from the Fathers' house for this purpose, accessed by a separate door near the sacristy. This door leads to the Sala Rosa which leads  to the Donati Chapel, made 1641-1643, which has its altar above the body of San Filippo, the only thing between the altar and the one in the Chiesa Nuova is the shared party wall.

Top right photo: The Cappella Esterna in the Chiesa Nuova.

Bottom right photo: The entry to the Rooms of the Saint.

---

[82] Connors, Oratory 44, 45. See Figure 84, no. 11. This stairway was on the far side of Casa and may still be accessible through the government archive offices.
[83] Connors, Oratory 44, his words.
[84] Downes, Opus 91.
[85] Id. Borromini takes the time to create this fairly exhaustive list.

The oval staircase I made, the Lumaca, enables visitors to ascend to the upper levels of the Saint's chapels. In the little vaulted room on the second level, the Anticamera del Santo, Pietro da Cortona has painted the magnificent Saint Philip Discovered in Ecstasy.[86]

San Filippo-Pietro da Cortona.

In 1634-1635, the Cappelletta di San Filippo was transported from the Casa Vecchia to a room directly above the Donati Chapel. This room held great significance for the Fathers as the saint had said Mass in it every day for so many years.[87] I should note here that it was Padre Virgilio Spada who conceived the idea of locating not one but three altars over the body of the Saint.[88] The door I made in 1639 leading into the Cappelletta del Santo[89] from the Anticamera has an elegant dark green flecked marble frame, and a beautiful winged white marble cherub, smiling and looking up, together with flowers, at the ceiling picture by Pietro da Cortona. Please note the band just inside the outer moulding, and the ogees under the pediment and the curved band over the cherub. These I made of raw sienna marble, a beautiful light brown.[90] The gabled inner panel has a cousin in the one over the street door to the Oratory (Plate X in my Opus).[91] The inscription above the door reads: The room in which Saint Philip Neri daily in the last years of his life was accustomed to say Mass and for so long to engage alone with God. So that it should be made open to the veneration of all it was brought with the walls entire to this larger site.

The door to the Cappelletta di San Filippo Neri. The ogees under the pediment and the curved band over the cherub, who looks above to Pietro da Cortona's painting of the Saint. The ogees are of the beautiful light brown Siena marble. The dark green flecked marble frame surrounds the Siena.

---

[86] Id.
[87] Downes, Opus 79.
[88] Downes, Opus 405
[89] Connors, Oratory, Catalogue 55, 56, 229-231, see Figure 80, No. 30 on Figure 74. The Professor notes the conflicting evidence for the date of the door.
[90] Downes, Opus, quote 78, fn 132. The reference to Pietro da Cortona p. 78, 79, fn 130.
[91] Downes, Opus 78 fn 137. The inscription found here.

Latin: SACELLVM IN QVO S. PHILLIPVS NERIVS POSTREMIS SVAE VITAE ANNIS QVOTIDIE SACRVM FACERE ET DIV SOLVS CVM DEO AGERE CONSVEVIT VT OMNIVM PIETATI ESSET EXPOSITVM IN AMPLIOREM HVNC LOCVM INTEGRIS PARIETIBVS TRANSLATVM EST ANNO MDCXXXV.

I also decorated the vault above the former landing from the straight stairway that was replaced by my spiral staircase, using Filippini heraldry.

The Sala di Recreazione

I placed the Sala di Recreazione, or recreation room, directly above the refectory in an identical oval plan, and construction of this room began in 1640. This room was very important to the Fathers, as they set aside an hour for communal recreation after both their midday and evening meals, and thus the positioning above the refectory was essential.[92] As it happened, Padre Spada was defending the shape of this room against the concern of the Fathers that it was ostentatious as late as the date of the beginning of construction. I was becoming more and more attached to the patterns of interlocking curves that were inherent in these oval plans.

I designed the chimneypiece, installed in August 1641. Its oval hearth and convex mantel set into the concave wall was parallel to the design of the library balcony, which was under simultaneous construction.[93] The fireplace is eighteen feet long, is made of marble (except for the stucco top) from a single piece I discovered while we were excavating for the Oratory.[94] This coarse marble is white with greenish grey streaks that give it a fabulous luminosity in which the individual crystals glitter in the light.[95] I made it like a tent, with a convex oval that projects into the room and contrasts with the concave wall. I made a Doric frieze on the fringe of the tent, and placed in the metopes stars, flaming hearts and lilies, below which are little tassels. The elaborate fluted panels come from a drawing by G.B. Montano of a series of Roman columns.[96] Some have said that this is my grandest invention in room furniture. I must agree. I was able fortunately to overcome the cries of some in the congregation to remove the fireplace which did not meet the dictate for "prescribed modesty".

---

[92] Downes, Opus 121. Not generally available for viewing. Now a library study room.
[93] Connors, Oratory 43, See Figure 90. The Professor notes that Borromini raised the height to 44 palmi to achieve "satisfying proportions". The Professor's observation that Borromini was moving to "a consistent preference" for "patterns of interlocking curves". See also figure 91.
[94] Blunt 105.
[95] Id.
[96] Id. 41. Figure 31.

The oval hearth in the Sala di Recreazione, its convexity constrasting with the concavity of the wall. The marble lower section (the hood is stucco) is from a single piece. The coarse white and the greenish grey streaks create its luminosity. The doric frieze has stars, flaming hearts and lilies in the metopes, and little tassels are below. The fluted panels were also unique. My grandest invention in furniture.

I created a dignified vestibule for the recreation room with considerable height,[97] which has a pointed vault in a Gothic style. I set the vault of the salon above a cornice, since I could make this room as high as was visually pleasing, there being no need for good acoustics.

I made rooms in the triangles left over from the oval form of the room, and the northwest triangle was home to a well, wood storage, and also a bell.

The Brothers held the congregations of faults in the recreation room every fortnight. The general business chapter gathered at the sound of the bell. It was so convenient to be able to ring the bell with the rope that passes through the triangle. The rope continues to the triangle one floor down where the refectory steward is able to ring it for table.[98]

---

[97] Portoghesi 60. The Professor describes this as the "Gothic upward pull of its pointed vault".
[98] Downes, Opus, Borromini's narrative, 121. Also see Downes, Opus Ch. 16.

The Garden Courtyard

The garden courtyard that is to the west of the refectory and the Sala di Recreazione is a difficult space because the Oratorian authorities decided to add an extra story to the building surrounding it. Because of this the aria colata or massing of the surrounding structure overwhelms and suffocates the inner court.⁹⁹ I created colossal composite pilasters here, with arches for the piano nobile, with small balcony gardens for each arch. I used five simple leaves in the capitals, smooth without relief cutting, without extra volutes,¹⁰⁰ in keeping with the Fathers' desire for simplicity. These giant pilasters which link the two levels of loggias are based upon Michelangelo's pilasters at the Palazzo dei Conservatori at the Capitoline.

The garden courtyard suffers from "aria colata" (suffocation of the space) because the Oratorians insisted on adding a level to the building. The colossal composite capitals have five simple leaves in the capitals (two abrupted on the side) in keeping with the Fathers' desire for simplicity. The model was Michelangelo's Palazzo dei Conservatori.

The Finishing Pieces

In 1641-1644 we made the portaria, the main portal, the guest quarters on the piano nobile, the library, the balance of the Oratory façade, the loggia on the south side of the south courtyard/cloister, and the entrance to the grand scalone or great staircase (which was not made for another twenty years!), and the first,

Center of the Garden Court.

or south courtyard/cloister that lies between the Oratory and the sacristy (made in 1642).

Going straight from the door of the House, before reaching the loggias of the first court and the sacristy I placed six large steps the full width of the passage and the loggia (18 palmi). Each of these is a monolith. The sides serve several purposes: first they act as seats, second they serve as a boundary to the portaria, and third they are a place of rest for noblemen's servants. Fourth, they are a place to set things down. These seats I call cavalcatoi, or mounting block for riders. They add beauty to the entrance without blocking the view of the loggia, some 413 palmi in length. The main level of the House is not raised more than 4 palmi above that of the portaria. The eye can see everything.¹⁰¹

---

⁹⁹ Connors, Oratory 45. See figures 25, 83. Professor describes aria colata: the stale darkness of light-well courtyards.
¹⁰⁰ Borromini's description, Downes, Opus 105. Professor Downes, Opus 104 fn 235 invites a comparison with the conventional Corinthian Order at the Pantheon.
¹⁰¹ Borromini's description, Downes, Opus 81. The loggia is not currently open in its length for viewing.

One of the seditori, or messenger seats, which I placed in the entrance hallway to the Oratory. The steps and seditori solved the problem of the different levels of the Oratory and the Chiesa.

The six steps to the first court. These are all monoliths, with the sides serving as porters' seats, convenient for servants and setting things down.

The portaria or porter's quarters lies between the Oratory and the Chiesa Nuova. For the corridor leading to the Oratory, the andito, I settled on a barrel vault, which I placed over a quite complex system of superimposed pilasters.[102] The guest quarters and reception areas for cardinals and other important guests were above the portaria on the piano nobile and I was allowed more liberty in decoration of these, as they were considered part of the public section of the Casa. I designed a large square camerotto (really a gathering room) for the cardinals and a narrower gallery for the gentlemen.[103] Then I placed two camerini (changing rooms) adjacent, and I gave each a mezzanine.

I delighted with the cornices and vaults in these rooms; I made them cut across the corners. The Fathers permitted me greater latitude in these public places. Corner-cutting had the effect of reducing the optical length and width of these rooms relative to their height.[104] If you look at one of these camerini you can see a quarter of a hidden spiral staircase that has bulged into the room at the level of the cornice. I created balance by repeating the bulge in the other corners.[105] I feel I acquired greater ability in elegance with these vaults, which I was to return to in my later style, where I tried to create the image of a Roman vault deprived of its corner columns.[106]

---

[102] Connors, Oratory 47, the Professor describes how the barrel vault with pilasters prevailed over a groin vault on columns.
[103] Connors, Oratory 48. The Professor relates that the "gentlemen of their suites" had use of adjacent galleries.
[104] Id.
[105] Id.
[106] Connors, Oratory 49. Professor Connors cites the Campanile at the delle Fratte, the entrance vestibule of the Propaganda Fide, and one of the Lateran ciborium projects as examples of Borromini's late style. Fn 34, 123.

The Library

The library. I used the very fine walnut bookcases from the Fathers' old library. I used giant balusters for the shelving, versus columns, to save on wood. I used panels from the old library to make the light railing above. The four spiral staircases I designed for convenience in the corners have regrettably been removed.

In the Library the Tribute to Cardinal Baronius, successor provost and historian for the Casa. The star of Filippo, laurel, palmi, and lilies. In the relief below symbols of his duties.

Giannini Plate XLII showing the cross section of Library and Oratory.

As these rooms and the south courtyard advanced, we were able to complete the library, which had remained in an unfinished state for four years. In 1642 we did the walls, in 1643 the shelves and ceilings, and in 1644 the furnishings. The main salone of the library was flanked by smaller rooms with collections, and three private studies on the east, while on the west were the librarians' rooms, a gallery of maps, and the like. I could not vault the salone because I had no lateral buttressing opportunity nor was there sufficient support from below. Thus I gave the room a wooden ceiling.

    The old library of the Casa had walnut bookcases in excellent condiditon, well designed and crafted, with drawers with drop down lids. I covered all four walls with these bookcases.[107] The windows of the library were dictated by the façade, and so I had to raise the shelving. I used giant balusters versus columns to save on wood and to increase visibility for searching in the lower shelves. This idea came from my friend from Florence, Filippo Arigucci, who was thinking, I believe, of the reliquary tribune over the main door of San Lorenzo, which is fronted by similar slim balusters, designed by Michaelangelo.[108] I think the balasters are elegant. We reused the flat wooden scrolls from the old library to make a parapet for the ramps. The balusters work well with the light rail I placed around the gallery. For this, I was able to use the panels from the old library. By reusing the final walnut, I believe I created some elegance for this library, which is simple at the wish of the Fathers. In keeping with this simplicity, I used parchment to line the shelves, made paintings in grisaille, and false travertine in the coffered ceiling. I located four little spiral staircases of wood in the four corners of this room. In this way a reader did not have to go far for a book! Also I made above the bookcases a passage around.[109]

    Please note that the bust of Cardinal Cesare Baronius, historian of the church, and the successor provost of San Filippo, is set in a beautiful wreath of laurel, with stars, lilies, and palmi, a narrow frieze of fleur-de-lis below, and a bas-relief with a Gothic thurible, papal tiara, cardinal's hat, bishop's mitre, crozier, a bell, books, a processional cross and above the dove of the Holy Spirit in a burst of rays.

    Regrettably, the western wall of the library was extended 1663-1665 because it was thought that the existing wall was threatening the vault of the Oratory below. This, in my view, harmed the three-dimensional quality and the verisimilitude of the original image, and caused me significant pain in the last years of my life.[110]

---

[107] Borromini's description, Downes, Opus 131.
[108] Downes, Opus 130 fn 342.
[109] Borromini's description, Downes, Opus 131.
[110] Quote, Connors, Oratory 56, Portoghesi 56. Professor Connors details the alterations and the efforts to "set the addition off from the original façade". Professor Portoghesi says that the alterations to Borromini's magnificent façade was "a pain that contributed to the dramatic psychological situation of the last years of his life".

The First Courtyard

The first courtyard or cloister, between the Oratory and sacristy, was made 1641-1644. Much of what I designed has now been obliterated. For the wall of the sacristy, I added nicchioni, or pairs of large niches, at both ends of the wall. I did this to combine the wall and the loggia on either side of the wall into a single theme, in the manner of a theatre. In all this, by the way, the building committee and Soprastante of the order watched over my shoulder to the point I could not breathe, from an architectal point of view. In fact in 1642 the Soprastante Padre Isodor Roberti resigned over his disagreements with me, when Padre Spada supported my plan.

The First Courtyard. Now radically changed from my original.

The sacristy, already constructed before I arrived, made it impossible for complete symmetry with the first cloister. The long or northern side of the court is terminated by the sacristy, which receives light from the court by three windows. These windows do not correspond to the centres of the five arches of the loggia. The centre of each arch answers to the nearest impost to the window within four inches. And so I conceived of the idea to double each window with a fictive one, with ornamentation making it seem like there was just one window.[111]

Palladio had used a giant order in the cortile at the Palazzo Porto- Colleoni at Vicenza in 1552. But my model here in the first court was Michelangelo's giant order at the Palazzo dei Conservatori. I used a giant order of pilasters for this court taken from the Capitoline palaces. Of course, I could not continue the pilasters on the wall of the sacristy. Instead I carried the string course over the lower order of arches across the top of the windows.[112] These rectangular two light mullioned windows are elegant in their simplicity.[113] Then I placed a splendid window with a flat arch above it in the middle of the top floor, also using bent horizontal bands. This I took from the central portal of the Palazzo dei Conservatori.[114] The window overlooked the public space of the court. Fathers who lodge in that quarter are able to see who is causing the doorkeeper to ring for them. I was able to bring some order to the disunity of the first courtyard, which had not been designed properly at the outset, by means of this central window which spanned both the rest and fictive windows below.[115] Regrettably, this window was removed after I left.

---

[111] Borromini's description, Downes, Opus 83.

[112] Blunt 98. Professor Blunt notes a difference from the Capitol: there both floors have "flat trabeations".

[113] Portoghesi 58. The Professor says this formed a flat arch recalling "late Gothic examples and endow this stark façade with a horizontal tension and a hitherto unprecedented organicity". Opus Architectionicum Plate LI shows how the courtyard looked before the removal of the central window.

[114] Professor Portoghesi's description. The central window was taken out in 1924 when reading rooms for the Library were added atop the Sacristy. Connors, Oratory 56.

[115] Paraphrase of Borromini's description, Downes, Opus 83.

I have already mentioned the staircase on the short west side (as I have pointed out, not constructed for some twenty years), which is of the usual Roman style where a single flight doubles back on itself, but at the upper stage I have the stairs opening with a wide vault which covers both flights.[116] This allows the visitor to go from a narrow dark space to a space far wider and lighter. I was to use this original motif again at the Palazzo di Spagna.[117]

I have already mentioned the curve in the corner pilaster piers. Others used half pilasters and quarter pilasters for corners. I eliminated the corner itself (Palladio had toyed with this in the interior of the Redentore). After I left the Casa for good in 1652, Architect Camillo Arcucci closed the arches I had placed on the piano nobile level of the Courtyard with window walls, and my recessed walls and balcony gardens were removed from the design, and long after that my elaborate balcony window was removed from the Courtyard, and the corridor on the upper level of the loggia was closed up.[118]

The Orologio

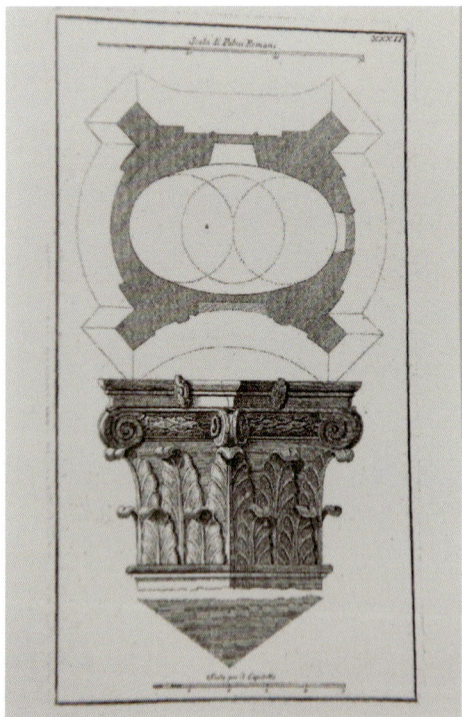

From the Giannini plates, a diagram showing the geometry at the Orologio.

The Orologio from the courtyard side. I used an internal oval which is followed by the two shorter sides. For the face a concave section. The corner pilasters are at a 45 degree angle. The oval parapet follows the curve of the two sidewalls. The cage atop follows the curves I placed atop the Bernini Baldacchino at San Pietro.

---

[116] Blunt 99.

[117] Id. Professor Blunt's description. Professor states that this was a "novelty in Roman architecture", but not unknown in northern Italy and is in the treatises of both Palladio and Scamozzi.

[118] For the discussion of the corners: Wittkower, Art and Architecture 225. Professor Wittkower states: "[t]his new solution soon became the property of the whole of Europe."

The front of the Orologio. After I left the project Pietro da Cortona inserted the mosaic. The star of Filippo on the left.

From 1644-1647 work had stopped on the Casa. Innocent X Giovanni Battista Pamphilj became Pope in 1644. Father Spada had to give up his post as Preposito of the Congregation when he was made the Pope's elemosiniere segreto, or secret almoner who saw to the needs of the poor. He also became the Pope's architectural consultant (to my good fortune since he had become my dearest and most trustworthy of friends).

When work resumed in May of 1647, I began my last project at the Casa, the Orologio and the northwest corner of the complex. I had in mind that as the visitor approached down the Via dei Banchi Nuovi he would be struck by the imposing Torre dell' Orologio, or clock tower, which would be a real presence on its own Piazza, and facing the Piazza di Monte Giordano. I thus added a tall bell tower and crowned it with Filippini heraldry (the twenty four pointed Neri Star) in wrought iron.[119] The weather vane and the cross and the bell and star resulted in a total height for the Orologio of some 135 feet. Here at the pinnacle the "swallows and the winds would reign" and in my mind a fanciful image and great height were required.

The cage atop the Orologio, with cross, weather vane (see the flaming heart of the Oratorians), crown, and bells. This all follows the crowning of the Baldacchino for San Pietro.

---

[119] Id. Portoghesi 56-58 Connors, Oratory 52.

I used an internal oval for the tower that brings together the opposing facades.[120] The two shorter sides of the tower follow this oval. On the face I designed a concave section and on the rear, not seen, a rectilinear section. On the corners I placed pilasters at a 45-degree angle. In my original design the face of the clock was to have had a flaming heart that was pierced by an arrow, which had as its head a fleur-de-lis. In the end after I left, Pietro da Cortona inserted a mosaic in the face. In the attic, the oval parapet follows the curve of the two sidewalls, all the way around.[121] The cage I placed at the very top follows the crowning of the Baldacchino at San Pietro. I should close here by noting that some eleven years later, courtesy of Padre Spada, the Neri Stars (actually they are the family star of Cardinal Peretti Montalto) were put on two candlesticks.[122]

I placed the clock tower above a three storied building, tying up the elevation with colossal pilaster strips. I used even finer brickwork than I used for the facade of the Oratory.[123] Then I reinforced these strong unbroken verticals with other strips which are broken above the piano nobile. From there I layered the wall into three planes. At the corner I made the middle pilaster concave (like the corner at the southwest corner of the Casa). You can compare this energizing treatment "of an otherwise" lifeless surface with the Master Michelangelo's façade and pilasters at the Palazzo Senatori at the Campidoglio and the outside of San Pietro.[124]

My Departure

The Orologio was my last project at the Casa. From 1650 until 1652 my situation with the Fathers worsened. I had had enough of the Fathers and they certainly had had enough of me. In November of 1650 I declined to arbitrate a dispute with the master builder Defendino Pascalli, since the former officers of the Congregation who knew the case refused to be involved. I probably went too far in refusing to release the book of measurements, as it was the only record of the work done and thus the payments due.[125] I felt, and still feel, that this refusal on my part was appropriate, but it put me at direct odds with my patron. Then lesions appeared in the vault of the Oratory and the library in 1651 and 1652, and instead of calling me in, the congregation turned to Cortona, Camillo Arcucci, and Pascalli for advice. The crowning blow occurred in October 1651 when plans were made to transform the Oratory altar, which I have previously told you about. Despite not only my opposition but that of Padre Spada, those plans went forward. In August of 1652 Arcucci, who honestly had no status as an architect, was named Architect, ostensibly because I had refused to continue.

---

[120] Portoghesi 56, the quoted phrase is Borromini's.
[121] Id. 57. Description of the original design is from Professor Blunt 107: "The bells were to have been suspended from an iron construction composed of fleurs-de-lys and stars, and the face of the clock was to have had in the centre a flaming heart pierced by an arrow with a fleur-de-lys head, which pointed to the hours".
[122] Downes, Opus, some direct quotes, 458 (fn 205), 459. Professor Downes notes Borromini had wanted these stars atop the Oratory facade as well.
[123] Connors, Oratory 52, Downes, Opus 459 for the description of the tying up function of the pilaster strips.
[124] Downes, Opus 459, quotes.
[125] Quotes, Downes, Opus 453. Professor Connors describes fully the alterations that occurred 1651-1924 at Casa 55-57. The Oratory was brutally transformed into a tribunal by the new civilian government in 1871. The garden courtyard was occupied by Neapolitan and Jacobin troops – 1798-1800. The whole Casa was confiscated 1871 and a courtroom structure added on the south end of the gardens. In 1871, or 1922-1924, the refectory and Sala di Recreazione were stripped.

In 1657 Padre Spada, who by this time, after the death of Innocent X in 1655, had returned as Preposito (his predecessor Provost Scarampa had died in the plague of 1656), proposed my return as architect to the Deputies (remember that he also took my side in Arcucci's disastrous redesign of the Oratory altar wall). Despite their agreement, the Congregation declined to have me return by a vote of twelve to four. They harbored too many bad memories. That refusal, coupled with other personal setbacks which I will describe to you dear reader, was a significant blow to my mental well-being and balance.

CHAPTER SIX

Santa Maria dei Sette Dolori

In 1641 Camilla Virginia Savelli, founder of the Augustinian Oblates, and wife of the Duke of Latera, asked me to design a church for her as part of the convent she began in the Trastevere, below the Janiculum hill, where the Via dei Panieri meets the Via Garibaldi, next to and below San Pietro in Montorio. At this time I was thoroughly involved in work on the Oratory and Sant' Ivo, but I agreed to the request on condition that I could use Antonio del Grande (he was the architect who later built the gallery in the Palazzo Colonna and the wing in the Palazzo Doria) for all the necessary measurings. Francesco Righi became my assistant in 1641 (born in 1621, he came with me at age 20 and became my trusted associate), and so I had now capable assistants and so I could take on projects such as the Dolori (Francesco was to set up his own practice in 1659).

The church was made 1642-1646. The interior stucco was done 1648-1649. Unfortunately work on the church was then interrupted, as the fortunes of the patron house of Farnese declined, and when work resumed in 1658 I was not involved, which led, I think you will agree, to disastrous consequences.

The brick façade. The convexity and concavity are mine, but others have made brutal alterations, like the doors. The convex section on the right reminds us of the tomb of Sergius IV at the Lateran.

The doors "brutally" inserted into the façade,[1] the chapel added to the atrium, the wing of the convent that is towards San Pietro in Montorio, and the staircase and loggia of the convent, are all attempts by others to take up my themes, but show great incongruity.[2] My drawings[3] show pieces of my original design. The façade was to have superimposed niches between colossal pilasters which interrupted a minor Palladian motif, and a concave center. The lateral projections were to return to a main rearward plane.[4] I actually kept a model of this church in my casa, but it does not survive. The alterations to these plans by others altered and I would say corrupted my original design. As these changes occurred in the period 1658-1666, they inflicted at a point late in my life great pain and anguish upon what was by that time my fragile mental disposition. It seemed like my enemies were conspiring to ruin the wonderful things I had begun, almost as if someone were deliberately trying to bastardize my original designs, to bring an end to what was a pure beginning. Subsequent restoration has done further damage, including the destruction of my white walls by the addition of bright colors, the use of sham marbling, and the addition of an illusion coffered vault.[5]

The vestibule, the church/nave to the left.

A look at the curves I made in the façade here. Like the Oratory and the Re Magi, the nave runs parallel to the façade.

The plan I made for the interior of the church was, I must say, very pleasing, a culmination of my desire to link my architecture with that of the architecture of the time of Hadrian. The basic form of the church is an octagon, or perhaps more accurately a rectangle with rounded angles. Over the years I had much pleasure in dealing with the rectangle and my abhorence of its corners. These were to culminate in the chapel of the Re Magi at the Propaganda Fide. Santa Maria was a very important statement in the progression of my rectangular plans[6] that led to that Magi Chapel. Santa Maria, like the Oratory and the Re Magi Chapel, has a deception in the relation of the facade to the interior- the door in the center of the concave bay of the façade leads into the vestibule, then the main axis of the nave runs parallel with the façade, and not away

---

[1] Portoghesi 62, quotes.
[2] Id. 62-63.
[3] Albertina drawings 645, 642, Portoghesi 62.
[4] Steinberg 194 fn 14
[5] Blunt 129, 130.
[6] Portoghesi 63.

from it as you, the visitor, expect on entering.[7] The nave is preceded by a vestibule, which is very similar in shape to the Cappelletta in the crypt at San Carlino.[8]

Detail from the atrium (it has been altered with the addition of a chapel), which is very similar to the Cappelletta in the crypt at Carlino.

The atrium I designed for Santa Maria with its "curvilinear-rectilinear perimeter" is based upon my study of the Room of the Small Baths and the central space of the Small Palace of Hadrian's Villa.[9] If you recall, I had this same room in mind when I designed the lower level church of San Carlino.[10] I also used the design of the small baths for the concave façade of Santa Maria.

I articulated the church with columns set in niches, also like San Carlino.[11] I continued the two columns which flank the entrance door by inserting scrolls that merge into the architrave of the main entablature, where this entablature rises in an arch over the entrance. You can see that in the middle I created an opening, which forces the scroll-architrave upwards, and I even cut across the frieze and made the scroll virtually touch the bottom of the vault. I am not quire sure why, but I never used this particular device again.[12]

The columns at Santa Maria are, of course, not freestanding as at the Canopus of Hadrian's Villa. I placed them in what I would call a "dialectic relation" to the wall, and so where the cornice rises up to form the arch,[13] I drew the wall back into what I would call the "shallow concavity" of the lateral altars or the sanctuary of the main altar.[14] By doing this, I changed what was essentially a two dimensional motif into a multidimensional motif which is especially positively impacted by the light here. What the Roman model had in height, the church here makes up for in depth.

---

[7] Blunt 130, 131. "[t]he axis of the church runs parallel with the façade and not away from it, as one is left to expect".
[8] Id. 130.
[9] Portoghesi 63. Professor Portoghesi states that "the atrium-church system marks the moment of the clearest tangency with the investigations of Hadrianic architects".
[10] Id. See 9, where Professor Portoghesi comments that the "Hadrianic instruction" of the Baths influenced Borromini in the concave façade and the atrium.
[11] Blunt 130.
[12] Id. Professor's words.
[13] Portoghesi 9. It is Professor Portoghesi who draws the comparison to the Canopus.
[14] Id. Quotes from Professor Portoghesi.

I used Serliana arches in the nave, and a cornice which I bent and curved without interruption as I have mentioned. I bent the cornice here at Maria and turned it into an arch without interrupting its continuity,[15] and for this my model was the loggia of the Canopus of Hadrian's Villa. The collonaded exedra of the Canopus had just been excavated and reconstructed. It impressed me immensely. Note that in the interval between the Serlianas of the nave, I was making a linking between them, as you can see by virtue of the fact that I omitted here the circular moulding, or astragal, at the base of the capitals. The rhythm was a-b-a-c-a-b-a-c, the "c" being the bay with no astragals. In the renovations, astragals have been added to these neutral linking sections through fictive painting, an abomination profoundly altering my intent for the rhythm.

At the cloister of San Carlino I used the curved angle corner to establish the correlation of a continuous rhythmic chain, but here at Santa Maria I carried the rythmn around the corner, much like the literary enjambment where the last sentence of a verse continues to the beginning of the next verse. This treatment of the corner is part of the effort made by all of us Seicento architects to create a fusion between the centralized and longitudinal type of church.[16] The Counter-reformation focused on the Eucharist, and a centralized plan was most conducive to helping the congregation turn its attention to the altar. The longitudinal plan, on the other hand, had so much to commend to it in terms of procession, and reverence and order.

For the ceiling of the Maria, I used a flattened cloister vault, completely smooth. The two sustaining arches came later and are not mine. What I designed utilized a system of ribs, which ran parallel to the two axes of the church, and which crossed at right angles. This vault decoration was prefigured in the refectory of San Carlino, strengthened at the Oratory, and finding its final form at the Re Magi.[17]

I should also point out that the oculi in the lateral chapels are mine, but not the other windows.

The façade at Santa Maria uses rough brickwork, which I intended to cover with stucco. Regrettably funds ran out and so we are left with the extremely rough façade we see today. The contrast with the fine brickwork at the Oratory could not be greater. I drew a very plain main entry door; the elaborate one you see today is not mine. I do especially like, though, the concavity in the simple setting of the rough brick and the two sharply edged piers flanking the bay.[19] I intended a crowning feature in the central upper zone to connect the projecting bays on right and left, and I was going to flank the projecting elements by another bay on each side. I would have had niches in these atop each other, to mirror the existing façade. In the right hand bay you can just make out one of these.

---

[15] Id. 63. Professor Portoghesi notes that the elongated plan of the church resembles the proportions of ancient thermal structures (1:25 width to length versus 1:2).
[16] Id. 64. The rhythm and comment about the fictive astragals come from Professor Portoghesi. 63.
[17] Id. Professor Portoghesi's description. He has a plan at 64 which shows Borromini's scheme.

Santa Maria was a place for my architecture to develop further. I only wish I had been allowed to finish it and that others had not been allowed to radically alter my designs.

The Nave. I bent and curved the cornice without interruption and used Serliana arches. I used a smooth flattened cloister vault, the sustaining arches are not mine.

CHAPTER SEVEN

Sant'Ivo alla Sapienza

The modest entrance to the courtyard, from the Via Rinascimento.

The courtyard. The concave exedra of Giacomo della Porta. My attic, flanked by the Chigi star and monti- the star also in the windows. A striking aspect of Sant'Ivo is that the exterior bears no resemblance to the interior, as you will see. The bulging exterior apses have no relationship to the hexagon- plus- bays inside.

Sant'Ivo has two special, extraordinary aspects to it. First you see on the outside my famous spiral – unique in Rome, its beauty and originality is without parallel. Then, when you enter the church, expecting the outside to be repeated, you encounter no repetition at all, but a gleaming white vault that soars to the sky. It is so breathtaking because by some miracle I have carried the groundplan – the lobed hexagon - all the way to the lantern up above.

This Church was begun in 1643. But the conceptual beginning is much earlier. In 1632 the Cavalier Bernini recommended me to Pope Urban VIII for nomination to the position of Architect to the Archiginnasio of Rome- which was to become the University of Rome, commonly called the Sapienza. The rector of the Sapienza, the lawyer Montecatini, formally announced that "the Cavalier Bernini has made known through the Cardinal Patron Barberini that, on behalf of the people of Rome, he has appointed as architect of the Sapienza, the most illustrious Francesco Borromini, nephew of Carlo Maderno."[1] I believe the Cavalier did this to usher me out of his enterprises at San Pietro and the Palazzo Barberini, but I do not know this for a fact. He could not have done it because of the skill I showed at dealing with small spaces, as at Carlino, as some have later said, since I had not begun my work there at the time of this nomination. If he did it because he truly appreciated my architectural skills, I thank him. In the event, the church I built here, Sant'Ivo, named for the patron saint of jurists, the French civil and canon lawyer, was not to be erected until 1643-1660.

To place the beginning of the building of Sant'Ivo in the context of my life and the life of Rome and the Church: I was 44 when work began in earnest on the church, the year 1642. I had finished the church proper of San Carlino, and the Oratorio of San Filippo, and so I had established myself in the city as an architect of skill. The Barberini Pope Urban VIII was nearing the end of his reign, which came 1644. The Cavalier Bernini was still in his highest glory, receiving papal commission after papal commission. In 1642 he made the Fontana Tritone in the Piazza Barberini, a work of great skill and a breakout so far as communal fountains are concerned. I deeply resented that my greater skills in architecture were not rewarded in the same way that his skills in sculpture were rewarded. I know that by this time I had become a difficult person with whom to work. I had always been difficult, but my successes, and my failures in being recognized, had made my attitude worse. My successes, my friendship with Padre Virgilio Spada, served me well so far as my reputation, but they did not serve to temper my loneliness, my paranoia with criticism, my shyness, my inability to interact with people on a social level, as Cavalier Bernini could do so well. I felt that Carlino had gone so well because I had been left alone, and that the Oratory had succeeded despite the fact I was never left alone.

The Church of Sant'Ivo, therefore, was for me extremely important. The Pope had made me architect here. The Sapienza was ultimately under the Pope's authority and I needed to show Pope Urban that in architecture I could be as creative and inventive as Cavalier Bernini was in sculpture, and that in this sphere I was both technically and artistically better than the Cavalier.

---

[1] Portoghesi 149.

The Short Chronology of the Construction

To allow you the proper perspective on my commentary, I must give you a short chronology on the building of the Church. This project, more than any other, involved three separate and distinct building periods, tied specifically to the three successive Popes who ordered and paid for the work: Urban VIII Barberini (1623-1644), Innocent X Pamphilj (1644-1655), and Alexander VII Chigi (1655-1667).

The architect Giacomo della Porta was engaged at the Sapienza complex from 1578 until his death in 1602.[2] The institution that would eventually come to be the University of Rome had initially been founded by Pope Boniface VIII in 1303 as the Studium Urbis. In 1432 Pope Eugenius IV arranged for the purchase of the city block between the Piazza Navona and the Pantheon. The existing structures were modified, extended, and renovated, eventually resulting in a basic palace formulation, which encompassed an interior courtyard surrounded by an arcaded portico on both sides with two floors. It was left to della Porta in 1581 to create the definitive parti, which was now a symmetrical, three story palace in the form of a U, which enclosed a two-story arcaded courtyard.[3] The main entry was on the west. della Porta planned a second entry on the east (the side toward the Piazza Sant' Eustachio), and a centralized church behind a concave exedra at the end of the courtyard.[4] By the time of della Porta's death the western façade, the majority of the courtyard loggias and the concave exedra for the church were finished. There matters sat, for Pope Paul V Borghese (1605-1621) stopped the work. I was appointed architect for the Sapienza in 1632, and I was to remain architect under the three Popes I have mentioned, until 1667, some 35 years. At the time of my appointment, the Church was unbuilt, and also the eastern third of the north wing of the palace, most of the facade on the side toward Piazza Sant' Eustachio, as well as all the hallways to that Piazza.[5]

The building programme was of course dependent on the interest and the funding of the reigning Pope. During the 35 years I was on the project, there were more periods of inactivity than activity. I did not even begin drawing until three years after my appointment. Then from 1635-1640 I was making the primary design of the church. I decided in my plans to replace della Porta's design, but to keep his concave exedra. I wanted to begin by reconstructing the west façade on Via Corso del Rinascimento, to create two portals left and right down which the visitor could appreciate the view of each of the interior arcades, to provide rustication for the wall, and to add height to the towers, with a second floor tempietto with concave sides.[6] I was not able to secure funding for any of these, and so, still today, the visitor encounters a fortress, forced to enter through the one portal placed along a stark and foreboding wall.

---

[2] Smyth-Pinney 316.
[3] Id. 315.
[4] Id. 316.
[5] Id. 316.
[6] Blunt 111.

Construction did not begin until January 1643 (the contract with the masons was entered into in September of 1642, the scarpellini were signed on in June 1643).[7] The foundations for the six main piers were laid in 1643.[8] It took a year to build the basic structure of the Church such that it reached up to the level of the drum. On the death of Urban VIII in July of 1644, the vault was not yet finished. Innocent X was elected in September, and the vault was finished in October 1644, but not on Innocent's initiative.[9] If you could have looked at the church's condition at this point, you would have seen the round drum with six apses, but no lantern or spire above it. The vault inside the drum was finished to a point, but not decorated. There was a large hole at the top, where the lantern would be placed. Next followed a long period of inaction, due to the fact that Innocent regarded the Sapienza as a Barberini project, and the Barberini he decidedly did not like. The Consistorial Advocates, the group of important Roman lawyers who controlled the faculty, took steps to protect the building from water damage, covering the cupola with lead in 1648-1649.[10] This group also petitioned the Pope to proceed with finishing the Church, and Carlo Cartari, the most influential of the Advocates, commissioned a perspective drawing of the Church and complex which he gave to the Pope.[11] Innocent in April 1649 issued a chirograph allowing the Advocates to obtain a loan to finish the Church. But, alas, no funds were forthcoming and the church sat for several years, unfinished. Then in 1652 when Innocent was about to begin the process of reconciling with the Barberini, with whom as I say he associated the Sapienza project, Innocent finally turned seriously to the completion of Sant'Ivo.[12] I had made drawings for the spire the last half of 1651. I was able to begin the lantern and spiral in March 1652. The work proceeded quickly. The iron superstructure was put in place and gilded October 1652.[13] The Roman building process was to stucco a building from the top down, taking down the scaffolding as the work progressed.[14] The spiral stuccoing was done this way 1653 on, including the bands of jewels and pearls I used to embellish the spire.[15] The inside of the lantern was also decorated during the reign of Innocent, including the fabulous Holy Spirit I placed at the top.[16] The other aspect of the work that occurred under Innocent was the shoring up of the Church due to the cracks that appeared almost as soon as I had the spire up. As I will explain to you later, I simply did not foresee the weight of the immense spire when I did my initial plans and projections.[17]

---

[7] Connors, The Spiral 670.
[8] Smyth-Pinney 321.
[9] Connors, The Spiral 670.
[10] Id. 671.
[11] Id.
[12] Id.
[13] Id.
[14] Scott 305.
[15] Connors, The Spiral 671, 672.
[16] Id. 672. Scott 313.
[17] Connors, The Spiral 671, 675.

When Innocent died, and the Chigi Pope Alexander VII assumed the chair of Peter in 1655, he at once commissioned me to make a misura e stima to detail what remained to be done on the project.[18] He had inherited, it was said, a body without a soul.[19] Alexander had me change many things, including a softening of the exterior of the drum with the addition of another pilaster (3 palmi wide versus the 2 existing pilasters 5 palmi wide) to each buttress, resulting in a triple pilaster cluster.[20] In 1659, I made changes to the Church interior (which I will discuss in more detail later), and completed the hexagonal rooms off the main area, the north portico, and the Alessandrina library off the north portico. The façade and entry off the Piazza Sant'Eustachio were also made in this period. The greatest part of the work under Alexander was the interior decoration of the vault, finished in time for the dedication on November 13, 1660. The pavement would be placed after this (I made the drawing in October 1660).[21]

There, I think keeping these three separate phases of the making of Sant'Ivo in your mind will help you as I take you into more detail: 1) the central main body and drum of Barberini Urban VIII (1643-1644); 2) the lantern and spiral of Pamphilj Innocent X (1652); 3) the decoration of Chigi Alexander VII (1658-1659).

A Personal Interlude

At this point, I stop you, dear reader, to cover significant events which occurred during the making of Sant'Ivo which greatly impacted my career, my life, and I must say the whole of my mental state. The first of these was exceedingly positive from my perspective - the election of the Pamphilj Pope, Innocent X, in 1644. Once the Pamphilj was elected, all of the Barberini left town, freightened that they would be arrested for fraud, for Urban VIII had left a bleak financial situation for his successor. All things Barberini were shunned, and this included the close Barberini confidant, the Cavalier Bernini. Moreover, Innocent made my patron Virgilio Spada his elemosiniere segreto (in charge of supposedly anonymous papal donations) and his unofficial adviser on all architectural matters. Under Innocent my professional life, though still difficult for me because nothing could draw me from my reclusivity, my shyness, and my difficult unapproachable manner, became very much easier. I could now look forward to papal commissions.

The second of these events seemed positive to me at the time, but in the end, significantly affected in a negative way how the Roman community viewed me. This event was the collapse, or imminent collapse I should say, of the southern belltower Bernini had constructed for the façade of San Pietro under Urban. As early as 1641 serious cracks appeared in the foundations of the tower. Cavalier Bernini had designed a tower of immense proportions, more than 200 feet high, far too heavy for the site (in fact, as I

---

[18] Scott, 304.
[19] A quote from Borromini's friend Martinelli, Scott 303.
[20] Connors, The First Three Minutes 49 fn 53.
[21] Smyth-Pinney 327, figure 24.

testified, three times higher and six times heavier than it should have been),[22] which had subterranean springs beneath it. In the summer of 1642 the Congregation of the Fabbrica of San Pietro ordered work stopped. After Urban died, and Innocent assumed the reign, he established a commission, of which I was a part, to investigate.

The Cavalier insisted he had relied on others who had made the appropriate calculations and certified that the foundation was sound. He even brought my great patron Carlo Maderno into this justification. I was very emphatic in my criticism of the Cavalier. He was responsible for the design, he could not shuttle this on to others, for any reason. He, after all, was the architect in charge of the project. I examined the site at great length. I made drawings of the cracks, of the foundations. There is no question in this matter- the tower the Cavalier designed was too heavy for the foundations. I said so, vehemently, and I was justified in doing so. The Cavalier had no business in architecture- he was a sculptor, of highest order to be sure. But he was technically grossly deficient. Had he accepted the blame, I would have left the matter alone. As it was, it was by no means certain that the deficient foundation would be remedied. Padre Virgilio, impartial a man as he was, and the Pope's principal reference in these matters, concluded that the Cavalier's error lay in placing the tower on top of two foundations (one the original, the second added by my patron Carlo Maderno, who had created and then filled in forty-two deep wells), which had settled differently. The Padre believed, erroneously, that once the settling finished, the tower would be fine. I was morally compelled to bring forth what I knew to be true, for not only would the façade on the south be threatened, but if Bernini had been allowed to proceed with the twin tower on the north, the entire façade would have come down. Innocent was a very cautious man. He could see the cracks. He heard all the conflicting opinions. One thing was certain to him, and that was the uncertainty. And so in February 1646 he decided not to proceed with the North tower and to tear the South tower down. I had won. But the victory was bittersweet, for now every friend of Cavalier Bernini was an enemy of mine. The brother of the Cavalier, Domenico, openly criticized that I would have declared publicly against his brother, in the Pope's presence, "with all his heart and all his strength". As if I should have acted timidly in defense of the truth! In any event, the outcome of this event would prove fatal to my fortunes. I was safe so long as Innocent and Virgilio Spada were present, in their absence I was at the mercy of the crowd.

The Genesis and Drawing of the Ground Plan

I drew the plans for Sant'Ivo 1635-1640. Though of course they were refined many times thereafter, the Church as built is remarkably in accord with those initial plans.[23] Although I was appointed architect 1632, and although the governing body of the Sapienza, the College of Consistorial Advocates (and especially Carlo Cartari, the key member – and also Papal Archivist – who was to become deacon of the Advocates in 1647) was pressuring Urban to proceed, money was not forthcoming and so I did not begin work on the plan until the last half of the decade of the 30's.

---

[22] Morrissey 155.
[23] Smyth-Pinney 314, 320.

With all that time, I was free to think about all the possibilities. I was influenced by many factors and many sources in making this plan, and I will try to take them in turn. Overriding everything was the allegory of Divine Wisdom and the nature of the Sapienza institution as one intended for teaching and preaching. Pope Sixtus V placed the inscription you see over the entrance to the cortile begun by Pirro Ligorio: INITIUM SAPIENTIAE EST TIMOR DOMINI[24] (knowledge begins with fear of the Lord). In all I did, this concept was present and all here had to be consistent with the purpose of the institution this chapel was to serve, and so it guided all aspects of the physical form of the church and its decoration.

In fact, in my first drawings, I had the Seven Pillars of Wisdom of the Old Testament behind the high altar (I later abandoned these as not in keeping with the upward thrust I accomplished in the dome). If you consult my plan of Sant'Ivo in the Archivio di Stato in Rome, you will see the three verses I intended for the frieze above the entrance door: Sapientia adificavit sibi domum; Excidit columnas septem, Proposuit mensam suam. Taken of course from Proverbs 9:1-2: wisdom has built herself a house, she has erected her seven pillars (remember I intended these pillars for behind the altar),….she has laid her table. I meant very much for this to be the House of Wisdom.

A second factor was the limitation of the physical site and the demands those limitations placed on the plan. The Church would sit at the end of a long cortile, and della Porta's concave exedra, which I did not alter, would have to form the front. The Church could not be freestanding, and had to fit within the confines of the width between the north and south porticoes of the Sapienza. And there was little room to the rear as the Piazza Sant'Eustachio came right up to the site. Thus, I had very little room to work with, and the Church would have to be tall, to reach the light, as there could be no entrant light for some 60 feet off the ground. The site also had an irregular dimension (definitely "out of square") with unequal sides for the north and south porticoes. Working with these width and depth and vertical conditions (the site was I say, tight, narrow, small, and crooked!) presented a great challenge, one which I completely relished.

A third factor was what I would call "the hexagon and the bee". All artists of my time worked within the framework of papal patronage and I was no exception. I began with wisdom as an allegory; I had a small circular space to work with, and I had a Pope to please. Although I was the architect for the congregation, that was no guarantee I would be retained to make the actual Church, and there was certainly no guarantee that the Pope would, in any event, provide funding for the project. Fortunately, this Pope had aligned himself with the concept of Divine Wisdom. Andrea Sachi decorated the ceiling of one of the reception rooms of the Palazzo Barberini in 1629-31 with the enthroned image of Divine Wisdom, placing all of the elements of the Barberini coat of arms in it – the family heraldic device of the bee, the Barberini sun impresa, and the laurel.[25]

---

[24] Scott 296.
[25] Scott 295.

And now I was thinking of these things and the geometric form I would select for the groundplan. Without question, the Sapienza as a place for preaching and learning required a centralized plan, and so my geometric thinking revolved around that. Geometry, as I have said, is the foundation for all proper architecture. Here at the Sapienza, I was of course greatly reinforced in this thinking by Fra Benedetto Castelli, a Benedictine who was professor of mathematics at the Sapienza, who became one of my few friends and who shared my passion for insistent geometry.[26] He was also a great influence on the Barberini court, which was helpful. He died in 1643, but he was very active with me during the years I drew the plans. And so, thinking of the proper geometric form for Sant'Ivo, I next consulted the ancient sources at hand. I was impressed with the great apsidal rotundas in the area, especially Minerva Medica, but more of this later when I discuss the drum of the Church.[27] For the floor plan, I was most influenced by the ancient rotunda of the late fourth or fifth century Mausoleum of the Calventii near the Via Appia, which was in the form of a hexagon, with six apses.[28] Here I must give credit to Baldasare Peruzzi, who not only drew this Mausoleum for the rest of us in Rome to see, but also he made a sketch for a triangular church in which you can see the germ for my initial drawings.[29] Both the Calventii and the Peruzzi sketch had lobes, the former has six semicircular lobes around the central area, and three semicircular lobes and two triangles "at the shoulders". The Peruzzi sketch uses a triangle for the center figure and not the hexagon, but the key concept of lobes and small triangles attached to a central core is here. I took from these the choice of the hexagon, although I did not use the central cylinder of the Calventii, but rather abandoned the central cylinder altogether in favor of all apses with no cylinder, but more about that later.[30] It was at this point that I united the concept of the bee (from the Barberini heraldic) with the geometric form of the hexagon. To this I added appendages to the sides of the hexagon. The bee is a six-sided shape. If you draw a bee, with four wings, a head, and abdomen, and six legs, and then imagine lines connecting the abdomen of the bees, you arrive at – yes – a hexagon. And so based on the ancient heritage and the Barberini bee, I struck on the idea of a central hexagon for the Church. The hexagon was perfect for the preaching and teaching role of the Sapienza – and the plan would be symmetrical about six axes.

Of course, the hexagon was not enough for the creativity and uniqueness I sought, and so, as I say, my plan from the beginning envisioned extension of each of the hexagon's sides. For these extensions I envisioned (like the Peruzzi sketch) alternating concave lobes and convex spaces, that would fill out the space of the exterior drum I selected. In these extensions you can picture the head and four wings of the bee (the main altar being the head). The door would be the sixth piece. The six ribs of the drum/vault would constitute the six legs of the bee.

---

[26] Connors, The First Three Minutes 51.
[27] Id. 48.
[28] Id.
[29] Id. 46-49.
[30] Id. 49.

The bee and the hexagon fit perfectly of course for the Barberini. Hexagons and honeycomb - like configurations were common in Barberini buildings, like the Casino Barberini at Palestrina.[31] The Pope himself was styled as "the King of the Bees".[32] The bee, its cell, honey and wax had long been regarded as embodying Divine Wisdom.[33] Wisdom herself in Ecclesiasticus cites the fruit of the bee: "For my spirit is sweet above honey: and my inheritance above honey and the honeycomb" (24:27).[34]

A final word about my selection of the hexagon. Now, architects for all time have avoided the hexagon. Why? Because with a hexagon the parts of the building can never conform.[35] With the square, the octagon, and the dodecagon, equal sides will oppose each other through the two main axes. But with the hexagon, one of the axes goes through two sides, while the other goes through two angles. This is most unsatisfactory when it comes to creating balance in the parts. The solution, when architects did design to use the hexagon, was to design the central hexagonal space as a main space, and then to design parts (chapels) as lower satellite spaces that would be placed in the angles of the triangle.

What I did at Sant'Ivo, which has (all modestly cast aside) been described as "revolutionary" and "outside all architectural tradition", encompassing the entire perimeter, including the six bays, with an "uninterrupted sequence of giant pilasters"- creating a "unity and homogeneity" of the entire area of the church.[36]

I created a "sharply defined crowning entablature" which I believe dramatically illustrates the star form of my ground-plan.[37]

Now it was time to put my pencil to the paper, and for my first drawings I did use graphite, switching to chalk only for the presentation drawing for the Pope. Here I first constructed my hexagon. I did not begin with an equilateral triangle, as I will explain to you.

I started with the arc of the della Porta exedra. I measured from the centerpoint of the circle which created that arc – it is 47 palmi in radius from the exedra. I intended the center of the Church to be 47 palmi from the exedra, to create proportionality. The Church site determined the choice of an axially symmetrical plan[38] (of main and cross axes), but that choice does not determine for me where to position the hexagon along the

---

[31] Scott 300.
[32] Scott 300.
[33] Scott 301.
[34] Scott 300. Although Professor Connors rejects the bee as a source (Connors, The First Three Minutes 49 fn 55), Borromini's emendation to Fioravanti Martinelli's guidebook, though it may be an after the fact rationalization, is that the chapel is founded upon the impresa of the Barberini bee. The Consistorial Advocate Carlo Cartari referred to the chapel "as if in the form of a bee". And S. Giannini's Plate X, (1720) reflecting the engraving Borromini had Domenico Barriere make for him, 1660, has the Barberini bee at its center. Borromini's presentation drawing had bees encircling the Barberini impresa of the sun. Scott 298, 299.
[35] Wittkower, Art and Architecture 206.
[36] Id. 208. The Professor compares the tradition Borromini avoided: "a hexagonal main space with lower satellite spaces placed in the angles of the triangles".
[37] Id. quotes.
[38] Smyth-Pinney 330.

main longitudinal axis, and so I had to select the figure's center point and the cross axes. Originally, as I say, I intended the center to be 47 palmi from the exedra. As it happened, initial calculations of the position of the east wall were "short" by 7 palmi, and thus the center ended up being 54 palmi from the entry door.[39] Once I had the center point fixed, I could draw a circle. I, of course, had to choose the radius for the circle. Here I had in mind creating the largest possible area for the central space, which I concluded was equivalent to a diameter of 35 palmi. At one point, I drew a plan with a radius of 36 palmi but this I concluded resulted in walls for the drum that were too thin[40] - it was structurally just too daring.

The plan was based on a series of interrelated geometric figures based on a common dimension of 35 palmi. I drew the main axis, then placed the centerpoint on it 54 palmi from the entry door, and then drew the cross axis. I then chose the circle's radius – 35 palmi. I set my compass at a radius of 35 palmi and drew my circle. Then without changing the setting or angle of my compass I moved my compass point sequentially on each of the two points of the cross axis and swung arcs to each side, above and below. The points of intersection with the circle gave me the hexagon's other four points on the circle's perimeter (when the foundations were laid in 1643 this was the exact sequence used by the workers).[41] I then added the radial lines from the center point to the hexagon's points and sides. From those points, I added the three semicircular lobes and three small triangles. I drew the lobes with a radius of 35 palmi (the lobe for the altar I dropped back a bit, the centerpoint is just outside the hexagon). The three alternating triangular areas, with the convex wall segments which "cut off" the triangle's points,[42] were somewhat more work. Here I swung an arc with a radius equal to the length of one of the sides of the hexagon, from the edge of the hexagon, along the radial line[43] (you can still see this arc on the northwest side in one of my drawings – Albertina 501). I then used the point on the radial line out in the north corridor to create the convex inward curve of the added triangular area. The controlling radii for these lobes changes for each scheme for the area and does not equal the radius used for the semicircular lobes.[44] This gave me the freedom to make the triangular convex areas as was individually appropriate.

There are those who think that an equilateral triangle, and not a hexagon, was the basis for my groundplan. Simply stated, it is said that I began with an equilateral triangle, then drew the semicircular apses by swinging an arc outward from each of the three sides, and then created the convex areas by cutting off the three corners of the triangles by arcs swung in from the angles. Triangle – plus – apses – minus – angles.[45] But this generation of the plan involves a construction moving inward, beginning with the triangle's point at

---

[39] Id. 318.
[40] Id. 319, 320. Professor Smyth-Pinney's term "too daring".
[41] Id. 330. Professor Smyth-Pinney cites Albertina 501 (at 319) and three plans now at the state Archives in Rome (figures 11a, b, c at 318), Borromini's earliest drawings, which show that he proceeded from a hexagon, not a triangle. The last of these three drawings (11c) corresponds, says the Professor "to an astonishingly accurate degree" to the church "as built". 320.
[42] Id. 320.
[43] Id. Professor Smyth-Pinney's description of Borromini's drawing of the arc is at both 320 and 330.
[44] Id. fn 17. Professor Smyth-Pinney describes in her text on 320 accompanying fn 16-18 Borromini's "consistency in fundamental geometry".
[45] Connors, The First Three Minutes 38.

the entry door, the other two points of the triangle determined by the given width of the site. From there, I would have had to bisect the triangle's sides, and draw the radial lines inward from the edges of the triangle to give me the center point of the figure. From that I could create a circle and hexagon, for use simply as a check for accuracy. This outward-in approach makes the center of the plan unimportant, while for the church the center is all important.[46] The ability to modify the figure's position was very important to me in the development of my design and the fact that the triangle's position could never vary theoretically was fatal to its use. The hexagon offered advantages over the triangle: when you make a plan drawing beginning with the center point and circle you achieve a substantial advantage in accuracy, compared to first drawing a triangle and then dividing the legs of that triangle.[47] The workmen on the site who need to lay the foundations and make the walls at full scale have no use for a plan with a single triangle. You will note, dear reader, that all of the plans consistently show the characteristic signs of the geometric sequence I have described above – I establish the center of the circle and the hexagon first. It is true that the triangle, with its points hovering outside of the site's actual boundaries, does achieve a certain subtle presence, but it is only as a secondary figure.[48] In my later drawings for the Chigi Pope, I did draw a triangle, but these were, in truth, fraudulent, made, as I will explain later, for two reasons: to hide the thinness of the walls of the drum which had experienced cracking, and to move away from the Barberini hexagon – bee to the triangle, a Trinitarian triparte figure, that would be more acceptable and "ownable" by the Chigi.[49]

---

[46] Smyth-Pinney 331.
[47] Id. Professor Smyth-Pinney politely points out at 320 fn 16 that Professor Blunt's diagram at Blunt 115 (83) is "doubly flawed": neither the two triangles nor the equality of the six circles is accurate. She has the benefit of the accurate measurements. See 335 fn 11, figures 4(314), 5(315), and 9(317).
[48] Direct quotes. Smyth-Pinney 320.
[49] Smyth-Pinney 330.

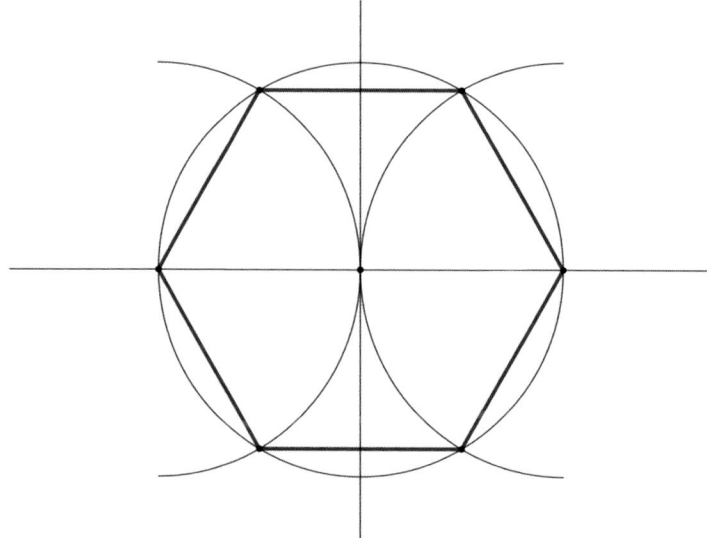

I drew the main axis, placed the centerpoint (54 palmi from the front door), then drew the cross axis, then chose the circle radius of 35 palmi, then drew the circle with my compass. Then without changing the setting of my compass I set the point on each of the two points of intersection between the cross axis and the circle and swung arcs up and down to give me the other points of the hexagon. (Professor Smyth-Pinney provides this step by step process at Smyth-Pinney 330. Hopefully I have not changed her meaning. The drawing here is by Taylor Hemmesch).

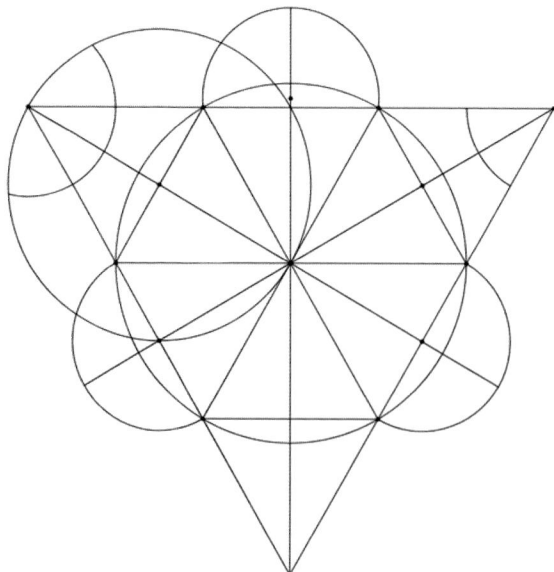

I drew radial lines from the centerpoint to the hexagon's points and sides. For the two lobes adjacent to the front door I used a 17.5 palmi radius centered on the hexagon's edge. For the apse the center was back a bit, slightly stilted, creating a horseshoe. For the two triangles adjacent to the apse, I first set my compass point on the point of intersection of the radial line and the side of the hexagon, and then made a circle with radius equal to the distance of the radial from the center to the point of intersection with the hexagon. From the point of intersection of this new circle with the radial line, I then swung an arc to the "inside" with the radius of the generating circle being 17.5 palmi (the same as the radius for the lobes). I used this arc to "lop-off" the end of the triangles to create the convex bay. (Smyth-Pinney 330). (drawing by Taylor Hemmesch).

The Interior Vault / The Main Body of the Church

Left top photo: Another view showing how I carried the floor plan straight into the vault.

Right top photo: The cornice envelopes the nave, following my floor plan. The pilasters here have irregular fluting – alternately broad and narrow.

Bottom photo: What I did at Sant'Ivo was revolutionary and outside of all architectural tradition, for I encompassed the entire perimeter, including the six bays, with an uninterrupted sequence of giant pilasters, creating a one of a kind unity and homogeneity for the entire church. Note the floor here, done last, consisting of two rhomboids, one white, one grey.

The dome of the vault, intended to mimic the silk tent that is placed over the tabernacle. I shrunk the ground plan all the way up to the base of the lantern. By using pilasters and not columns I established sharp edges for the bays, enabling the gathering together at the point of the lantern. The convex sections actually have straight elements where the vault springs, above the window I transitioned to a single concave curve. The Chigi star and monti of Alexander VII. The eight pointed star alternates with the six pointed star of knowledge - the star of David. Above the uppermost of the six pointed stars in the horizontal column, I placed a little cross in reference to the Chrismon. I alternated the Chigi symbols with wreath and palm surrounding the shield. Note the three crowns around the Chigi mountains which symbolize the Trismegistos.

The interior vault is, in my view, one of the most glorious vaults in all of Christendom. I meant this to represent a tent, replicating the silk tent covering that was placed over the tabernacle of the altar. Unlike at San Carlino where I used a transitional structural feature- the pendentive- to fasten the dome onto the body of the church- the two being of course dissimilar- one an oval, the other an octagon, here at Sant'Ivo, I chose to continue the form of the church proper right into the dome and to the top of the lantern. I did this in keeping with the theme of wisdom- always rising, always reaching to the Pentecost. I also did this to create something extraordinary. Yes, there were other buildings where the ground plan is continued into the vaulting. All previous circular and oval churches, however, followed the type of dome Michelangelo gave to Saint Peter. Here I broke the vaulted surface into differently shaped units, continuing the shape of the ground plan and not turning to the rounded dome. What I did at Sant'Ivo, though unique, was simply to make the dome by a simple process of shrinking the ground plan all the way up to the base of the lantern, just like a tent, as I have said.[50] By using pilasters and not columns I established sharp edges for the bays, enabling this gathering together at the point of the lantern.[51] I do confess that the vaulting of the Serapeum at Hadrian's Villa gave me some precedent. There too the vaulting is broken into separate planes.

---

[50] Blunt 116. Professor Blunt's description of the tent.
[51] Id.

The colossal order of pilasters created the sharp corners I needed to carry the floor plan through the cornice into the dome up to the lantern. I used irregular wide and narrow fluting. In the capitals are the Chigi Rovere acorns.

You may ask, how I was able to unite these separate planes into continuity, once they reach the lantern? For the bays below are alternately convex and concave, and the convex bays have three different sides- flat, convex, and flat. The vaulting for the semicircular bays was easy- I could continue the concavity on the same plane and you can see that the entablature is semicircular. For the convex bays, though, the entablature is straight-convex-straight- and so I had to practice some deception. The spring of the vault, if you look closely, actually consists of three straight elements! The side sections are quite narrow and the middle has the open space of the window. This, fortunately, does not define any plane, and so I could have another straight element, that you the visitor overlook. At the top of the window, I gathered these three straight elements into a single concave curve, which I then continued all the way up to the ring around the lantern:[52] ingenious, and beautiful.

For the six alternating bays of the nave, I enjoyed the three convex the most. For these I created a gallery for the upper level. I made this with a round-headed arch- subsequently someone has- contrary to my thoughts- placed a flat trabeation with its corners cut off by little quadrants.[53] I then put in a balustrade of my style (as at Carlino and Filippo Neri, the balusters are three sided, and the thick and narrow ends alternate). Someone subsequently removed these as well.

---

[52] Id. 120. This is Professor Blunt's description of Borromini's ingenious method.
[53] Blunt 118. Professor Blunt's observation of the alterations.

I created twelve niches; two for each bay, and the twelve apostles were once here, in keeping with the theme of the Pentecost and knowledge. They too have been removed.

The stucco over the doors in a concave lobe. I used the palm tree to symbolize the Holy Spirit, the paraclete.

For the main altar- the central semicircular bay- I ultimately decided on a solid backing for the altar, with light supplied from a window I placed above on the east façade of the building. Cavalier Bernini has rightly been credited with the most consummate skill in using this type of hidden lighting- especially his Cornaro chapel for Saint Therese. Unfortunately, this window was removed after I left, and this whole bay was massively altered. The coffered arch you now see is not mine and does not belong here.[54]

The first thing that strikes the visitor when entering is the bright light of the church- the gleaming white. Many now ask if this is how I originally designed it, and they suggest that perhaps I broke up the uniform white with shades of off- white and pale grey which have been taken down. The answer is no. I believe architecture should be allowed to speak for itself. If color is needed to attract attention, then the architecture must be deficient since it cannot stand on its own. The reason that the visitor may be overwhelmed by the whiteness lies in the windows. I provided ample lighting in the vaulting and in the lantern (supplemented originally by the window behind the altar). When originally constructed these windows were more heavily leaded than they are now. They let in considerably less light, and so the white I had in the church was not nearly as predominant as it is today.

Again, my theme for this church was wisdom. And I also had to include the Pope's heraldic symbols (and very much wanted to, in the hope that I might receive a future papal commission). All the decoration occurred after Alexander VII began his reign in 1655, and thus his monti and star throughout. In the vaulting, above the windows, I placed the crowned monti, with the Chigi eight pointed star. These I alternated with wreath and palm surrounding the shield. At the base of the lantern I placed the monti, alternating with the della Rovere oak branches (which Julius II had allowed the Chigi family to borrow from the Rovere arms).[55] Then I put the acorns in the capitals of the pilasters (again a Rovere symbol). In the narrow sections of the dome I alternated the six pointed Star of David (symbol of wisdom) with the eight-pointed star of the Chigi.

---

[54] Id. 122.
[55] Id. Professor Blunt provides the surmise about off-white and pale grey colors above, and the leading.

A seraphim with its six wings at the top of the vault in the dome. The flowing hair, brilliant eyes, and the puffed cheeks, chin and nose of a young child.

The Temple, the Holy of Holies, is an historic part of the theme of wisdom. And so you see here not only the Star of David, but the palm trees over the doors leading to the side chapels. In the dome I placed the palm with the winged cherub's heads to form a ring below the lantern. In the vault, please see how I placed three crowns around the Chigi mountains, an allusion to the Trismegistos. Also see how, with the uppermost stars with six points, I placed a little cross at the top in reference to the Chrismon.[56] I tried to evoke the cosmic symbolism of the vault of heaven[57] with the stars and the two superimposed circles formed by the cherubim of the windows and the seraphim at the top of the vault. These two classes of angels were nearest to the throne of God.[58] For the windows of the vault I inserted palmi, wreaths of oak, laurel and olive, which I took from the praise of Wisdom in Ecclesiasticus. Detail, detail, and more detail. Note that I used irregular fluting in the pilasters.
 – alternately broad and narrow – novel, yes, but also with a classical tradition seen in the Augustan Temple of Apollo Sosianus.[59]

The irregular fluting of the pilasters.

---

[56] Portoghesi 157. See his figure 88.
[57] Id. Professor Portoghesi's descriptions and references to the vault of heaven.
[58] Id.
[59] Blunt 39.

Here, I must acknowledge the link to San Pietro: the stars encircling the lantern, the Seraphim which are around the stars, the lower order of angels that are in the roundels, and the descending line of stars, all repeat the design of Cesare d'Arpino, executed at San Pietro's dome for Pope Sixtus V in 1590.[60]

From the plates of Sebastiano Giannini. In this drawing you can see how I repeated in the vault of Sant'Ivo the design of Cesare d'Arpino at the dome of San Pietro with the descending line of stars.

The Plan for the Drum / Its Execution

The design for the exterior drum was contemporaneous with my design of the plans for the interior – they go hand in hand. Here there were two influences upon me – the ancient Imperial rotundas and the accommodation necessary for the interior vault. I wanted a drum like the Minerva Medica and the Mausoleum of the Calventii, both examples of apsidal rotundas. I designed my drum with six beautiful but powerful apses, "a quisa d'una rosa di sei foglie",[61] like the six petals of a rose.

---

[60] Scott, 315, Portoghesi 182. The Professor's list of linkages to San Pietro.
[61] Connors, The Spiral 670, fn10.

When you first see the drum of Sant'Ivo from the courtyard, and then you enter the church, you are I am sure stunned by the difference between the outside and the inside. The six bulging apses of the exterior drum give the viewer the impression that the interior will correspond and he will see six similar apses when he enters.[62] My interior, however, is based on a hexagon; the paradox here is that the hexfoil drum reveals nothing of the plan within the church.[63]

Albertina 500.

The drawing nearby shows the relationship between the church and the drum.[64] For a simple rotunda like the Pantheon, the cupola follows the cylinder of the walls. Where a ground plan becomes more complex, like a cross, the cupola must retreat and it is drawn as a small circle inside the main figure.[65] A pendentive is then used to unite the cupola to the supporting walls. The cupola for these complex plans is, then, smaller than the generating figure and inscribable within it.[66]

One of the windows of the drum, the Agnus Dei above.

But for my Sant'Ivo, even though it has a complex groundplan with hexagon and six attached lobes, the cupola is larger than the hexagon, and in fact is circumscribed around it. I drew the six lobes with centers that I set on each of the sides of the hexagon.[67] As I have already related to you, I communicated all of my floor plan into my vault. If I had followed the historical precedent of inscribing the cupola inside the generating figure, the interior span would have been only 72 palmi in diameter, versus the 92 palmi I was to use. The design taking the entire floor plan into the vault allowed me to build a very, very large cupola. The diameter of the exterior is 102 palmi.[68]

---

[62] Connors, The First Three Minutes 38.
[63] Id. 47. The Professor's description of the paradox.
[64] Id. Figure 14, Albertina drawing 500.
[65] Id. 47.
[66] Connors, The First Three Minutes 47, quotes. The Professor's explanation of the retreat, the pendentive, and the making of the cupola. The Professor includes squinches with pendentives as available to "bridge the gap" between cupola and supporting piers or walls.
[67] Id. direct quotes/paraphrase. "Three of these lobes are concentric with the three apses of the interior and easily fit around them." This results in windows with normal jambs. The other three lobes don't "mesh" with the points of the triangles and their arcs. Here the window jambs are "abnormably thick."
[68] Id. 68,69. Professor Connors words: The Professor notes that the power of the drum comes "not only from its shape but its size". 48.

I retained the exedra of Giacomo della Porta, adhering strictly to his ground plan, primarily because the exedra was tied to the porticoes, to which I was committed.

I did plan an unusual front portal with a double pediment, but in the end I abandoned it for fear it would alter too greatly the concept of the arcades and courtyard. The lower section of the interior of the church is hidden behind the exedra. The convexity of the drum presents the usual contrast I required between convex and concave; della Porta's hemicycle with closed arcades presents a great contrast with my drum. My overall goal with the dome was to present a momentous upward thrust, knowledge and wisdom flowing towards heaven and back. The dome, if you will, has five parts, six if you count della Porta's hemicycle: drum, pyramid, lantern, spiral, and cusp.

I added the Chigi star and monti to the attic after Alexander VII ascended the throne. The six pointed star of knowledge of David below. The Chrismon Monogram above under the cornice.

The inclined bass relief of the Lamb of God above the central door, seated upon the book with seven seals, from Revelation 5.

For the drum, I followed the Lombard tradition (as at Carlino) and used a cylinder of masonry, which encapsulates the interior dome. This mass, as I say, does not correspond to the interior; it serves to absorb the lateral thrust, substituting for buttresses. The drum is divided into six convex sections, each with two small side bays and one larger one in the middle, with a window. This arrangement does not, of course, match the alternation of ("convex" and "concave") bays inside.[69] At the point where the sections meet, I strengthened the order.[70] In my drawings, I had an architectural panel in the side bays, but for economy I eliminated these. You will note the Pamphilj dove in the medallion above the window (a garland surrounds it), and the six-pointed star of knowledge in the voluted capitals of the pilasters of the drum. In the soffit of the jambs of the window of the drum, I inserted a bas- relief of the Lamb of God, standing on a book upon which you can see the seven seals from Revelation 5. I inclined this relief toward you as you enter.

---

[69] Blunt 123.
[70] Wittkower, Art and Architecture 210. Professor Wittkower's description of the strengthening which he says "enhances the impression of vitality and tension".

I superimposed the pilasters at the junction of the apses. Here two lines of acanthus leaves, and volutes surrounding a small laurel wreath enclosing the six pointed star of knowledge.

Where the order is strengthened at the junctions note that I superimposed the pilasters on each other, and so I ended with three capitals here. I always want to have unusual capitals, and here I have acanthus leaves, one line above another, and then volutes surrounding a small laurel wreath enclosing the star. Below the cornice is one more of my specialties- the little cherub head with wings- substituting for the egg and dart motif you usually see. By calling these out for you, I am shamelessly impressing upon you my great attention to every detail. No element is too small for the attention of a true architect. Also, please note that I placed the Chrismon Monogram within a laurel wreath above the large lateral windows of the drum.

One of the capitals on the exterior. The Pamphilj dove and olive branch.

The stepped pyramid. Here I proceeded in my usual geometric fashion. The steps are not concentric, but were drawn from arcs of circles of the same radius, with each of the centers moved back by the width of a step for each succeeding circle. I placed low buttresses above the pilasters of the drum, concave, to contrast with the convexity of the steps, then used the Michelangelo pier/merlons.

Above the cornice of the drum, I created a pyramid, with steps like the Pantheon and the dome I did at Carlino. The stepped dome I made, I must say, is no simple element. Like everything I did, I proceeded in geometric form. The steps are not, as you might at first think, a series of concentric circles. I drew arcs of circles of the same radius, with each of the centers moved back by the width of a step for each succeeding circle.[71] This area is slightly convex,

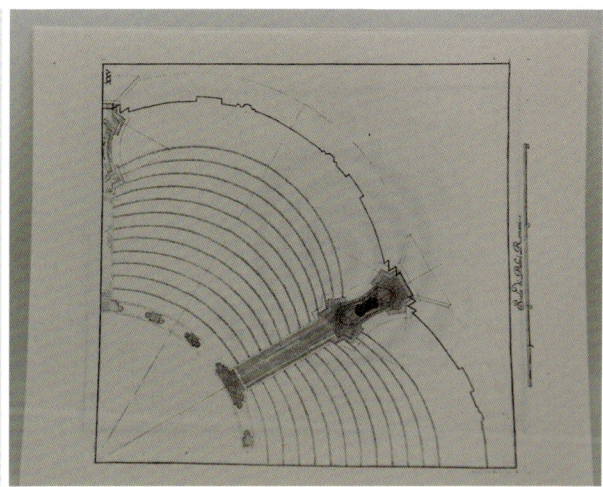

Diagram 1472 From the Giannini plates. The pyramid. The arcs of the steps have circles of the same radius with each center moved back by the width of a step.

matching the interior at this point. Then I placed low buttresses that are above the pilasters of the drum. These are concave, providing the contrast with the convexity of the steps. I placed piers at the ends of the buttresses, using Michelangelo's Porta Pia Ionic motif.[72]

The paraclete, symbol of Divine Widsom, surrounded by a swag of laurel, the cherubs and wings in the cornice substituting for the usual egg and dart (taken from the Landi chapel at Santa Lucia in Selci).

The merlons, taken from Michelangelo's Porta Pia.

---

[71] Blunt 125. Professor Blunt also notes that "the lines of the Porta Pia motif all meet on the circumference of the lowest step." See engraving no. 89.
[72] Id. 154.

SANT'IVO ALLA SAPIENZA | 157

The stepped pyramid, Michelangelo's merlons, the lantern, the spire, the cusp. In the lantern, patterned after the Tower of Baalbek, I used a scalloped cornice, and triple clusters of columns on each pier.

The Genesis and the Making of the Lantern and Spire

Innocent X inherited from Urban VIII in 1644 a completed ground plan, drum and vault. But the Church was unusable because it lacked a lantern, windows, and decoration.[73] Urban was not inclined to proceed with the Sapienza because it was a project of the despised Barberini.[74] I found the way to instigate him to action, and it was the lantern and spiral. Innocent wanted to impose his image on the skyline of Rome, and he was less interested in the interior.[75] And so I designed a magnificent and unparalleled spiral which would sit atop a grand lantern. As I will describe later, I erred in estimating the impact of its great size on the drum; when I constructed the drum I did not anticipate a lantern and spire of this great size. I will describe for you shortly the additional work I had to do to resolve the cracking that ensued because of my error.

I called my exotic lantern and spiral the "tempietto sopra al tempio della Sapienza".[76] I began the design only in the latter half of Innocent's reign, in 1651, construction began in March 1652.[77] The ziggurats of Mesopotamia, which I had seen in the engravings of Martin van Heemskerk, and especially the Tower of Babel were dominant in my plan. I used double columns here with concave recessions between them. To show you further that everything fits into my geometric patterns, I call to your attention that at the higher level of the lantern I drew

Detail from the exterior of the dome. The Pamphilj dove and olive branch. The torch, a symbol of knowledge. I placed fleur-de-lis and rosettes below the cornice of the lantern. On top of the cornices, on the convex pieces, are what I would call torches, which sit atop pedestals with volute legs, again symbols of knowledge.

all the elements of the concave bays by using arcs of circles drawn from centers that were on the outer perimeter of the entire lantern. My drawings for Ivo still have the holes I made from the leg of the compasses, showing how I made these arcs. Pay special attention to the quite detailed capitals I gave these columns, which have volutes springing from acanthus leaves.[78]

---

[73] Smyth-Pinney 322.
[74] He did put his Pamphilj arms over the door of the University. Connors, The Spiral 670, 671.
[75] Id.
[76] Connors, The Spiral 668, fn 1.
[77] Id. 669, 672. Figure 45, Appendix C, no. 1.
[78] Blunt 125, 126, Albertina 509.

And now for the spiral and the finial atop it. There are so many explanations for my idea here, all but one are false. It was not the stinger end of a bee (to design that for the Pamphilj would have been professional suicide), nor is it the Tower of Babel, nor is it a conch, though I was fond of conches and had one in my home and though my close friend Virgilio Spada was an avid conchologist.[79] Nor is it the spiral of the Old Testament Pillar of Fire, nor the Lighthouse of Alexandria, nor Dante's Mount of Purgatory.

The famous spiral. The tempietto sopra al tempio della Sapienza. In order to make each turn of the spiral appear to rise by the same amount, curves at the top are semicircles generated from the center while those at the bottom are generated by a center 1 ½ palmi up and to the left. The spiral makes three turns to mimic the papal tiara. The globes here are a symbol of totality. The columns I inverted. The panels are predominated with small pyramids. Atop is another torch. I have the torches here as flames of the symbol of charity, and the chief attribute of wisdom— the central theme at Sant'Ivo- is charity.

For my conceptual starting point, I began again with the allegory of wisdom. I also had a burning desire within me to create the most original, the most daring, spire in Rome, and I settled on a spiral, which was in my mind from the famous Ziggurat and also the Mosque of Samarra. What did I intend the spiral and its finial to represent? "Wisdom is a gift from God",[80] whose chief attribute is charity, which is symbolized by flames. With this conception of charity, I linked the papal tiara. I was to have the spiral make three complete turns[81] and these I meant to recall the triple-crowned papal tiara.[82] The Pope's charity in sponsoring the University, I felt, exemplified the highest wisdom.[83]

---

[79] Scott 308, fn 99.
[80] Scott 303. Professor Scott's description of charity as the chief attribute of wisdom.
[81] Scott 304 fn 78. Borromini wrote "Si resolve di redurre tutte tre le girate" on a cross section drawing of the spire, Albertina 510, Scott figure 11.
[82] Portoghesi, "Borromini decorate" Bollettino d' Arte, XL, 1955, 28-29, Scott 304 fn 79.
[83] Scott 303.

The decoration of the interior of the lantern occurred in 1653 under Innocent (the decoration of the vault was later, under Alexander). Here I continued to use the themes of wisdom and charity. We placed a dove (now fallen!) with an olive branch in its beak. Then we placed a glory around it – with 15 flaming tongues – "linque infiammate".[84] I note here that Sant' Ivo had experienced a miracle when a tongue of fire appeared above him as he used his fiery lawyer's tongue in defense of the poor. This too, symbolized the Pentecost, another link to Divine Wisdom (there were 15 disciples present for the Descent of the Holy Spirit).

The lantern. The Dove of the Holy Spirit- the Paraclete- was suspended here, with an olive branch in its beak. It has been lost over time. A glory of fifteen flaming tongues surrounded the dove. At the base, the Chigi star and monti of Alexander VII. These alternate with the Rovere oak branches (Julius II had granted permission to the Chigi to use this in their emblem). Acorns are in the capitals. The cherubs are, of course, individually modeled.

Above the lantern, the spiral springs from the torches of the lantern. Geometrically, the spiral consists of two series of concentric semi-circles. I placed globes, symbol of totality, squinched in between the ends of inverted columns, which climb the spiral here. I placed panels with multiple geometric forms but predominated with small pyramids. At the top there was another torch- this one all the way around. As you observe the spiral, please pay attention to my concern here for optical illusion, "l'inganno dell' occhio", for I had to deal with the problem of how I could have each of the turns of the spiral appear to rise by the same amount. I did this by having the curves at the top half be semicircles generated form the center, but having the curves at the bottom half generate from a center that is 1 ½ palmi up and to the left.[85]

---

[84] Scott 313, note 122. The 1655 misura e stima commissioned by Alexander notes the olive branch: "Per la palomba fatta nel campo in mezzo a detta corona che porta il ramo d' olivio agg. bozz. e stucca…".
[85] Connors, The Spiral 673. The Professor notes with this language that Borromini's spiral is not a true spiral "such as a geometer might have drawn, but a false one constructed out of arcs of circles".

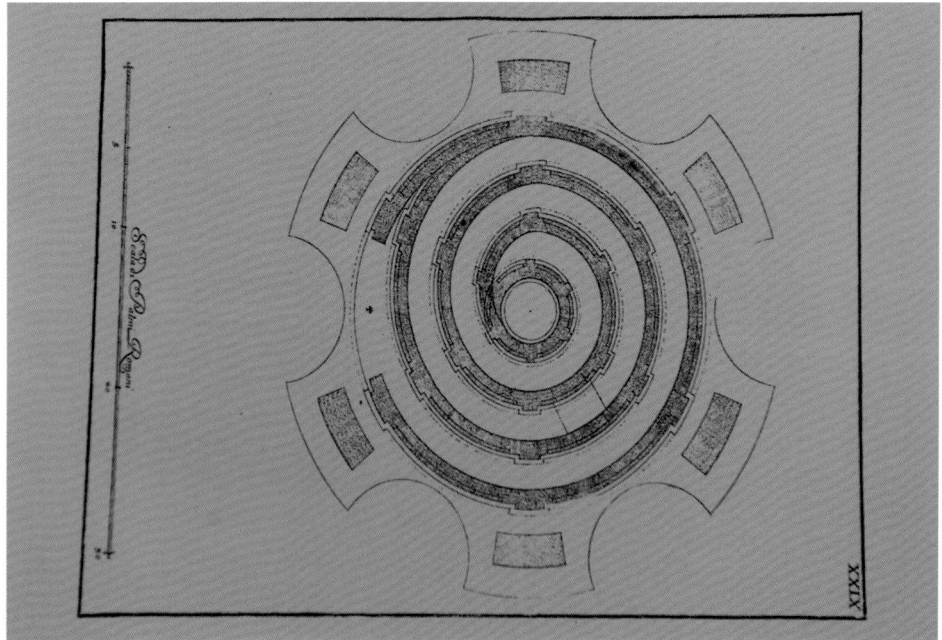

My drawing of my creation of the curves of the spiral, "l 'inganno dell' occhia".

The ironwork superstructure finial, in place by October 1652, has an open onion dome, an orb, a flat metal Pamphilj dove, and a lily-pointed cross. All these represent knowledge, taken from the Iconologia of Cesare Ripa Perugino.

The Ascent Through the Spiral

Let me now speak of the ascent I created through the spiral to the very top of Sant'Ivo. Favored visitors to Rome at this time were guided to the roof of the Pantheon, and to the copper ball at the top of Saint Peter's lantern. The Pope, of course, wanted to add Sant'Ivo to this itinerary. We thus designed a passageway to ascend to the top of the spiral for these same favored pilgrims. Several staircases already led to the loggia scoperta. We created two flying buttress bridges from the side wings to the roof, from north and south. Then the stepped roof on the drum gave ascent to the level of the lantern. Climbers, after they crossed the bridge and reached the stepped vault, could walk along the base one quarter turn, through the porticella "Porta Pia" buttress, to ascend the steps to the balustrade of the lantern which has an opening on the front for this purpose.[86]

Then, I made a tiny well in one of the piers of the lantern, just 3 ½ palmi wide, and I placed 37 iron rungs enabling you to reach a chamber some 10 palmi high and wide, contained in the mass of the spiral.[87] Now you, the visitor, were required to step outside,

---

[86] This description of the ascent of the spiral that Borromini made comes from Professor Connors. See Connors, The Spiral 677, fn 36.

[87] Id. From the Professor's detail. See his figure 58, a 1692-1699 pen and ink by Gilles-Marie Oppenrod showing this chamber with climbers resting in it.

and actually walk along the spiral, using the curving path between ridges of the crown, touching the giant jewels and pearls. After 3 ½ turns, you must go back inside into the manhole I made for you, which is 3 palmi wide and some 9 palmi high. As you stand in this well, you can pull yourself up to actually situate yourself into my "fiery travertine crown", to have a fabulous view of the city.[88]

This ascent I thought of as "a wreath made up of laurel leaves and berries and wrapped in a ribbon." I had the lambent flames drawn together in groups of threes for this purpose. The flaming laurea and the triplet flames give a sense of the divine; this is the laurea, the doctorate, final goal of the university curriculum.[89]

The Additions to the Drum Made Under Innocent X

As you will remember, the Barberini Pope Urban VIII at his death left the church finished only up to the ocular of the drum. It was left to Innocent to add the spire, and also the finishing of the top of the dome of the drum. I divided the stepped vault into separate "gores", each of which I had rise to a central platform, which was already in place.[90] What I added under Innocent was the six buttresses that "curl down" from the lantern like ski slopes, the contraforti orbicolati, and the six arched counterweights with balls on top, the porticella (which I took from Michelangelo's Porta Pia).[91]

Innocent also had me make the attic storey on the exedra of della Porta, including four oval windows, and two round platforms on top of the attic. The Chigi Pope was to later have me decorate this with his Chigi Monti![92]

The Additions to the Drum Made Under Alexander

Alexander was unhappy with what he regarded as the heavy Minerva – Medica look of the drum. Consequently, he had me change the double pilasters, which separated the apses, into triple pilasters, and also had me add two panel pilasters to each of the windows.[93]

The Cracks Occasioned by the Addition of the Spire

I had not planned on the great size and weight of the spire when I designed the drum. The six primary piers for the structure were "L" or "V" shaped, placed at each of the Church's six angles. I did not design the Church structurally as an "equally loaded, bearing wall

---

[88] Id. 677-678, quotes.
[89] Id. 678, quotes, attributing this interpretation to Oppenrod.
[90] Id. 670, figure 43.
[91] Id. Professor Connors' description.
[92] Id. 675, figure 53, fn28.
[93] Id. 675.

building".⁹⁴ The thicker ribs rise "three dimensionally" upward to the oculus of the dome.⁹⁵ The walls in between the ribs are relatively thin. Because of this I was able to make whatever openings in them I chose.⁹⁶

The additional weight of the lantern and spiral caused cracking in the dome which appeared almost immediately. The problem was made worse by the failure to complete the palace's north porticoes and the hexagonal rooms on the north.⁹⁷ Then too, as I explained to the Consistorial Advocate Carlo Cartari, movement in the original structure became a risk due to variations in the groundwater level as the foundations were built.⁹⁸

I took a number of corrective actions. I pleaded for the north portico to be finished, unfortunately although six foundation pieces were put in place in the summer of 1653, nothing had been done as late as 1655.⁹⁹ Most importantly, I installed in May of 1652 an iron reinforcing chain around the base of the drum. This chain had to draw the ribs inward without crushing the fragile lobes, and was a great engineering feat in and of itself.¹⁰⁰ This chain weighed 949 pounds and I designed it to contain the hoop thrusts that were created at the base of the dome by the great weight of the lantern.¹⁰¹ I was an expert at these chains, and also at hiding them, and I would have made such a chain and hidden it when I initially made the drum for Urban VIII had I properly anticipated the weight of the spire. My chain unfortunately did not eliminate the cracking, and in 1655 the Consistorial Advocates delivered to me a formal letter requiring me to accept responsibility, which I did, conditioned on completion of the north porticoes.¹⁰²

---

[94] Smyth-Pinney 321, quotes.
[95] Id.
[96] Id. Professor Smyth-Pinney describes Borromini's point-loaded strategy and its advantages at 321, 322: it "placed the major weight…on the ground…comfortably within the constricted available site" while allowing Borromini to push the "inner membrane walls outward to their absolute maximums".
[97] Id. 322-323.
[98] Id. 327 fn 55.
[99] Id. 322, 323.
[100] Id. 327 fn. 53. Professor Smyth-Pinney notes the largest crack still exists left of the altar and is continuously monitored.
[101] This chain is still in place and you can see it at the level of the pilaster bases. Connors, The Spiral 671.
[102] Smyth-Pinney 327.

The Fraud I Committed in My Later Drawings

From the Giannini plates. In this drawing, I increased the mass of the walls. They are actually much thinner. I had to convince that the building was structurally sound, despite the cracks that had appeared.

As I have described, the walls of the vault I made between the buttressing were very thin. The use of six piers to bear the load allowed me to make a large dome with great visual impact by pushing the thin membrane walls outward to their absolute maximums.[103] This enabled me to have the widest possible interior and the most expansive vault within the small space allotted to me. After I placed the drum and lantern and spire and the cracks began, and the Chigi Alexander VII began his reign, I had to find a way to convince Alexander to execute the remainder of my plans and not to become concerned about the integrity of the structure. Because the Barberini and their bee and hexagon were not viewed favorably by the Chigi (any more than they had been by the Pamphilj), I needed to hide the hexagon as best I could. It was at this point that the triangle emerged in my plans. The triangle is a symbol of the Trinity, and the Chigi could identify with it. I was also at this time (1658-1660) beginning work on what I intended to be a publication of my drawings (made by Domenico Barriere) and the triangle was useful in explaining my work in mathematical and geometric terms. By redrawing the initial plan and making it smaller, I could mask the thin walls and also call attention to the triangle that was in reality completely subservient to the hexagon. I also wanted to mask the thin walls of the Church and the fact that they were not intended to be bearing walls.[104] I visually increased the thickness of the walls in the drawing.[105] I had to twice enlarge the niches

---

[103] Id. 321, 322.
[104] Id. 327, Professor Smyth-Pinney discusses the importance of the triangle and the Trinitarian symbolism at 330.
[105] Id. 325.

at the triangle's points and I stilted the two lobes adjacent to the entry.[106] In all this, I was successful, for Alexander proceeded forward, and I was able to promote better the notion that my work reflected master manipulation of the geometry of the triangle.

The Chigi Changes

A half section of the dome.

The third and last building phase (save the pavement) occurred 1658-1660. This programme was to include the completion of the north wing, the entrance from the Piazza Sant'Eustachio, a public library (the Alessandrina), and the hexagonal spaces on the north side.[107] The project began in March of 1659 and was complete by the dedication on November 14 of 1660. The drum was changed to make it lighter and more elegant, the Chigi Monti were added to the attic above the exedra, and I walled in the twelve niches on the piano nobile to further address the issue of the cracking.[108] I also added two choir lofts to match the one over the Church's main door. As part of the work toward the Piazza Sant'Eustachio I added the two concave wings framing the cupola for the view from that Piazza, the mezza luna.[109] In addition to all the changes to the prior work, the main part of the program of Alexander was the interior decoration, which I discuss elsewhere.

---

[106] Id. 324, quotes.
[107] Id. 323, 324 fn34.
[108] Id. 324.
[109] Connors, The Spiral 674.

Other Sides of Sant'Ivo

On the east façade of Ivo, I had already placed two portals on the axis of the cloisters (what I had tried to do for the west façade), and placed large windows over them, making slightly curved pediments interrupted by the arch of the windows. I had intended to place herms as support for the pediments, but in the event I used Michelangelo's consoles.

For the portals, I placed an oak wreath, a symbol of dialectics, and winged crowns of laurel, to symbolize poetry, and the scale and the sword to symbolize justice, and the serpent looking in the mirror, a symbol of prudence and medicine. All of these were, of course, the subjects of study at the Sapienza. Pay special attention to the fact that in the large window of the portals, I made soffits with deep arches decorated with coffers highlighting their depth, with the Chigi acorns hanging from consoles like earrings from the lobe of an ear (watch for these again at the Propaganda Fide).[110] The soffit of the cornice here is incised in an alternate rhythm ab-c-ab-c with wreaths, rosettes, and elongated leaves, enclosed in coffers of variable width. Incidentally, the Cavalier Bernini copied these portals at his Sant'Andrea al Quirinale!

The portal of the east side, with Michelangelo's consoles. The oak wreath symbolizes dialectics, the winged crown of laurel poetry. Above note the Chigi acorn hanging from the console like an earring.

The Barberini Impresa of the Sun: pay attention to the volute mask.

On the south side on the Via dei Canestrari, I placed on the lateral façade a marble plaque, with the radiant sun and the laurel wreath of the Barberini. As I am sure you can see by now, Sant' Ivo's building stages fully reflect in the heraldry the successive reigns of three Popes.

---

[110] Portoghesi 154.

The Floor

I finished Sant'Ivo with the floor and the Alessandrina Library. For the floor, made in 1660, I made a mistake. I decided early on to use the most common type of marble unit; this consisted of two rhomboidal sections, one white, one grey. If you put these together such that the longest side is in common, all the angles will be of 45 degrees or 135 degrees.[111] I proposed two alternatives to the Rector- the first had all the slabs running parallel. This was rejected, probably correctly, since the pattern ran contrary to the centralized design. The second proposal, which was accepted, was to have the units flow from the center. My mistake was to use what was in essence an octagonal device for a church that was in the shape of a hexagon. There are eight sections, of course, in an octagonal plan. Unfortunately eight does not equal six, and the church has six bays, and the result was that the lines of the eight sections emanating from the center have an intersection with the periphery, which does not correspond to the articulation of the wall.[112] To counter this deformity, I put straight lines of grey marble across all of the openings of the six bays, and then I paved the bays with slabs that I set parallel to each other. Not completely satisfactory, but a partial solution to the problem I created for myself.

The Alessandrina Library

The Library of the Sapienza came last, built under and named for Pope Alexander VII, the Alessandrina. Work began in earnest in 1665, and three sides were completed in 1666. Carlo Rainaldi was brought in after my departure to finish the fourth side.[113] He failed to place the columns for this wall towards the Dogana Vecchia, and consequently the book case structure for the Library is not synchronized.[114] Some would say he was getting even for the fact I replaced him at Sant'Agnese. I

From Eberhard Hempel.

---

[111] Blunt 121. The Professor's analysis here.
[112] Id. The Professor's explanation of how Borromini partially solved the problem.
[113] Portoghesi 150, his description set forth here.
[114] Id.

designed the Library in three fields, in which I placed sail vaults that are tied with an inscribed ring. The bookcases I placed within these large structural bays.[115] The wall pilasters are aligned with the bookcases. The narrow balcony interrupts, only slightly, the pilasters, which link the bays in a continuity.[116] The pilasters as you can see, support the vaulting. I then subdivided the two lateral walls into sub-unities. I tried to create an ascending tertiary rhythm here: a-b-c-b-a and then in the upper zone a-c-a.[117]

I should tell you that when others subsequently did a restoration of the Library and removed the shelving they found my drawing out on the wall- in full-scale mind you- of the outlines and mouldings of the book shelves.[118] I can assure you that I spared no attention to detail- and that I did not leave this work to assistants or students.

Sant'Ivo did so much for my spirits. You can see how my favorite devices developed here. First, the continuing pervasive contrast of convex against concave, the elimination of the corner, the simplicity of the white decoration, the volute, the precise adherence to geometric principles, the rhythm of the bays, the spectacular cornice, the cherubim, the brilliant lighting, the ever present curve, movement in all aspects, and symbolism in every detail. Others have used terms like spatial invention, mathematical precision, originality but not capriciousness, fantasy of the form, inventiveness but not whimsicality, and always eminent practicality. I, of course, love and agree with all of these terms and praises!

---

[115] Id. 158.
[116] Id.
[117] Id. 159.
[118] Blunt 128.

CHAPTER EIGHT

San Giovanni in Laterano

The nave which I restored by removing one out of every three of the ancient columns and imbedding the remainder in new piers. I planned to vault the nave with crossribs, as I did at the Re Magi, but Innocent would not permit (nor finance) it. I created twelve magnificent niches for the Apostles which extend themselves well into the nave.

April of 1644 brought the election of Giovanni Battista Pamphilj. The next nine years were to be the busiest of my career. One of Innocent X's highest priorities was the restoration of the Lateran Basilica, the Mother Church of Rome and the world, which had been allowed to fall into ruin, while lavish attention had been continuously focused on San Pietro's. In April 1647, the Pope placed my good friend and benefactor Padre Virgilio Spada as the superintendent of this project, and I was chosen as architect. I proposed a plan for the complete reconstruction of the church. When this was rejected by the Pope for reasons of economy, I proposed a renovation which would preserve the parts of the church which could be salvaged, and permit completion of the renovation by the time of the Jubilee year 1650. This renovation was to include the apse (I wanted to place a colonnade round the apse of the kind you see at San Carlo al Corso), and the left and right transepts, the nave and side aisles, and importantly I wanted to vault the ceiling, in the manner I was to use at Re Magi: a "flattened vault with a pattern of diagonally interlaced ribs" which would originate above the canted pilasters.[1] In the end, and to my great disappointment, we accomplished only the nave, the side aisles, and all the tombs of the side aisles. What we did accomplish was quite successful, and we finished in November 1650 (the tombs came later), in time for the beginning of the Jubilee Year.

The Basilica was in exceedingly dilapidated condition. The north side especially was literally about to fall down. The walls of the nave were fully two feet off center at their top. The columns had become so weak and off center that they had been encased in brick to keep them standing. I redrew plans to suit the Pope's demands and limitations, and feverish work began. Remember that at this time I was thoroughly engaged in the project at Sant'Ivo. I was also working on the Orologio at the Oratory. I was thoroughly happy to be so busy. Finally my work was being recognized. The commission at San Giovanni was, if not the equivalent of the commission of Carlo Maderno at San Pietro, then certainly very close to it. The commission, being one that pertained to the Mother Church of all Christendom, was certainly the most important Papal commission then extant. I lived simply in my casa off the Via Giulia near the Fiorentini, with but one servant. My rooms were full of books. I spent my entire day at my work, drawing, supervising at the sites, reviewing work orders, answering questions, and taking measurements. Evenings I spent reading. I did not drink and I did not carouse. I had few friends, though they were good ones. I was consumed by my work, and my work consumed me. I was happy, because I was productive and inventive, all to the greater glory of God and His church, and finally, I was recognized.

---

[1] Echols 159 fn 51. Professor Echols harbors doubts about Borromini's intention.

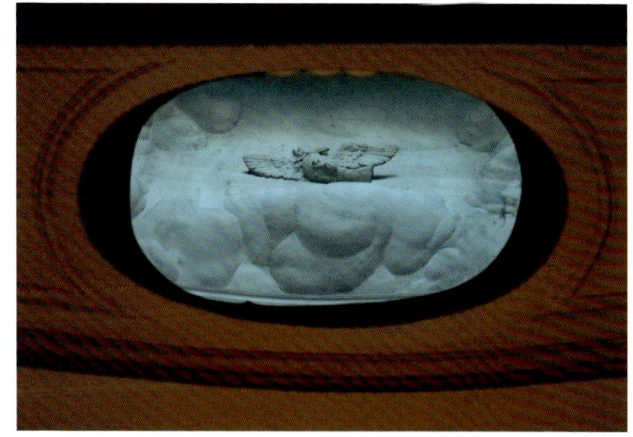

Top Photo: The nave viewed toward the entrance. The reliefs of Old and New Testaments above were directed by Alessandro Algardi.

Right Photo: On the inside of the main door, looking up, an oval aperture and a cloud with the Paraclete. Not many people stop to see this.

The Nave

The reconstruction was, to be modest, a remarkable feat of engineering, because I had to cut into the walls of the nave to create new arches, even while the old roof and ceiling (which some thought was the work of Michelangelo) had to be left standing above.[2] I even had to chain the leaning north wall to a new outer wall as work progressed, so that it would not fall. My task was to produce a modern baroque basilica while preserving the pre-existing structure.[3] The Pope put significant restraints on the project. He limited the restoration to the nave. I was to preserve so far as possible the original form of the basilica and the walls that had originated with Constantine. I believe I was chosen because the Pope knew I could create an imaginative new design and he (and Padre Spada his advisor) knew that I was a skilled builder who could safely complete the goal of preserving the Constantinian structure.

As I began, I discovered that the Renaissance architect of the ceiling of the Laterano had left beams that protruded more than 5 palmi beyond the clerestory wall.[4] I was able to hang a plumb line from these beams and then to build external walls in the plumb line to the roof. I then attached the old walls with clamps to the new walls. Finally, I "shaved off" the remaining bulge in the interior.[5]

The ovals of the nave are now filled with prophets (added in the eighteenth century). At the Pope's request I had these open to the wall behind to show the ancient structure; "come gioria nell anello, accio resti e perpetua memoria la fabrica fatta da Constantino".

For the nave, I created sidewalls with ten bays. I first enclosed consecutive columns of the old church inside one broad pillar,[6] then I framed each of these pillars with a colossal order of pilasters which were throughout the whole height of the nave.[7] I left the ovals (they now contain the prophets) open to show the old walls, in keeping with the Pope's desire to retain the visibility of some of the old parts (I decorated these with a beautiful floral border).

---

[2] Connors, Borromini 255.
[3] Wittkower, Art and Architecture 212; Connors, Borromini 255.
[4] Echols 154.
[5] Id. quotes. The Professor's description of Borromini's skills in saving and restoring the walls of the nave, "without disturbing the sixteenth century coffered ceiling".
[6] Wittkower, Art and Architecture 212.
[7] Id. quotes.

Then I made a niche of colored marble for statuary into the face of each pillar where before there had been an opening between two columns. In this scheme, as you can see, I created an alternating rhythm of large and small units- smaller bay with niche, then larger bay with an arch. The arches over "open" bays I made cream-colored to contrast with the dark colored tabernacles in the niches- these tabernacles break through the plane of the wall and project significantly into the nave.[8] I enclosed the niches (each of which has a marble door in the rear, suggesting the Heavenly City of Jerusalem, which the Apostles entered through the twelve doors) in verde-antico columns, which I actually took from the side aisles of the old Basilica. I used twenty-four of the thirty-six columns of verde antico that had supported the roof.[9]

One of the open bays which carry into the side aisles.

The Apostle Simon in one of the niches I made for the nave.

---

[8] Id. quotes. The Professor's description of how Borromini created the rhythm for the bays (AbAbA…for the high bays of the pillars and the low arches, and aBaBa…for the low tabernacle niches and the high arches). Professor Connors notes that Borromini intended these niches to protrude "like a human breast". Connors Borromini 255.

[9] Connors, Borromini 255.

The central door with the canted bays I used to tie the nave together. Note the irregular fluting on the joined canted pilasters and the extravagant capitals. Two of the Apostles below in my niches which carry forward into the nave.

The bases and pediments in these tabernacles are of dark grey marble, which I used to create a strong contrast to the white of the piers and pilasters. Note that I decorated the sides of the piers with crisp bands of laurel and palm–leaves, and the gray marble bases of the niches with the same style of garlands of palm-leaves.

The richness of the niches is a thing of which I am proud. The Apostles Peter and Paul come forth into the nave in these extended places.

I made the windows of the nave alternately oval and rectangular; for the pediments over the rectangular windows I used my trademark windows at the Palazzo Barberini, except for those in the very middle bay; in these I used the form Michelangelo used at the Capitoline palaces,[10] the form I used in the first cloister of the Filippi Casa.

---

[10] Blunt 139.

Another angled view of the wall of the nave, and the niches for the Apostles. The bases of the pilasters have a richness described as Michelangelesque.

I carried the rhythm and alternation of pillars and open arches across the corners of the entrance wall, which has the effect of making the nave into a single enclosed space.[11] I used the Capitoline palace type window in the shallow curved bay of the entrance wall.[12] I turned the bays of the nave nearest the entrance so that they go across the corners at a 45-degree angle (remember my rule about corners). I also made the entablature break forward slightly over each pair of coupled pilasters here.

You may ask, dear reader, why I did this. The answer is in my plans for the spectacular vaulted ceiling of the type I made later at the Re Magi Chapel.[13] Only through this ceiling vault could I continue properly the logical continuation of the articulation of the nave.[14] A pair of ribs would have sprung from the central pilaster astride the entrance; these would

---

[11] Wittkower, Art and Architecture 212. Professor notes that the rhythm of pillar and open arches had been well known since Bramante and Alberti's days, it was for Borromini to "carry it to the corners of the entrance wall".
[12] Blunt 139.
[13] Id. 141. Professor Blunt explains Borromini's change in plans to turn the bays of the nave nearest the entrance to accommodate his grand vault. He goes on to explain the problem Borromini would encounter at the other end of the nave at the crossing, where Borromini would have had to cant the pilasters to accommodate the ribs of the vault. He surmises Borromini abandoned the cant here after the Pope refused to fund the vault.
[14] Wittkower, Art and Architecture 212.

178 | SAN GIOVANNI IN LATERANO

have ended on the second pair of pilasters on the other side of the nave.¹⁵ This would have required a similar scheme where the nave reached the crossing. For the ceiling, I should also note for you that I actually had two alternate plans for the ceiling- one a classical barrel vault, the other the vault I have previously discussed which was similar to what I did later at the Collegio di Propaganda Fide Re Magi.¹⁶

The work of the nave went rapidly, the structure completed in 1647, the roof in October 1648.¹⁷ Then when I reached the capitals of the pilasters the Pope decreed that I could not take down the existing ceiling! The effect here is thus not complete because the high pilasters need to run on into a vault and not end at the flat ceiling. And also the nave is not properly connected to the transept and choir.

---

¹⁵ Blunt 141.
¹⁶ Connors, Borromini 255. The Professor notes that Borromini had begun buttresses that would have taken the thrust from his vault.
¹⁷ Blunt 134.

The bay over the entry door with the armorial shield of Innocent X. Adjacent are the bays connecting to the sidewalls of the nave and they are canted at 45 degrees. I did this first to eliminate the corners but also to hold the crossribs for the vault I was never allowed to make.

The Side Aisles

One of the side aisles, arcaded, decorated with a multitude of my white stucco cherubs.

The outer side aisle where I imposed a flat ceiling. This follows the tradition of early Christian churches where the side aisles descend in height. See how the cornice is curved at the corners. My cherubs support the beams in the piers.

In the side aisles I faced no problem of an existing ceiling, and I did not have to incorporate earlier masonry.[18] I did, however, have to follow the alternations of larger and smaller bays that I had established for the nave arcade.[19] I placed windows between the side aisles; this let me bathe the larger bays of the side aisles in light, creating a great contrast between the large and small bays. I built the two inner side aisles with alternating barrel and sail vaults. As I say, I used "light boxes" to convey light from the nave.[20]

---

[18] Id. 141.
[19] Id.
[20] Connors, Borromini 255.

Vault of the side aisle. The cherubs, and bands of laurel and palm leaves are the most crisp I executed. Notice the absence of corners in the piers and cornices.

At this point, I want to discuss with you the system I devised to fill the inner aisles with light, an achievement that truly stunned my fellow architects, who believed that there was not enough room between the aisle roofs to provide light. First, I built large windows which "sit at the spring of the flattened vault of the outer aisle". Since the roof of the outer vaults now descended from the outside to inside, I needed to keep the rain from flowing into the windows, and thus I made two wing walls from either side of each window out to the center of the outer vault. I then made a vault to span these two walls and all of this I made high enough and wide enough such that you cannot see them from inside the church.[21] Regrettably all of the exterior windows have now been closed.

Ceiling in the side aisle.

---

[21] Echols, 154, 23. Professor Echols takes this from Virgilio Spada's Relatione (Güthlein, "Quellen", 1979, 213).

These side aisles, by the way, had been so low and inconveniently arranged that I had to pull them down completely and start over. The height of the inner aisle of each pair of side aisles was dictated by the height of the nave arches;[22] not so for the outer aisle, which I made much lower and where I imposed a flat ceiling, covered by flat architraves. This scheme of stepped aisles follows the pattern of the early Christian basilica. It also provided buttressing for a vault over the nave, if one of my successors might convince a later Pope to make my vault.

Top photo: More detail in the vault at the end of the side aisle.

Right photo: One of the side aisles, full of my favorite winged cherubs. The side aisles have rightly been described as "delicate".

---
[22] Blunt 141; Connors, Borromini 255.

It was my intention to carry the order of the second nave around the presbytery, as at San Carlo al Corso, to accommodate the Holy Week procession. This regrettably did not come to fruition for lack of funds.[23]

The Door to the Lateran Palace

Top and right photo: This is the bay in the right aisle whose door leads to the Lateran Palace. See the arms of Innocent X. The swags with the Pamphilj dove and the leaves over the windows I repeated at the Villa Giustiniani.

Please do not miss this bay, and the arms of Innocent X. I repeated the swags with the Pamphilj dove on the side walls and the leaves spread over the ceilings above the windows, almost exactly, at the Villa Giustiniani.[24] On the other side of this door, in the Palazzo del Laterano, which is the south end of the west arm of the cloister, I made in 1650 special stucco sculpture. Innocent's arms in an orb are carried by an angel with two wings that serve as curved pediments, his other four wings support the orb of the world. See especially the angel's fingers which are over the mouldings separating the two doors.

---

[23] Portoghesi 161. Citing Bianchi Lombardi, who was writing in connection with his project for the façade of Laterano.
[24] Blunt, Baroque Guide 55, 183. Professor Blunt notes that the stucco work on the Lateran Palace side "is a beautiful example of Borromini's use of sculpture to perform the function of architecture", like the façade niche with Carlo Borromeo at the Carlino.

The Overall Decoration

I am so especially proud of the decoration of San Giovanni. It is of great beauty and I can assure you it was very carefully thought out. I made the bases of the giant pilasters from a light grey marble; I sought to be bold here, like Michelangelo, and to give the decoration a baroque fluency. I varied the width of the fluting of the pilasters, as I did at Sant'Ivo, but you can see the effort is gentler and less emphatic.[25] For the niches, I was equally original, and I made the dark grey marble bases firmly curved, making them project at almost right angles to the planes of the wall. I made the mouldings round the back panels as rich as the doorjambs in the Oratory.[26] Around the Apostles, I made laurels and palmi with the same nervous crispness I gave the laurels and palmi over the doors at Sant'Ivo. For the railings, which separate the chapels of the outer aisle, I again used the baluster I first used in the cloister of San Carlino, except that I interrupted the effect by alternating their pointed edges and their flat sides forward.[27]

One of the cherub herms above the side door at the entrance. Notice the Chiro in the capital above.

Right photo: In the side aisle, a stucco medallion for Pope Innocent X Pamphilj held by two of my four winged cherubs. A cornice with no corners, a beautiful conch and ribs which attach to a scroll in the vault, scrolls above the windows with a swag through the volute.

---

[25] Id. 141, 142.
[26] Id. 142.
[27] Blunt 144.

In the right aisle the Cappella Orsini. Here the variation on the famous Carlino Cloister baluster. To the alternation in vertical disposition of the bulge I added this: the flat face and sharp edge are alternated to the aisle. This makes it seem like the balusters are twirling as you walk past.

I placed winged cherub heads everywhere, especially in the aisles, where I have them supporting the flat entablature of the lower openings. They hang like bats to the vaults of the inner aisles.[28]

Outer right aisle. I especially like my supporting cherubs here.

---

[28] Id. Connors, Borromini 255 (where the Professor talks about "the early space [has been] invaded by an intense angelic presence").

186 | SAN GIOVANNI IN LATERANO

Every cherub is different.

Top photo: In the inner side aisle, in the flattened vault, four of my white four winged stucco cherubs, each individually modeled with different hair. See the Pamphilj dove with olive branch in its beak.

Right photo: A supporting cherub in the side aisle.

Bottom Photo: Detail of a capital. Left the keys of the Pope, right beautiful palms.

I focused on all three elements from the Holy of Holies; in addition to the cherubs, I have pomegranates and palmi. For the capitals of the nave pilasters, I replaced the eggs in the egg- and-dart mouldings with pomegranates.

Although in most of the arches of the nave I decorated the sides and soffits with bands of laurel, I replaced these with palmi on the two middle arches and also the arch over the door.

By October 1649, the nave and side aisles were ready (a new cosmatesque floor was added in 1650). The Church is truly a masterpiece.

More detail of the delicate and detailed stucco work at one of the entrances, inside. Notice the variety of fruits and flowers.

One of the cherubs of the side aisles.

Another Personal Digression

I need to mention here two events, which occurred in this Laterano renovation time period. These were very negative events against this backdrop of a very successful period of my professional career. Innocent had based his family in the Piazza Navona. Here was the family Palazzo, here he was to also place the family church, Sant'Agnese. It was now home to the first family of Rome.[29] During his reign, Pope Gregory XIII had had Giacomo della Porta make a fountain at the southern end of the piazza (to become the Fontana del Moro after Cavalier Bernini placed the Moro in the center) and had water brought from the Aqua Vergine aqueduct that fed the Trevi Fountain. della Porta also intended a fountain for the northern end but funds were only available for the basin. Innocent now planned a fountain of the highest order in the center to replace the simple drinking trough there.[30]

I was at this time held in the highest esteem by the Holy Father. My San Carlino, my Oratorio, and my Sant'Ivo were acclaimed. I had been the most professional source of authoritative advice on the towers at San Pietro. I was about to begin the complete renovation of the Lateran. And so Innocent came to me to ask me to extend the Aqua Vergine to the Piazza Navona in sufficient quantity of water that it would sustain a grand central fountain, and also the two fountains on the north and south ends that Giacomo della Porta had made. I did this with great success, and also removed the

---

[29] Morrissey 201.
[30] Id. 202.

steps to the della Porta fountains in favor of additional water basins. I went further to suggest to his Holiness that the design of the new fountain should focus on the four great rivers of the known world- the Nile, Danube, Ganges, and Rio Plata. Since Rome is the center of the world, having the four rivers of the world empty into this fountain would represent allegorically this centrality. Innocent thought this was a capital idea. In April 1647, Innocent had found an ancient obelisk that Caracalla had brought to Rome, which had made its way over time to the Circus Maxentius on the Appian Way, and he determined that this obelisk would stand in the center of the fountain. Innocent asked me and several other architects/artists to submit designs for the fountain. He did not ask Cavalier Bernini, which pleased me but at the same time caused me to back away from an aggressive involvement. This project would largely be a sculptural, and not architectural, project. Sculpture was not my forte, architecture was. I knew that the others who were participating in the contest, particularly Alessandro Algardi, were far better sculptors than I. In fact, Algardi produced a plan based on the allegorical figure of Roma,[31] placed on a tall squared base, with four river gods on the corners. Contrary to what some have said, in the end I did not submit a design. The design some have attributed to me, one with a fountain of four unremarkable sides, with shell like apertures with grotesque lion faces which serve as spouts for water flowing into a low stone basin, is, I think you will agree after seeing it, far too pedestrian to be mine.

    After relying on the fact that Cavalier Bernini was not allowed to submit a plan, I did not submit a plan (as I say, the plan with an obelisk and four lions spouting water has been attributed to me, but is not mine). Then, the Cavalier Bernini did submit a model, secretly, and he won the competition in July of 1648. Had I known he was going to be allowed to submit a model, I would have submitted one too. The Bernini design without question reflects extraordinary skill, beauty, and inventiveness. I know that I could not have produced anything of this order. But the Pope went against what he told me he would do- not allow Cavalier Bernini into the competition- and Bernini did steal my concept of the four rivers, and the water I had brought to the Piazza. I could not control my temper.

    I refused to continue at San Giovanni. I had my workers, including the stuccoists, leave the site. Here even my friend Virgilio Spada abandoned me, for as superintendent he kept the work going by engaging a company of stuccoists to replace my men. I have to say that my workers almost came to blows against this substitute company. Swords were everywhere. Fortunately for all of us, Padre Spada managed to calm us all down.[32] The new workers were dismissed, the old workers returned to work. I returned to San Giovanni. But the episode of the fountain of the four rivers was now heaped atop all the other affronts I had suffered. My mountain of woes continued to grow.

---

[31] Id. 204. Professor Blunt, in his Baroque Guide, at 233, 234, tells us of Borromini's contribution to the north and south fountain and also of his simple plan for the central fountain.

[32] Wittkower, Studies 161, Connors, The Spiral, 682, note G.1. Connors, Defence, 85. Professor Connors states that, in fact, Borromini expected to receive the commission for the obelisk fountain on the Navona. fn 54.

The second incident injurious to me occurred as the renovation work at Giovanni was coming to an end at the beginning of winter 1649-1650. In December 1649, I personally came upon a wayward cleric, Marc Anotonio Bussoni, "in flagranti"; he was damaging the marble ornament, smashing up, sitting on, and disfiguring some slates of stone.[33] I had no choice but to order punishment for this man, who had deliberately brought destruction onto the first church of Rome, and Christendom. And so I ordered my men to bind and beat him. This they did. Unfortunately, they went too far, and the man died, a death I had not ordered, nor desired, nor planned. I was brought in, and I was very close to being tried and hanged for this clear case of manslaughter and possible case of murder. Fortunately, the Pope accepted that I was in a state of extreme fatigue from my round the clock work at San Giovanni; Padre Spada was very supportive. Whether it was understanding, or pity, or gratitude for my success at San Giovanni, I was pardoned in August 1651 and required to leave the city for Florence for some months. But again, a deep emotional scar, one well deserved.

I was returned to the Pope's favor by year-end 1651, when he gave me a large gratuity and then later a knighthood (July 16, 1652, bestowed on me by Virgilio Spada).[34]

The Tombs

I was brought back ten years after the Jubilee renovation of 1650 by the Chigi Pope Alexander VII to restore the tombs in the side aisles. Here one of my cherubs, above the Chigi monti and eight pointed star, on the tomb for Sergius IV.

I will now describe for you my work on the tombs and monuments of the side aisles at Giovanni. After the nave was finished in 1650, the only other work accomplished was the laying of a new cosmatesque style floor, and these tombs. Innocent refused to proceed with a new ceiling, as I have said, and the restoration of the apse was never begun. Innocent had me begin the project of the tombs, but almost all of this work was done under the Chigi Pope Alexander VII, who brought me back to the Lateran some ten years later.

---

[33] Wittkower Studies 160, 161, fn 77.
[34] Connors, The Spiral 682, note G.1.

You can see the Chigi heraldic symbols everywhere. I should really save this description of the tombs for later, as this work was done in the last part of my life. But I cover it now so that the material about Giovanni is all in one place. But remember this material well, for my work on these tombs demonstrates emphatically that I was in full control of my working faculties throughout my life, despite all of the mental and social problems that became increasingly problematic in the last ten years of my life.

The armorials of the Chigi Pope Alexander VII.

For the tombs, I began with a problem of incongruity, which lay in this- we had to remove all the medieval tombs of Popes and Cardinals and Bishops from the side aisles in order to reconstruct the building. These dismembered tombs were stored in the cloister. Innocent wanted them replaced once the reconstruction was complete. But these were medieval tombs with medieval works in them, and I could not simply place them as they were into this now beautifully modern baroque church. I determined, correctly, that what I would do is take the relics of the departed, and significant other pieces from the medieval tombs, and create a new baroque tomb of my own design, and insert the medieval pieces into them. The result will certainly offend the medieval purist, but the tombs are nonetheless of great beauty and fully congruous with the Church. And they are not, despite what the Pope had to say, "chimeric". Yes they do have Gothic elements, and yes there is an illusionist perspective aspect, but the tombs are well rooted in the traditions my architecture carried forward from the classical and the Michelangelesque.[35]

I begin with the three tombs of the Popes- Sergius IV, Alexander III, and Boniface VIII. There was a third tomb I made for Sylvester II, but that was destroyed regrettably in the nineteenth century. The tombs of the Popes were placed against the piers that separate nave from the right aisles, and so I did not have an issue with fitting the tomb around a window, a problem I had with the Cardinals in the outermost aisle which I will describe shortly. For Sergius, I used from the old tomb the half-length bas-relief of the pope giving a blessing. This I surrounded with a frame of eight-pointed stars- from the Chigi arms. I "piled" these on top of each other, giving this the look of a starfish colony. Single stars alternate with paired stars. I placed outside this two column-herms. I placed the wings of the cherubs so that they cover almost all the column.[36]

---

[35] Blunt 146. Professor Blunt says "[i]f the monuments are considered as re-creations of Borromini they are of great interest and, in their singular way, of great beauty".
[36] Id. 152. Professor Blunt's description of the "piling on" and herms.

The tomb of Sergius IV. I salvaged the relief of the Pope giving a blessing. I surrounded this with all the Chigi stars piled on top of each other—it looks like a starfish colony. Single stars, then paired stars.

SAN GIOVANNI IN LATERANO

The herm on the tomb of Serius IV. The hair locks are some of my favorites.

Monument to Alexander III in black and yellow marble. The cylinder reminiscent of the panel at Carlino. Unique bases and capitals.

For Alexander III, I was really not able to find an acceptable piece from the old tomb. Here I made a beautiful oval cylinder, much like the aedicule of the façade of San Carlino or the façade of Sette Dolori. I put the cylinder inside a simple curved niche, supported by four columns. If you look at the bases and capitals you will see that they are unique, some would say unorthodox. The Chigi monti and star are above.

For Boniface VIII, I began with the precious fresco made by Giotto of Boniface's election. I created a beautiful small pediment and garland border for it. Here I made an exquisite frieze and populated it with the acorn from the Chigi arms. The Gaetani shield above is made in the strapwork popularized at Fontainebleau.[37] The convex, concave curvature and angle positioning of the cornices is, I think, extraordinary.

---

[37] Id.

The Tomb of Boniface VIII with the fresco of Giotto.

Detail from the tomb of Boniface VIII.

When I came to the Cardinal tombs of the outer aisle I had to deal with the oval windows of the side walls. Here I met the problem head on, instead of attempting to avoid or disguise, as most architects would have approached the problem. I ended up using the window to my advantage, since it helped me create a false perspective, which added additional depth to these tombs placed against the outer wall. I began each of these tombs at the oval window. I added a pair of winged cherub heads above the windows as a frame of sorts. Then, with great inventiveness, I believe, I placed the architecture of the monument below the window. I used columns in some cases, in others canted consoles with the Chigi monti above.[38]

I begin with Cardinal Giussano in the right aisle. Here, where I used a still more unique solution, the only thing left from the old tomb is in the inscribed tablet. The panels with Gothic tracery came from the altar in the chapel of Saint Mary Magdalene. These panels inspired me to place over them a cusped architrave where the side pieces rise up. Thus I made the curves of all three sections play against the oval window. Then I made four hooded herms (a sign of mourning) to support the architrave, and each of these carries a basket of pomegranates, the symbol of eternal life. As you can see, this creates an illusion of perspective. The viewer- you- is led to see this as a Gothic shrine surrounded by three very flat arches. The middle one you see frontally. The two side ones are seen in very deep perspective. I made the inner pair of herms much smaller than the outer pair in order to make this perspective clear.

---

[38] Id. All of the description here taken from Professor Blunt's discussion.

The pale grey marble tomb of Cardinal Casate, Conte di Guissano, in the right outer aisle. Here I had to work around the oval window, actually using it to my advantage to create false perspective, creating new needed fictional depth. The only thing from the old tomb I was able to restore was the tablet. The Cosmati panels came from the Chapel of Mary Magdalene taken down in the restoration. Then I created a cusped architrave, added four hooded herms (the inner two are smaller) (they carry the pomegranate, symbol of eternal life). All of this leads the viewer to see this as a Gothic shrine surrounded by three very flat arches.

Next I take you to the Cardinal Acquaviva monument also in the right aisle. The oval of the window required me to make the mouldings of the parapets behind the horizontal figure of the deceased or the entablatures of the colonnades curve downwards toward the middle. I used this downward movement to create the perception of recession. This illusion is of course not as great by any measure as the colonnade at Palazzo Spada (to which I speak later), but it is like the partial illusion in the loggia windows at Palazzo Barberini, and in the half-domes at the church and refectory at San Carlino. In the Acquaviva monument, I made the inner columns lower and thinner than the two outer columns (a total of six columns in the Colonnade) and placed them closer to each other. Here, I think, the perspective effect is very great. Also in the right aisle, the tomb of Cardinal de Chaves, where I added only the frame.

Tomb of Cardinal de Chaves. Here the tomb was intact. I added the frame.

SAN GIOVANNI IN LATERANO | 197

In the right aisle, the tomb of Cardinal Giulio Acquaviva (d 1574), in which I incorporated the statutes of Temperance and Prudence which were made by the Renaissance tomb sculptor Isaia da Pisa for the tomb of Cardinal de Chaves.

For the Cardinal Annibaldi tomb in the outer left aisle, I added some figure sculpture of my own, namely a figure of death, with a crown and smile, and also a snake crawling across the back of
the tomb.[39]

In the left aisle, near the entrance. The tomb of Cardinal Ricardo Annibaldi della Molara (d 1274), the recumbent Cardinal made by the great Renaissance pioneer Arnolfo di Cambio. The famous "funeral procession" that was part of the tomb is now in the Cloister.

Also in the left aisle, I did the monuments to Cardinal Bernardo Caraccioli (where I was able to use his recumbent figure from his original tomb), and Cardinal Gerardo Bianco (which has the incised slab from his original tomb).[40]

In the left aisle, the tomb of Cardinal Bernardi Caroccioli (d 1255) which includes the figure of the Cardinal from his original tomb.

---

[39] Id.
[40] Blunt, Baroque Guide 56.

Here I should tell you that as Architect of San Giovanni, I was contracted to redo the high altar and to make the bronze doors, but because I was removed as Architect at the Oratory, I left these works at the Laterano. Pietro da Cortona finished this work.[41]

San Giovanni was in many respects my greatest success, for it demonstrated my architectural abilities in a very large setting, the most important church in Rome, and let me show the City that I was first among the architects in technical skill, able to rescue a tottering building in a short period of time, and creating what was to become one of the accepted masterpieces of baroque decoration. Here, more than any other place I think, my stucco decoration is sublime and supreme.

In the left aisle, the tomb of Cardinal Gerardo Bianco (Corrado di Sabina) (d 1062), with the incised slab from his original tomb.

If only I had been allowed to make the vaulted ceiling. What we did achieve was to set the stage for its ultimate construction. The vault would have, I hoped, the kind of Gothic ribbing I was to place at the Re Magi at the Propaganda Fide. And so the foundations of the basilica were made ready to support a vault. Toothing was even left above the aisle vaults for the attachment of buttresses. You can still see the strips of rough brick I inserted for these, on the outer clerestory wall. And I placed additional bases above the entablature, over the colossal pilasters, for the attachment of the vault ribs, which you can also see. Alas, it was never to be.[42]

---

[41] Morrisey 5,6. Professor Morrisey states that Alexander VII removed Borromini as Architect at the Lateran, replacing him with da Cortona.
[42] Echols 156 fn 35, 38, quotes. Professor Echols cites Thelen and Hempel here.

CHAPTER NINE

The Piazza Navona and the Palazzo Pamphilj

Innocent X Pamphilj began work on his family Palazzo on the Southwest corner of the Piazza Navona almost immediately after his election in 1644. Eventually this work was to extend to a large portion of the western half of the Piazza, to include a new church to replace the small shrine over the site of the martyrdom of Saint Agnes. The Pamphilj family had built their Palazzo here in 1491-1497. From 1645-1648 the Pope rebuilt that palace.

The several years after the election of Innocent were perhaps the most satisfying of my life. The Cavalier Bernini was held to account for his towers at San Pietro, I was selected as architect for the restoration of San Giovanni, and the Pope sought me out for his plans for the Piazza Navona. The significant negative during these years, as I have mentioned, is the Pope's engagement of Cavalier Bernini for the Fountain of the Four Rivers in 1647.

When the Pope began in earnest on the family Palazzo, he selected Girolamo Rainaldi and his son Carlo as architects, as he was proceeding cautiously and the reputation of this father and son team was one for caution. I did sit on a commission the Pope appointed to oversee the work. In 1646 the Pope, through Padre Virgilio Spada, asked me to take a more active part. I began meeting weekly, on every Thursday, with a group consisting of the architects, Mastermason Ludovico, and a representative of the Pope's notorious sister in law Donna Olympia (she was di nauseante ingordigia, "disgustingly greedy"). Donna and her son Camillo had bought up property next to the family Palazzo, and it was to be consolidated into the Palazzo.[1]

As part of this consultation, I focused on antique consular diptychs containing imperial circus loggias, and I made several of my own designs for the new palazzo. My final plan was inspired by the mannerist form of the Collegio Romano with its blunted angle.[2] As part of my plan, I would have used a long court with apsed ends- a reflection of the oval of the Piazza- which would have included a giant order and an open loggia or viewing box on top of the roof.[3] The Rainaldi plan was executed as more in keeping with the Pope's conservative inclinations. I was, however, able to resolve the problem of the covering of the grand room between the two courtyards of the Palazzo.[4] In 1647, I was at the Palazzo for but a brief spell, but during that time I was able to design not only the salone, but also the doorcases inside it, and the larger one at the entrance from the staircase passage,[5] and I spread the Pamphilj dome and lily throughout (see the oval panels in the internal doorcases). I must say that here I made a very spectacular tiara for the large door. I am especially proud of the ceiling decoration in the salone, with the stucco oval to mimic the Piazza. I designed the salone to be made cove, as the sidewalls could not be raised high enough for the projected height of the vault, without taking air from the courtyards. I cemented tiles over the upper part of the vault, with the same slope as

---

[1] Morrissey 185.
[2] Connors, Borromini 256, Portoghesi 181.
[3] Connors, Borromini 256.
[4] Portoghesi 180.
[5] Downes, Opus 285.

the roof. Padre Spada believed my treatment here was revolutionary, defying all the critics who insisted it would fall. He referred to it as volta reale a schifo, a vault of bricks laid upright, in the form of a boat (that is, a hipped barrel vault).[6] In 1647, I also constructed the Galleria on the north side of the palazzo, adjacent to the church of Agnese, which I had run the entire depth

The Galleria, from Eberhard Hempel.

of the palace from west to east, from the Via dell'Anima to the Piazza Navona. The idea here is that of a viewing box with a Serlian motif for the facade.[7] Pietro da Cortona was to place his masterpiece- the Story of Aeneas- on the ceiling of this room. I used two Serlian arches (we also know them as Palladian) with a continuous entablature for the ends of the Galleria. On the columns of the Serlians I used a vine decoration that plays with the light to create a very minimal vibration.[8] The Serlian arches viewed from the exterior serve to project the internal longitudinal space.[9] I would like you to pay special attention to the large Pamphilj coat of arms above the window. Here I turned the papal keys upside down. I also made the cornice of the arch bend into volutes in the interior, while on the exterior I made a continuous arch that bends without interruption. This exterior Serlian arch is then repeated on the north side of the façade of the church.

The doors I used in the Galleria are based upon drawings made by Pietro da Cortona, as you can see from the scrolls ending in volutes that I positioned over the tops of the doors- directly from Cortona's style. However, these door surrounds are nonetheless, I think, perhaps the best and most memorable of those I designed in my mid to late career.[10]

---

[6] Downes, Opus 98-99 fn 211. Professor Downes notes Padre Spada's praise and that the Mastermason raised a protest through a notary that "such a vault could never be sustained".
[7] Connors, Borromini 256. The Professor notes that the imagery of the gallery façade comes from the papal benediction loggia in Raphael's Fire in the Borgo and also the imperial circus loggia on late antique consular diptychs.
[8] Portoghesi 181. Professor Portoghesi speaks of Borromini's "personal stamp" in the coat of arms and the continuous cornice "that bends in an arch without interruption".
[9] Id.
[10] Wittkower, Art and Architecture 225, 226.

CHAPTER TEN

Sant'Agnese in Agone

The nave. From the Rainaldi plan. I widened the piers, added the whole columns to the edges of the piers. I intended the church to be all white, except the altar and the red marble of the columns. I made a very high drum and elevated the curve for the dome to accentuate the verticality of the church.

And now we move onto the Church of Agnese, I believe one of my greatest successes, but also perhaps in the end my greatest failure and certainly a source of great agony. The old church of Sant'Agnese was taken down in December 1651; the Rainaldis were hired in 1652 as architects, they being the favorites of nephew Camillo. The foundation stone was laid on August 15, 1652. The Rainaldi family embarked on a Greek cross plan with four squat arms.[1] The pillars of the crossing had broad levels, which then opened into large niches framed by recessed columns- the pillars and niches derived from St. Peter, the recessed columns were from Cortona's SS Martina e Luca. The design had a heavy, low dome. The exterior would have two short bell towers and a high, flat façade reminiscent of Master Maderno's at San Pietro. Many, including me, felt this design too lackluster;[2] this was especially the view of the respected architect Martino Longhi. This was to be the church of the Pope's palace; he would not accept that it was not worthy of praise. Probably what finally doomed the design were the stairs, which when built clearly intruded too far into the Piazza. It was also a problem that the façade covered much of the cupola.[3] Some said the cupola rose like the moon at the horizon. And so in 1653 the Pope determined to discharge the Rainaldis and to have me assume responsibility. I accepted much of the interior, then finished up to the cornice, but I tore all the façade down. Cavalier Bernini had finished his fountain in front of the church, and I wanted especially, graciously I felt, that the façade be accepting of the fountain (hence, for example, the central concavity). In addition to this, I very much wanted the church to create an "open skyline" for the Piazza.[4] The cupola and two campanili would represent three key pieces of my effort to carry the view to the sky. The dome and cupola needed to be completely visible and dominant, posed directly above the entrance, they should be like the face of a vertical rock.[5] Work began under my plan in August of 1653 and progressed rapidly.

The Nave

With what were really minor alterations, I radically, in my view, changed the character of the prior design. I took out the recesses designed for the columns, and I beveled the pillars so that the columns appear to be detached from the wall.[6] The piers I designed were based on convex curves, which I then proposed to continue into the concavities of the arms.[7] However, I ultimately had to abandon this idea, but I did manage to modify the spatial effect by widening the piers through the addition of columns, making them more monumental, with the addition of whole columns to the edges of the four main piers.[8] This change, of course, had the effect of changing the shape of the pendentives from points (the usual for Roman churches) to broad bases. The body of the church was to be all white

---

[1] Morrisey 215, Wittkower, Art and Architecture 213.
[2] Morrisey 219, especially Martino Longhi.
[3] Portoghesi 168. Professor notes that Maderno had the same problem with the façade of San Pietro but that problem was the result of "extenuating circumstances and necessity".
[4] Id.
[5] Portoghesi 170, quotes. The Professor produces a drawing on 169 of what he believes Borromini's façade would have looked like if his plan had been fully executed.
[6] Wittkower, Art and Architecture 214.
[7] Blunt 157.
[8] Id.

except for the high altar. The balconies you see are mine, as are the portals at the sides of the altar in the sacristy. The altars are set into the main piers, and the gray of their bardiglio marble creates great effect.[9] The columns were of red marble. I created an unusually high drum and an elevated curve for the dome- both of which accentuated the verticality of the church and added to the focus on the crossing.

Here you can see my columns and pilasters and the verticality for which I sought.

The Façade and Dome

On the exterior, I started with a concave façade, eight tall columns framing the doorways, the center one of which was taller than the others. I designed what I think you will agree, if you look at my drawings, was a very special pediment. The pediment was driven by one of the four semicircular windows intended to flood the interior (three of these fortunately have survived). My pediment would have been connected to the lower cornice in a curve (you can still see residual fragments of this original pedimentation in the passageway behind the balustrade of the face).[10] I extended the width of the façade into the space of the adjoining palaces; this permitted me to use towers of impressive height. The campanili would be convex at the first level, concave at the second topped with the convex globe. For these campanili I designed many fanciful inventions, including a herm with a cap in the form of a volute,[11] a little open attic (similar to the one I was to put in the campanile at Sant'Andrea delle Fratte), and a heraldic pinnacle that would stand out against the beautiful evening sky. I crowned the lantern with a tiara. This façade would have been, I am sure, the most brilliant in all of Rome considering its setting in the Piazza Navona, and the backdrop of the western sunset behind it.

Innocent died in January 1655; most of the larger work on the Church was finished but only in the rough. The façade was finished up to the cornice. The dome was up waiting for my lantern. Work stopped, caught up in the intrigues of the Pamphilj family. Neither Donna Olympia nor her son Camillo liked me. I never appealed to them and their taste for the highly cultured. I was never obsequious to them. That was not my nature. Camillo now showed little interest in the church. I was much disheartened. My enemies would have you believe that I walked off the job, but in reality I was completely disheartened at this point and was not wanted. The new Pope, Chigi Alexander VII,

---

[9] Portoghesi 171, 172. Professor Portoghesi here describes Borromini's use of false perspective at the end of each lateral arm.
[10] Albertina drawing 599.
[11] Portoghesi 171, quotes. See Professor's reconstruction at 169 for the "fanciful inventions".

was a great friend of Cavalier Bernini and no admirer of mine. It is true I tried to get the Pamphilj to commit to this project by showing my own willingness to disengage, and yes I let myself be seen in the bookshops of the Piazza Navona rather than on the work site. The Pope was induced to form a Commission of Inquiry (does it not seem a coincidence that the Cavalier Bernini had been subjected to such a Commission over his falling tower after the election of Innocent?). I was formally discharged in February 1657. After that unsatisfactory changes were made to my church. Carlo Rainaldi was brought back, he reduced the height of the lantern, and he subtracted eight columns from the sixteen I had planned for it. He took off all the grand crowning features I had designed for the lantern and replaced them with the stark structures you see today. He simplified them and took away their glory. He added a story to the campanili. Missing from my design are many special elements: all the "fanciful inventions". These included fantastic pinnacles, and a tiara on the lantern, and a volute made with a capped herm. The low curved steps I planned were never made; these would have ended in an oval landing, a place where you could have viewed the statue of the Rio Plata in the fountain.

Ironically, Cavalier Bernini was brought in a decade after I left, after the death of Camillo in 1666 and the entry of his widow Donna Olympia (Aldobrandini), and he made further significant changes to the interior and exterior.[12] He completely abandoned my extravagant and beautiful pediment (he thought it was, no doubt, "chimeric") and gave the Church the plain pediment you see today, enclosed in the attic. My pediment would have drawn your eye up to my dome. For the interior, he made a much heavier cornice and took out the parts of the attic which were over the main order that was below the pendentives, the purpose being to create space for a fresco. After this, artists frescoed the dome and placed gigantic high reliefs with colored marbles over the three altars. None of this, of course, was in keeping with my intentions. I would have used white stucco, and the interior would have been composed purely of architectural forms. Architecture speaks for itself.[13]

Despite these deletions and alterations, Sant'Agnese takes a unique position in baroque architecture. It really is the High Baroque form of the centralized plan that almost happened at San Pietro. My dome was dependent on the dome of Michelangelo. Ever since the late sixteenth century, domes had lost weight and volume, and drums had risen in height "at the expense of the vault".[14] This resulted in grand additions to the city skyline. This development, this movement, reached its finality, I am proud to say, in the dome of Sant'Agnese. If you stand opposite the entrance, the dome seems part of the façade. The dome is strongly connected to the façade, with the double columns at the sides of the entrance continued into the pilasters of the drum and then the ribs of the vault. Whereas at San Pietro the collapse of Cavalier Bernini's towers prevented Michelangelo's dome from appearing between two grand towers, here at Sant'Agnese I fulfilled that concept.

---

[12] Blunt 159.
[13] Id. 160. Professor Blunt's ultimate assessment: "as a work of architecture it is confused and full of conflicting elements."
[14] Wittkower, Art and Architecture 217.

Before this, the pilgrim did not have the opportunity to view at a glance a group of towers and a dome- here the concavity of my façade, and above the great convex drum bring the pilgrim beauty and joy.[15] Many have noted that I here repeated the motif of the façade at Sant' Ivo, only reversing it. That is no accident.

Though others modified my plan after I left, the façade here is largely mine, the principal feature being the grand dome flanked by the two campanili, with a curved façade. This was unique for Rome. The pediment you see is not the grand one I designed, which had four windows to flood the interior with light. Those who followed me also removed the inventions I had planned for the top, including a capped herm, an open attic, and a heraldic pinnacle. Nonetheless, when the sun sets behind the church, it gives us perhaps the most beautiful silhouette in the city. On either side of the façade, in the adjoining palaces, I inserted a Serliana window to appropriately balance the scene. I should also note that it was I who added the water basins, in place of steps, in the fountains in the Piazza Navona!

---

[15] Id. Professor Wittkower obviously does not share Professor Blunt's outlook, stating that Sant'Agnese "occupies a unique position in the history of Baroque architecture".

The doorway to the ramp.

CHAPTER ELEVEN

Palazzo Carpegna

I was engaged by the Carpegna family as early as 1635 to design their palazzo, which sits on the block to the east/northeast of the Fontana Trevi, which was to become the home to the Academia di San Luca. Unfortunately my plan was not executed, and today you can see only my spiral ramp and the loggia on the ground floor. I made several dozens of drawings for this palazzo, the most special of which carried the building over the Vicolo Scavolino. These unexecuted drawings anticipated the development of the European palazzo of the eighteenth century, and were, for me, a way to carry out what I had not been able to do at the Palazzo Barberini. In these plans I was able to experiment, within the confines of a very fixed and difficult shape of the property, and the oval courtyard, the large vestibule, and the juxtaposition of the various axis all reflect, in my opinion, brilliant new approaches to the form of the palazzo.[1] My plans were extraordinarily original, I must say, and had features that were quite unknown for the time, such as semicircles and elongated octagons for staircases, vestibules, and small courts. Roman palaces had round square or rectangular courts, and circular courts were rare.[2] Some of this I took from Hadrian's Villa of course. Perhaps the most original idea was the design of two flights of stairs on either side of the oval court, meeting on a common landing (previously unknown in Italy, Camillo Guarino was later to use this idea for the Palazzo Carignano at Turin).[3]

I took this from Ripa's Iconologia, a hanging garland of fruit and flowers, a metaphor of welcome.

The thing I did make (around 1643)- the loggia/staircase- is small, but special. For the loggia, I used vaulting with depressed arches, taken from Michelangelo's second story of the courtyard at Palazzo Farnese. For the vault, I placed a double band which carried to the ground. I used only the corona in the cornice of the pilasters in order not to interrupt the downward movement. I created "delicate" diagonals in the cross vaults. I created further contrast to the double bands with the series of arches along the open side of the loggia.[4] I used here a metaphor of welcome, a hanging garland of fruit and flowers, taken from the symbolism of hospitality in Ripa's Iconologia.[5] I placed foliate garlands in high relief into the soffits of the arches; these continue the convex shape of the column shafts. Here

---

[1] Wittkower, Art and Architecture 227.
[2] Blunt 166.
[3] Wittkower, Art and Architecture 227 fn 47. Professor Wittkower states that Borromini made a drawing of a similar idea, which is at Uffizi, published by Professor Portoghesi in Quaderni (1954), no. 6, 28.
[4] Portoghesi 176, quotes.
[5] Downes, Opus 467, figures 43, 44.

you will note how I replaced the classical archivolt with this garland that I have rising directly from the capital. I took this idea from the Medici monument made by Leone Leoni in the Duomo at Milan.[6] The capital of the pilasters, the architrave segment, and the cornice combine to create a sort of vise around the capital.

At the end of the loggia I created a richly decorated doorway, which masks the spiral ramp behind it. Around the columns I wove a "knot of forms" that may seem almost mystical. I was proposing an allegorical motivation for the prince of the house: a rule of life if you will taken from Caesare Ripa:[7] watchful prudence in the form of the shield with the hydra, the promise of "satisfaction and riches" in the cornucopia, and in the hanging festoon, sunflowers represent the "renunciation of false riches", and the roses representing the "fleeting and ephemeral things".[8]

The ramp is oval, like the one I did at Palazzo Barberini, but I set it with the long axis across the line of the loggia, so that you are not aware of it until you turn right at the statue in the niche. I made a ramp versus a stairs, of course, so that the owner could ride on horseback to the piano nobile.

---

[6] Portoghesi 176.
[7] Id. Professor Portoghesi's words.
[8] Id. Professor Portoghesi's words.

CHAPTER TWELVE

Tombs

The Tomb of Clemente Merlini

Clemente Merlini, who died in 1642, was a legal official at the papal court. He was given a tomb in the dark chapel to the left of the tribune of Santa Maria Maggiore. I used red and white veined marble; the red stands for Merlini's strength in administering justice, the white for the purity of his character.[1] I participated in this work; I was not responsible for the project and I must say the work does not reflect my usual theme and practice.[2]

Top photo: Left of the Tribune. Although I participated, this is not representative of my work.

Right photo: The Ceva tomb/wall tablet.

---

[1] Blunt 154, describing Fioravanti Martinelli's description.
[2] Id.

The Tomb of Cardinal Francesco Adriano Ceva

Cardinal Ceva commissioned me to make a tomb for him at the Chapel of San Venanzio at the Lateran Baptistry, which I made in 1650. Here I made a flat wall-tablet of black marble, in low relief but with the Ceva family emblem and status in three dimensions,[3] with a frame of "peach colored" marble decorated with roses, in the same material. The mouldings I used here have the same stilted semi-circles as I put in the Sala Rosa at the Casa and the cornice at Sant'Ivo. They wind into scrolls and have my trademark flat pastry-like form.[4] I made palmettes of extraordinary elegance, done in pavonalezza, which is a cream-colored marble with slight purple markings.[5] Then I made the coat-of-arms in black and yellow marble. The cherub has two pairs of wings, a small pair above the shield and a main pair which curve around and out to form a half-oval shell, which I intended to be an impresa of the Holy Name. I could be a punster on occasion, and the black and yellow marble (grallo rosato) bands suggest a rather "raffishly vested torso" for my cherub.[6] Don't you like the cardinal's hat, and tassels, which I made in rosso antico? The monument was framed against a white stucco background which has now been removed regrettably.[7] There are those who say that in my maturity my decorative features became more severe and taut,[8] and that this tomb illustrates this. I am not so sure, I leave it to you to discern. A final note to you here: I have left a note on a preliminary drawing for this tomb in which I tell you that I used roses – the symbol of brevity of life - because the cardinal died young, and I used palmi to symbolize the fame of the cardinal's works of charity.[9]

---

[3] Downes, Opus, quotes, 493.
[4] Id. quotes, 493.
[5] Blunt 154. Professor Downes says these are of giallo chiaro from Numidia. Downes, Opus 493
[6] Downes, Opus, the description is the Professor's, 493.
[7] Downes, Opus 492 fn 324.
[8] Blunt 154.
[9] Blunt 155, 156.

CHAPTER THIRTEEN

*The Palazzo Spagna,
The Palazzo dello Spirito Santo*

A small note about the Palazzo Spagna, which the Spanish ambassador commissioned me to remodel in 1647, during the period of my glory after the election of Innocent X. Innocent had been partial to the Spanish as his predecessor Urban VIII had been partial to the French. I had always been partial to the Spanish too, as they were rulers of Milan when I spent my years there. This partiality actually led me to dress in the black attire of the Spanish.

My drawings were so appreciated by the Spanish king that he made me a Knight of the Order of St. James of Compostela. Unfortunately, very little of my plan for the Palazzo was carried out in the end. I think you can see my work in the vestibule leading to the staircase of the Palazzo (the staircase I made was damaged by fire in 1738 and rebuilt). I divided the vestibule into three aisles with a colonnade of Tuscan columns, these I then linked with an abacus-architrave. I used a similar colonnade at the cloister at San Carlino. I made the columns here humbler and thinner.[1] I used depressed arches for the vaulting, as in the Michelangelo corridor in the piano nobile of the Palazzo Farnese. For the side aisles I made asymmetrical openings, just like those in the entrance vestibule of Palazzo Farnese. The vestibule and staircase (now destroyed) was like the one I planned at Palazzo Carpegna. I made the staircase so that it leads at right angles to the axis of the vestibule, in this way a visitor coming off his coach would see the first flight in front of him.[2]

I was commissioned in 1661 by Virgilio Spada to make for him (he was commendatore) the Ospedale di Spirito Santo (to become a Palazzo). At the Padre's death in 1663, the building was in an unfinished condition (to be concluded after I left). I had worked on the court and made what I think was a clever arrangement with "superimposed arcaded loggias", plus the exquisite arrangement of the vestibule leading to a fountain in the left hand bay of the main façade of the court.[3] Today, mostly blocked off.

---

[1] Blunt 173. Quotes. The Professor notes that it is not certain that Borromini designed the vestibule, but he notes the several features he describes here "which suggest that it was designed by Borromini". The Professor here also notes the repetition at the Carlino cloister.
[2] Id. Quotes. Professor Blunt's astute comparisons to the Carlino and Farnese. His phrases here.
[3] Blunt, Baroque Guide 198, 199. The Palazzo is in the Piazza di Monte Giordano. Professor Blunt whose description of Borromini's work I set forth here, notes that the exterior of the palazzo was completely remodeled in the 19th century, but that the vestibule and the elements of the vestibule he describes are "reminiscent of his [Borromini's] method of designing".

CHAPTER FOURTEEN

The Palazzo Spada

I made the currently famous false perspective colonnade here in 1652-1653. Some have placed the date I made this earlier, and although I was on site 1635, some three years after the Spada family had acquired the property from the Mignanelli, the date of the colonnade is proven by the obvious similarities to the Collegio di Propaganda Fide, especially the heavy Doric columns. Once again, I must say, I made use of limited space and displayed my ingenuity. But I must be honest. The perspective idea here really came from an Augustinian priest, Giovanni Mariada Bitonto, who in turn was replacing a painted perspective by Paolo Maruscelli. Padre Spada's brother, Cardinal Bernardino Spada, was influenced to have me make the Colonnade due to a false perspective structure I had made for the Quarant'Ore, or 40 hours devotion, of 1646.[1]

The optical illusion at Palazzo Spada.

The area for the colonnade, which was positioned between the court and the southern boundary of the palace, was limited, certainly less than forty feet. I therefore needed to elongate the colonnade without actually elongating it. I did this by making the two sides of the colonnade converge and by reducing the height of the columns as they recede from the front. Donato Bramante had used this technique in the choir of Santa Maria presso San Satiro in Milan, and Antonio da Sangallo the Younger in the entrance at Palazzo Farnese, but neither did it in the grand scale I accomplished here.

Someone has altered the colonnade after I left, since my vault was interrupted at three separate points on the right side to admit light (see my Albertina drawing number 1157). These are now gone, and so we no longer have the alternation of light and dark

---

[1] Blunt, Baroque Guide 196, 197. The Professor notes that as to the Quarant'Ore of 1646, we "unhappily have no record". 197. Professor Portoghesi, in contradiction of Professor Blunt, puts Borromini's work into the 1632-1637 timeframe, and perhaps earlier. Portoghesi 172.

which gave an illusion of greater depth and of a space amplified by light;[2] instead we have a dark tunnel. I wanted the colonnade to be masculine and I certainly accomplished that, with a simple and massive Tuscan order. Please note, dear reader, the fluted consoles on the façade facing the court. These are echoes of those in the Ricetto of Michelangelo's Laurentian Library in Florence.

The illusion I achieved is complete: only 8.6 meters in actuality, it represents a gallery 37 meters long, a multiplication of four times.[3]

I also intervened in the main staircase leading to the Sala Grande (since changed in its steepness). Here I did the framed stars that decorate the barrel vault, the corridor vaults and the lateral walls and the pavement. The stars, which I made very large, have ten points, and also a second ten-pointed star inside of them, with "claw-like" points. I took this form of "negative relief" from the Egyptians.[4]

The unorthodox entablature in the court is also mine.[5] Also, I made two small spiral staircases in the Palazzo (one circular, one oval).[6]

Entrance to the rear courtyard.

I was also involved in the rear façade on the garden and its connection to the projecting wings of the palace (my adaptation here was never finished). See the splendid concave wall and the aedicule that supports the balcony. The sturdy structure of the portals is, I think, impressive. I gave these jambs "enriched telemones", reminiscent of Mannerist tastes. I turned the panel motifs in the archivolts of the portal "inside out" (these are found again on the entrance on the Via Polverone and on the aedicula below the balcony on the rear façade). See the ring of leaves beneath the capitals of the aedicula.[7] I needed to add these to provide the necessary height to the shafts of the columns already in place here when work began.

---

[2] Portoghesi 173. The Professor's description of the lighting.
[3] Professor Portoghesi provides these numbers, Portoghesi 173.
[4] Portoghesi 173.
[5] Steinberg 268, fn 2. Professor Steinberg says these are "probably" Borromini's.
[6] Portoghesi 174, figure on 174, figures 134, 135.
[7] Portoghesi 174. Here Professor Blunt and Professor Portoghesi seem to diverge: Professor Blunt seems to credit Paolo Maruscelli with the garden area "which he laid out anew on a much grander scale". Blunt, Baroque Guide 197.

CHAPTER FIFTEEN

Three Other Places of Note[1]

---

[1] For the Palazzo Guistiniani, Professor Blunt notes in his guide that the Guistiniani arms over the door have been removed, Baroque Guide 182. For the Villa Giustiniani, see Blunt, Baroque Guide 215, for the attribution and the notation of the similarities to other stucco work of Borromini. For the plan at Villa Pamphilj, see Cod. Vat. Lat. 112578; Portoghesi 179, 180.

The Palazzo Giustiniani

The entry to the Palazzo.

This palazzo is across from San Luigi dei Francesi. The Marchese Vincenzo Giustiniani kept a great art collection here and I was asked to make plans for a complete remodeling, which I did in the period 1650-1655. Alas the only part ever executed was the main door, and though it is said to have grandeur it does not have the great vivacity I gave most of my work.

The Villa Guistiniani

There is below the windows of the upper story of the Casino a frieze with the Giustiniani eagle and the Pamphilj dove who sits atop garlands of laurel. The decoration I made here is described as subtle. It is like the palmettes and ribbons at Palazzo Falconieri, the laurel wreath at Sant'Ivo and the Oratorio, and the leafy brands, Pamphilj dove, and gardens in the vestibule from the Laterano to the Palazzo Laterano.

The Casino of the Palazzo del Bufalo

I made a splendid door here, destroyed for the new Via del Tritone. A drawing and engraving survive, and they show a plan with Ionic capitals and lions' heads below the volutes. The curved pediment had an oval window, with swags of laurel. I like the buffalo's head (symbol of the family) on the top of the door.

The Plan for the Villa Pamphilj at San Pancrazio

It must be so with all architects that their best designs never left the paper, and so it is with me. My plan for Pope Innocent's proposed villa was a study in practical mathematics. My description of the plan, set forth in my letter to Innocent, corresponds to the sketch at the Vatican Library.

CHAPTER SIXTEEN

The Palazzo Falconieri

The façade.

The Falconieri family acquired a palazzo on the Via Giulia in 1638, just behind and a little to the south of the Palazzo Farnese. Then in 1645 they purchased another house to the north of this, and in 1646 I was commissioned to enlarge and remodel this complex of buildings. After my work, which I completed in 1649, considerable destruction was done to the complex and the courtyard by the building of the Via Lungotevere along the river. I accomplished my work here during my glory years, during the remodeling of the Laterano. It was a most happy time in my life. One thing I greatly enjoyed about working on the Palazzo Falconieri was that I was so close to my casa, just to the north off the Via Giulia: a comfortable walk to work.

The falcon atop one of the piers.

I worked on three separate pieces of this palazzo. First, I worked on the façade on the Via Giulia, then the Belvedere facing the river, and finally the decoration of rooms in the north wing. For the façade, I restrained myself at the request of the patron, and I followed the pattern of the sixteenth century façade. This I extended from seven to eleven bays, the formerly eight axes of windows became eleven axes of windows, enabling me to create a "bipolar rhythm".[1]

I also added a second door (since blocked up).[2] I added pilasters at the ends of the façade, which widen at the top; I took these from Michelangelo's pilasters in the Medici Chapel in Florence. Here I added a very striking and unusual element,[3] the falcon-headed herms, these I inserted into the angular pilasters (their angular nature also contributed to the bipolar rhythm) that rest on a base of roughly worked travertine.[4] I had actually contemplated exotic palm trunk columns,[5] but the patron thought this went too far and so I used the falcon, an Egyptian theme that fit the family name.

---

[1] Portoghesi 177, quotes.
[2] Blunt 170.
[3] Portoghesi 177, figure 139, 140.
[4] Id. See Portoghesi figure 141.
[5] Albertina drawing 1063, Portoghesi figure LXXX.

Detail of the cornice.

The soffit of the cornice with the falcon.

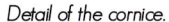

Soffit of the balcony over the main door on the Via Giulia.

For the cornice of this façade, please note that I used consoles grouped in threes which also had the effect of emphasizing the bipolar rhythm. Unfortunately, after my work, someone has added a thin stucco rustication to the upper stories.

This view from below shows the unusual fluting (you can also see the falcon). These were patterned after those of Michelangelo's pilasters at the Medici Chapel in Florence.

For the new south wing I created a "silvery façade", which falls within the category of my most "light" and "delicate work".[6] There was to be a U-shaped courtyard open to the river (see my Albertina drawing number 1059), and the façade would have been the inner side of this. Regrettably this courtyard was never made. The courtyard would have had a balustrade on its open side, sitting on a pyramidal base, and a fountain would have jetted water directly onto the river! For this new wing, I progressively increased the height of the four stories. This was directly contrary to the established classical architectural rules, and results, of course, in reversing the traditional gradation of the order.[7] I divided the ground floor by simple broad bands. I used the same motif for the next story, but I added stronger relief. Then on the third story I used Ionic pilasters. Then above this I had the recessed columns of the loggia. And so, as you can readily see, from the ground floor up the wall divisions grow in importance and also "plasticity" whereas in the classical tradition these diminish from the ground floor up.[8] I will admit here that this façade and the loggia are unconventional and contrary to the classical.

---

[6] Portoghesi 177, Albertina drawing 1059.
[7] Wittkower, Art and Architecture 225, quotes.
[8] Id. quotes. Professor Wittkower, in this text notes that Borromini was "welding old and new parts together into a new unit of a specifically Borrominiesque character".

I was feeling quite confident from 1645, basking in the approval of the Pope, Padre Spada, his advisor, and the acclamation I received from San Carlino and the Oratorio and so I became a bit extravagant here. For the belvedere, I was very much aware that from the other side of the Tiber, the viewer would see both the loggia of Palazzo Farnese, made by della Porta, and my loggia here at Falconieri. della Porta's loggia is, I believe, rather dry, especially in the mouldings. It has three arches separated by thin pilasters, all enclosed in the main mass of the palace façade dominated by Michelangelo's grand cornice. I made my loggia here to stand free of the rest of the Palace, above the neighboring buildings. I crowned the belvedere with a balustrade with Janus herms. These are double-faced in the Janus- Jana tradition where the head of a man is backed by that a woman.[9] The allusion I sought was to the succession of the seasons- a cosmic symbolism. Here, again, the motif of Michelangelo's merlons of Porta Pia.[10] All of this intended to create a grand silhouette against the sky.[11] I used a rich Serlian arch with very narrow side openings. I created main piers with tall and full columns in front. Finally, my personal note: I gave the ends of the loggia a "sharply concaved" form.[12]

The two-faced Janus / Jana atop the roof seated on merlons.

---

[9] Portoghesi 178. The Professor notes that the Janus-Jana tradition was to be repeated at the delle Fratte. The description of the contrast between the Farnese and Falconieri loggias is by Professor Blunt. Blunt 171.
[10] Id. Portoghesi figures 137, 138, 396.
[11] Blunt 171.
[12] Id.

Finally, for the interior: I built a chapel and decorated it, regrettably now destroyed. But here I believe I made my best ceilings for the piano nobile and rooms on the ground floor. The rooms here are small with modest height, and I decorated them entirely in stucco. Much of the stucco has now been painted in bright colors, and in two rooms the ceiling has been frescoed. My original work was all white, with a touching of gold. I am not sure I fully appreciate the additions. Here I resorted to "abstract symbolism of surrealistic taste".[13] I spread a low relief decoration on the cloister vaults, which has been descfribed as "laid upon the surface like a foamy net", using geometric frames of various rectilinear and curvilinear outlines.[14] These are of neo-classical sharpness, and I think harbor a great vitality. The two small square rooms, which face the Tiber, are the best of the rooms; here depressed spherical domes rest directly on the walls. In the angles I placed flat squinches, or ceiling corners. I pushed all the decoration to the edges of the vault, keeping the central area free and light. On one of these ceilings I placed a ring of laurel leaves, and within that a symbolic chain of Florentine lilies and palmettes, completely surrounding the vault. Please note the delicacy here and the very subtle effect of transparency and reflection. One of my drawings,[15] unexecuted, has the Pamphilj dove in the center.

---

[13] Portoghesi 178. All of the description here from Professor Portoghesi, who describes Borromini's work as reflecting "a completely new sensibility".
[14] Id. The Professor's description.
[15] Albertina drawing 1040. Portoghesi figure LXXXII. For the "push back" discussion, Professor Portoghesi draws a likeness to Francois Çuvillés.

One ceiling has now been named the "ceiling of the coat of arms"[16] because it has the heraldic insignia in the center of a triple framing device. Note the connecting concave volutes, the oval garland which captures the entirety of the crest, and the concave elements of the frame. The outermost frame is open in the corners- the "spiral chain" motif proceeds into a diagonal channel. From there these spirals continue around the vault at its base, to join up with spirals that escape from the other ceiling corners. The complexity here is, I submit, novel and completely free of boredom.[17] I placed this imagery of vegetables, fleur-de-lis, lilies, sunflowers, palmettes (note that I also used these over the central window of the Oratorio), much of which is symbolic of Florence, from whence the Falconieri originated, throughout these rooms.[18] If you consult the Hieroglyphica of Piero Valeriano (1556) and the Emblemata of Junius Hadrianus (1585), you see this imagery. My favorite image is the snake eating its tail, the symbol of eternity, around which I hung a laurel wreath, and through the circle of the snake I placed a scepter, atop which I made an eye. The snake equals eternal glory of fame; the scepter equals justice; the eye equals vigilance.[19] All three symbols I used for Orazio Falconieri, the patron, who was an official of the Vatican justice apparatus. In the room next to this I placed in the center of the ceiling three interlocked laurel wreaths, which you can see in Julius Wilhelm Zincgrief's Emblematum Ethico-Politicorum Centuria (1648). Both Zincgref and I took this motif from an earlier source, Valeriano or Hadrianus.

Photos on pages 238 and 239 are of my ceilings. From Eberhard Hempel.

---

[16] Kuntsgewerbe Museum 1038.
[17] Portoghesi 179, paraphrase/quote. The Professor describes all of this as a sort of "ideal checker game, played by the architect and the observer" to combat "the great enemy: boredom".
[18] Professor Blunt says the ceilings are among Borromini's "most remarkable achievements in interior decoration". Blunt 172. All this description from Professor.
[19] All from Professor Blunt's analysis. Blunt 172. See figure 126, at 172.

CHAPTER SEVENTEEN

Sant'Andrea delle Fratte

In 1653 the Marchese Paolo Bufalo engaged me to complete the church of Sant'Andrea delle Fratte on the Piazza begun by Gaspare Guerra in 1605. Sant'Andrea was the church of the Scots in Rome, built amid the orchards, or woods ("fratte") and was given by Sixtus V to the Order of the minims of San Francesco di Paola after the Scots became Protestant. The Marchese Paolo Bufalo, son of Ottavio, offered to complete the church for the minims in 1653 and commissioned me in that year. I began this work in the vigor of my most happy and prosperous time, but I was to end the work only in 1665, when I had begun a rapid descent into deep melancholy. 1653 was the same year that I took over the work at Sant'Agnese from Carlo Rainaldi. I never finished this project, unfortunately, and no one else took up the work after I left it, leaving the exterior in the unfinished state you see today.

Signor Guerra had finished only the nave of the interior; I was compelled to follow his design for the transept, choir and crossing, and so the interior bears none of my style, though I executed this work.

For the dome, I wanted to create an oval, but I was compelled to stay with the circle (this is the cause of the lack of any character to the crossing). Otherwise, I was given a free hand. The model I had in mind for the dome was the Conocchia, the late Roman tomb near Capua. The precise shape of the dome, with its diagonal directives, I took from the cross of Saint Andrew. At the Conocchia, however, the frontispieces project on a rectangular plan whereas here I curved these sections, establishing a "continuous double S-curve".[1] I was to use the sinusoidal curve again at the façade of San Carlino.[2]

A double S curve (repeated at Carlino façade), the brickwork is beautiful, but it was intended that it be encased in stucco. The drum has four equal faces—convex bay followed by a narrow concave bay for the buttress. The thin bricks in the capitals were designed to grasp the stucco. The cupola and lantern were never built.

[1] Blunt 196, quotes.
[2] Portoghesi 290, 291.

I used the same Lombard form of dome encasement as I used at San Carlino and Sant'Ivo. The brickwork you see is, of course, very rough, for the stucco I intended was regrettably – and surprisingly - never added. I used four widely projecting buttresses which "jut out" diagonally from the drum. This resulted in four equal faces- each one has a large convex bay of the drum itself, and then a narrow concave bay for the buttress. I more or less repeated this rhythm for the façade of San Carlino. I used a monumental order of composite columns (the capitals are made of thin brick-like tiles, which stick out, intended to grasp the stucco), which has the effect of ensuring coherence to my unique and extraordinary design.[3]

The companile was built between 1653 and 1659. The topping device has both the arms of the minims and the Bufalo family (a buffalo with a ring through his nose).

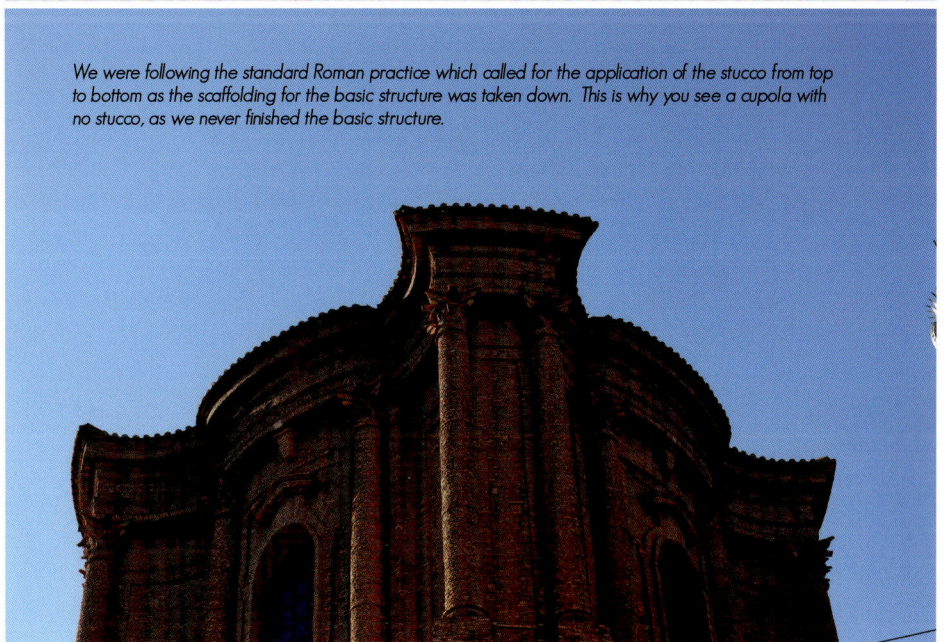

We were following the standard Roman practice which called for the application of the stucco from top to bottom as the scaffolding for the basic structure was taken down. This is why you see a cupola with no stucco, as we never finished the basic structure.

I had intended, if funds permitted, a second story for the cupola, below what was to be a large crowning lantern. If this second story had been built, the curves would have been even more audacious than those at Sant'Ivo. This second story would have channeled hidden lighting down into the interior, providing illumination for four windows that had the "charitos" motto of the minims on them.

---

[3] Wittkower, Art and Architecture 219, quotes. The Professor notes that the "plan of each face is….similar to the lower tier of the façade of [Carlino]." Professor notes that "[o]nce again Borromini worked with spatial evolutions of rhythmic triads".

A view from below, left is the campanile, with its classicism, on the right the drum showing its grand curvature.

One of my drawings[4] shows the second story and lantern that I planned which was never executed. In my mature and old age I continued to design based upon mathematics, as I had done throughout my career. Here at Fratte I designed the drum and lantern based on a series of concentric circles.[5] The largest of these defined the convex bays. I placed the axes of the four piers of the drum on diameters of the circles which bisect the angles between those of the four openings. Then I had each pier and each opening occupy an angle of 45 degrees. I used my usual system for the oval circles of the convex bays of the drum- I drew tangential circles. The curve of the concave bay of the lantern is then an arc of a circle that has as its center the point of contact for the first two circles. As you view this drum today, without its intended crowning lantern, with no stucco, you are drawn to believe this is an ancient ruin in the Campagna. Without the lantern and the stucco I am afraid you cannot have an appropriate perspective on my dome here. I will say that the convexity and concavity arc certainly present in abundance, and that the sinusoidal form for the exterior (from which, as I say, I took the final form of the façade at San Carlino) is very, very special. But the lantern with its concave bays would have magnificently contrasted with the convexity of the drum.[6]

I designed the tower, or campanile, with deliberate intent to create a great contrast with the drum.[7] The lowest section of this campanile I designed to really be seen as part of the church to which it is attached.

---

[4] Albertina drawing 108, Connors, Borromini 258. Also see Portoghesi 290, which reproduces the drawing in the margin.
[5] Blunt 196.
[6] Id. 196, 197. This paragraph from Professor Blunt's description of how Borromini, with his usual "extraordinary consistency" set out his pans in mathematical fashion. Hopefully I have not altered the Professor's explanation.
[7] Wittkower, Art and Architecture 218.

This view from the small alley behind the church.

The second level, without its intended stucco revetment, has "diagonal indication" in the column which I placed at each of its angles.[8] The projecting cornice above these columns is oriented externally on the bisecting line of the angles of the structure.[9] The next cylindrical section has been characterized, rightly, as the most classical structure that I ever made.[10] I intended to create a great contrast to the complex forms of the dome and the intended superstructure above it.

I designed the capitals of this central belfry (it has been described as "temple like") based upon the symbol of Janus. On two sides of every capital I placed a masculine young head and a masculine old head. According to the convention of the time, this expressed the past and the future.[11] On the side of the capital I placed a five-petaled rose and two upside down volutes. This I intended as an allusion to the third face of Janus, the present.[12] You will note, please, my attention to detail. I placed the youthful heads to the open sides of the columns while I placed the aged heads on the sides of the capitals to either side of the segments of the enclosing wall: that is, the past is already written while the open future is the time of liberty.

Look closely at the heads of Janus in the capitals. One old, one young, to represent the past and the future. The five petaled and two upside down volutes represent the third face of Janus, the present.

---

[8] Portoghesi 291. Professor states that while the drum has the "aspect of a ruin" the campanile has the "fineness of a jewel". Figures 182-189.
[9] Id. Quotes.
[10] Blunt 198.
[11] Portoghesi 292. Quote from Portoghesi 291. Professor contrasts this with the Falconieri (Janus - Jana - seasons).
[12] Id.

SANT'ANDREA DELLE FRATTE | 245

For the next higher level I used eight herms-a circle of eight seraphim; the biblical tradition is that these seraphim support the divine throne. These are much like the ones I used on the tomb of Sergius IV at the Lateran.[13]   I humbly consider myself the inventor of these cherub-herms-- a form far removed from any classical model theretofore. I placed narrow curved recesses between these herms. Above this is a narrow buttressing cylinder.

Above all this I made a fabulous, striking crown. Here I placed four inverted volutes that have been said to be beautifully elastic.[14] On these I placed a crown- at this level you can see the buffalo's head of the patron's family, the coronet of a Marchese, and the diagonal cross of Andrew.[15] I also hinted here, in the tentacles, to the status of Andrew as a fisherman, and to the serpents which came to be associated with Andrew's life.[16]

The eight herms. The biblical tradition is that eight seraphim support the divine throne.

---

[13] Blunt 198.
[14] Wittkower, Art and Architecture 219. The Professor credits Borromini with the invention of cherub-herms. See his fn 28.
[15] Blunt 198, Portoghesi 292.
[16] Portoghesi 292.

Regrettably, this wonderful campanile (best seen dear pilgrim on the Via Capo le Case- capo le case, by the way, means end of the houses and le fratte means the hedges. These names were given to these streets as this was the edge of the habituated part of Rome in medieval times) is dominant at delle Fratte, whereas I intended the dome with its lantern to present a brilliant urban theme for the cityscape. It nonetheless has the "fineness of a jewel".[17] I am so so sorry that I had to abandon this project and leave it in the unfinished state you see today.

Top photo: More detail. Bottom photo: More detail. Capitals in the drum.

---
[17] Id. 291.

CHAPTER EIGHTEEN

*The Falconieri Chapel in the Choir of
San Giovanni dei Fiorentini and the Crypt*

Signor Orazio Falconieri engaged me for a burial chapel for his family at the church of the Florentines, very near my home. Work began on this chapel in 1634, when Pietro da Cortona was commissioned for the High Altar, which was to be the centerpiece of the chapel. Unfortunately, Signor Falconieri lost interest and Cortona's design was not executed.

Then in the 1660's, late in my career, I was brought in to execute Pietro da Cortona's plan. I was able to make substantial progress, but left the project incomplete and Ciro Ferri of Cortona's school actually finished it.

Central altar. The compound pediment is mine. See the Chiro I placed in the soffit.

Altar to the right of the main altar. The three dimensional work in the lower portion is mine, the arch in one plane above is not mine. This altar draws on the monument to Boniface VIII at the Lateran.

THE FALCONIERI CHAPEL | 251

I significantly altered Cortona's plan by removing the attic above the altar and continued the columns upward. I placed the two outer columns forward of the others.[1] I then created a compound pediment, and increased the size of the window in front of the pediment (which Cortona had intended to be within it). The concavity made for the light has my prints on it, as does the soffit of the pediment, where I placed a medallion with the monogram of Christ between four six pointed stars, flanked by pomegranates in rhomboid frames (like the cornice of the Propaganda Fide).[2] I inserted the complex fluting I had initiated at the Sala di Recreazione at the Oratorio into the red marble columns of the chapel. The sculpture, of course, is not mine nor in keeping with my style or devices. The window above the altar is by Ferri. I had a part in the monuments on the sidewalls of the chapel. I made the curvilinear base and the oval niche enclosed by columns- these are in keeping with my later style and much like the monument to Pope Boniface VIII at the Laterano. The simple arch in one plane above is not mine and not in keeping with my three dimensional work at the bottom.[3]

I was also involved in the funeral chapel/crypt under the choir (look for the entrance behind the altar), though Ferri finished it. The almost flat low dome is mine (there is a drawing I made for it at the Kunstbibliothek in Berlin). In my later style I used Doric columns without bases and you see these in this crypt (I did this also at the Collegio di Propaganda Fide).[4]

---

[1] Blunt 202.
[2] Portoghesi 297. Professor Portoghesi refers to the "felicitous imprint of Borromini's hand" in the concavity created for the light. See the Professor's figure 227 for the "pomegranates in the rhomboid frames" he describes.
[3] Blunt 204 quotes. Professor Blunt in his text describes more fully how aspects of the altar are clearly not Borromini's. Professor Portoghesi refers to the niche as "an aedicula of oval matrix, carved out from the wall mass so as to produce deep channels of shadow". 297.
[4] Id.

The Crypt.

CHAPTER NINETEEN

*The Spada Chapel in
San Girolamo della Carita*

My name is associated with this chapel. In fact Padre Virgilio Spada designed it, and my contribution was in reality, not significant.[1] In 1660 I drew some plans, but they were always to document/detail Padre Spada's design. I would like you to see here in the pavement the serpent biting its tail (symbol of time and eternity), the rose (brevity of human things), the sunflower (riches), the daisy (love), the convolvulus (lost hopes), the carnation (ingenuity), and the primrose (comeliness).[2] Also notice on the walls, above the onyx fields, heraldic daggers of the Spada family, placed in leaf-form frames. There are five different combinations: a dagger between two stars, two daggers crossed and pointing down, three daggers converging, three parallel daggers, and two daggers crossed and pointing up. The apparition of the angels holding the tablecloth is an allusion to the "inviolable and the sacrosanct".[3]

---

[1] Blunt, 205, 206, figure 148. Professor Blunt refers to the chapel as "the fantastic invention of a talented amateur (Padre Spada)".
[2] Although Professor Blunt is of this view, Professor Portoghesi believes, I think, that Borromini did play an important part in Padre Spada's work. Portoghesi 292-294.
[3] Id.

Actually Padre Spada's work here.

CHAPTER TWENTY

San Giovanni in Fonte;
San Giovanni in Oleo

At the Lateran Baptistery I made a frieze around the outside for Alexander VII. This is made of trophies and the heraldic symbols of the Pope- the monti and the oak tree.

The Frieze for the Chigi Pope.

At the end of the Via Latina, just before the Porta Latina, an architect from the school of Antonio da Sangallo the Elder made a chapel in 1509 at the location where Saint John the Evangelist survived an attempt to martyr him in a vat of oil. In 1658 Cardinal Francesco Paolucci retained me to restore this chapel. I used the existing walls, did a straightforward redecoration inside (Lazzaro Baldi, a pupil of Pietro da Cortona, frescoed the walls), but I designed a new roof. I originally intended to give the chapel a dome with ribs consisting of palm branches, in light of John's martyrdom. Then I designed a stepped dome, but settled on a high attic with a low "conical" roof.[1] I took this from the circular temple beside the Tiber, and the relief (now in the Uffizi) that was also an inspiration for the campanile of Sant'Andrea delle Fratte. The patron's heraldic device included palmettes and rosettes, and so I used these in the attic. On the top I placed what you might call a strange structure,[2] which is like a lantern but not a lantern, and which I made out of the ends of palm-leaves. Then I placed here a cube comprised on each face of a heraldic rosette.

---

[1] Blunt 198. Quotes / paraphrases. This is taken directly from the Professor's description.
[2] Blunt 198, 199, figure 143.

Giovanni in Oleo.

The "lantern".

CHAPTER TWENTY ONE

The Collegio di Propaganda Fide and the Chapel of Re Magi

In 1646, again in the period of my ascendancy, Pope Innocent X appointed me as architect to the Collegio di Propaganda Fide, the seminary for the training of missionaries. The Cavalier Bernini had made the chapel of Re Magi here, and also worked on the southern façade. I drew plans in 1647, which included a larger chapel due to the increasing enrollment. This meant, of course, the taking down of the Cavalier Bernini's chapel, which many have attributed to my animosity towards the Cavalier, but in truth the original chapel was too small. Work proceeded very slowly. I was very busy with the Lateran, of course, but the congregation here at the Collegio was simply not sufficiently motivated. Innocent, too, had many other projects on his mind. Only in 1654, after an impetus from Innocent, did work really begin. It was then that the old chapel was torn down (it was across the street, by the way, from Cavalier Bernini's home). I completed the façade by 1656. The chapel of Re Magi was finished by 1664.

The façade of the Propaganda Fide. Those who felt that my work was affected by my mental state in my late career should pay special attention to the maturity of my style here.

The Seminary Rooms

I should discuss my work at Propaganda Fide in three parts. First, the rooms of the seminary. The staircase and the first floor corridor have my characteristic stucco work. I call your special attention to the room on the upper floor originally an oratory that has come to be called the Newman Chapel, for John Newman said his first mass here.

Chapel of Saint John Newman where the saint said his first mass.

The room is an irregular rectangle (if I may abuse the term). The plain unadorned walls[1] are interrupted by blind arched niches which rise up. These niches "curve" the cornice and then form six large lunettes within the cloister vault. I placed pointed vaults above this. I then divided the soffits of the arches over the niches into very plain coffers, very shallow. I feel these add great delicacy to this surface.[2] I feel that here I expanded greatly my treatment of the vault, that I had begun so many years before at the refectory at San Carlino. At the refectory, I joined the lunettes and their pointed vaults with a "figurative motif" which held together the "detached and unrelated membratures".[3] Here at the Newman Chapel, I imposed what I would call a "syntactic" structure directly on these membratures:[4] I had these surge along the intersecting angles of the vault, and come together, forming a "geometric" motif where pointed angles interpenetrate. Then I had these lock in the center of the ceiling in a large frame with my favorite concave- convex contour.[5]

The cherub in the center of the vault in the chapel of John Newman in the seminary.

---

[1] Portoghesi 287.
[2] Id. The Professor's words: "delicately structuralize their surface".
[3] Id.
[4] Id. The Professor's discussion of Borromini's motifs and structure of the membratures at Carlino and the Newman Chapel.
[5] Id. Quotes. This is directly from the Professor's description. See figure 174.

In places of the upper floors you will find other traces of my intervention, especially the decoration of the vault, where I made some delicate framings. I want you to see especially the small vestibule of the library.[6]

Vestibule of the library in the seminary.

I placed the ceiling here on six arches, with an order of flat pilasters in the angles and then I placed strong projecting pilasters at the center of the four walls. On the longer walls I made two dilated pilasters, which form a large niche for a door.

I ask you to look carefully, also, at the fine doors throughout the piano nobile. If you are a student, you may be interested in my drawings (unexecuted) for doors, windows, and fireplaces in this area, including one based on Signor Vignola's fireplace in the Palazzo Farnese, another with the inverted curved pediments created by Signor Buontalenti for the Porta della Suppliche in the Uffizi.[7]

The Façade

I turn next to the façade of the Propaganda. Innocent died before this was completed, and you will see the insignia of the new Pope, Alexander VII, in consequence. The facade would be seen on a very narrow street, the Via Propaganda Fide, with houses tightly placed on the other side. Thus I had to think of foreshortening, and also I had to limit my projections.

---

[6] Id. Quotes. Figures 170, 171. The Professor describes Borromini's work here as "a complex spatial articulation", the result of an "exceptional simplicity of means".
[7] Blunt 189, 191. See figures 137, 138.

I determined to use giant pilasters for the order, very simple,[8] and not conforming to any established order. These I made in an unusual, and some have said inverted fashion, for the shafts are unfluted, but into the capitals I placed very narrow slits, with very fine mouldings. For the entablature, I used only a cornice, with medallions that I recognize are placed in what seems an irregular manner. The pomegranates in the rhomboid frames are all different.

For the side windows, I used two types, and I am so proud of these. One, placed in the middle, has a concave curvature with a four columned Doric aedicule.[9] I split the entablature for these, turning the top mouldings of the cornice up, so that it ends in a scroll, which carries the pediment. I created a "discontinuous" pediment, which I have breaking forward in the middle over a cluster of four guttae. Then I filled the pediment with a circular opening that I surrounded in palmi.[10] The frieze, with triglyphs, has palmettes and rosettes, and guttae below, above the Doric order.

For the side windows adjacent to the middle side window, I used round-headed arches, slightly stilted.

Left photo: Façade window flanking the central window on one of the sides, in turn flanking the central portal. I then placed a pilaster and column on each side of the window.

Top and right photo: Windows of the façade.

---

[8] Id. 191.
[9] Portoghesi 288. See figures. Professor Portoghesi states that in the façade Borromini "has left one of the strongest imprints of his artistic will". 287.
[10] Blunt 192. Quotes. Professor Blunt's description here of how Borromini "split" the entablature, and made the cornice and "discontinuous" pediment.

This aedicula is more deeply recessed. Here I made really three structures: an outer arch supported by the two pilasters, a second arch to which I connected two columns, which are diagonally disposed.[11] Then I made an opening where I made an architrave that is supported by two almost completely hidden pilasters.[12] I placed triglyphs throughout, with guttae. Note that the architrave and frieze seem to disappear behind the column; I have this reappear to form the central part of the niche.[13] I placed a band of laurel around the window.

For the middle, central bay of the façade, I created a concavity, but in the central field above the portal I used a convexity for the window (I was always to use this concave/convex contrast, as I have so often related to you) (this is reminiscent of the balcony at the façade of the Oratorio). Really, for this central window I was inspired by Michelangelo's work over the portal at Palazzo Farnese. For this window I used some of the same features as I used for the side windows, the basic difference is that I placed this whole central window against the concave wall of this central bay.[14] I placed two columns on either side of the window, separated by a broken pilaster, setting the outer column and the outer half of the broken pilaster against the curve of the wall.

---

[11] Blunt 192, Portoghesi 288. Quotes. Professor Portoghesi's description of the "concatenation" of three structures.
[12] Portoghesi 288.
[13] Blunt 192. Quote. Professor Blunt notes that "[b]elow this level (arch) the arrangement is unexpected".
[14] Portoghesi 288 (likeness to Farnese), Blunt 193.

Top photo: The convex window over the portal.

Right photo: The central portal to the Collegio, concave in the upper cornice, concave and convex in the window frame, and concave and straight in the cornice over the door. Beautiful mouldings in the door frame. My unusual fluting in the pilaster/columns which are inverted—smaller in width as they descend.

You will see, though, that with the break in the pilaster I began a convex curve running through the entire central section, enclosing an oval space. I decorated the covering of this oval space with a stucco image of the Holy Spirit (you must look from below, into the soffit). These columns I set orthogonally to the curve, thus they are not quite at right angles to each other. I made the entablature over the columns follow the curve of the niche, adding what I believe you will agree is a further wonderful intricacy.[15]

For the central door (over which I placed tender and sparkling cherubim), I used a hood that follows my famous window at Palazzo Barberini, and in a three dimensional form that parallels my door to the cloister at San Carlino.

The column of the central portal, with no capital, unequal fluting, and piers narrowing to the base, as at Michelangelo's Ricetto at the Laurentian Library. The piers have two slightly concave half sides.

---

[15] Id. Quotes. This is Professor Blunt's description of the central window over the portal. I cannot locate the Holy Ghost the Professor cites. Professor Portoghesi states that there are at least three lines of direction here: diagonal expanding (projecting columns that close the order), rotary (curvature of cornice), and frontality (detached pediment). Portoghesi 288, 289.

The hood over the portal, following my famous window at the Barberini Palazzo. My festoon here is asymmetrical, wrapping around the conch.

I placed two piers (not columns nor pilasters) that, like Michelangelo's piers in the Ricetto of the Laurentian Library, are narrower at the bottom than the top. The piers have two sides, and two half-sides of a hexagon, each of which I made slightly concave. This, I will admit, introduces a Gothic feel here. I added my own device of making the flutings unequal.[16] In the tympanum of the portal I placed an "asymmetrical" festoon, which I wrapped around a shell. Above the cornice I placed an attic, and here I used windows of a fairly complicated design.[17] I repeated the theme of the windows of the piano nobile: the first, third, fifth and seventh windows follow in a simpler way the second and sixth below, while the windows in the even bays follow generally the theme in the uneven ones of the piano nobile. Then in the fourth attic window I used a pediment where I brought two window movements together.[18]

---

[16] Blunt 194.
[17] Id. 192, Portoghesi 289.
[18] Wittkower, Art and Architecture 228. Professor Wittkower compares the façade at the Oratory with that at Propaganda Fide and states that they illustrate the "deep change between Borromini's early and late style". Gone: "mass of detail", "subtle gradations of wall surface and mouldings", "joyful motifs"; now "mass and weight [have] grown immensely".

The Chapel of Re Magi

The Re Magi chapel.

Finally, the chapel of Re Magi, finished before the end of my career, except for the final stuccoing. This, of course, was one of my last works, and it reflects the culmination of my thinking about the vault. In fact the vault I made here is the one I wanted to place in the ceiling at San Giovanni in Laterano. It is like the ribbing I made at the Oratorio, but more sophisticated, more sublime, as I shall describe for you. It does have the strain of the Gothic in it, I do admit.

I settled on a rectangular chapel for the Magi, after first toying with the oval. As at the Oratorio, the dictates of the site at the Fide required that the axis of the chapel parallel the façade, so that you must turn to the left after entering the main portal of the Propaganda Fide, to enter through the portal to the chapel. I find this arrangement satisfactory here, because the seminary sits to the right of the portal, balancing the chapel to the left (I originally began the façade with five bays, but I extended this to seven bays so that the façade completely "covers" the chapel).

The beautiful vault of Re Magi, with diagonal ribs. The final perfection of my vault style. This is the vault I intended for the Lateran.

The arms of the Chigi Pope Alexander VII at Re Magi.

THE COLLEGIO DI PROPAGANDA FIDE AND THE CHAPEL OF RE MAGI | 273

The nave of the Re Magi.

When I designed the vault for the Magi, I had in mind the Milanese church of San Maurizio, which I had visited many times in my youth. I had studied the rectangular matrix for so many years; finally here at the Magi I think I solved all the problems. My geometric scheme was pure: width to length 1:1.62, equivalent to the Golden Section; width to height in a longitudinal sense 1:1; proportion of width to height in transversal sense, height measured to the top of the architrave 1:1; proportion of total length to total height, height calculated from the top plane of the pedestals, equivalent to the Golden Section.[19] What I made here, between the geometric schemes of two sections, is a "reciprocally inverted relationship". And the openings of the lateral chapels and the intermediary openings have a proportion of width to height of 1:2. I made the rectangular areas above the lateral chapels containing windows square.[20]

The exterior of Re Magi with windows opening onto the second floor passageway that extends on three sides of the chapel.

---

[19] Portoghesi 286. All numbers the Professor's.
[20] Id.

At the Oratorio, I cut the corners of the room off (remember no corners for me) through the use of "short straight facets",[21] and single ribs spring from these on their way to the central oval panel in the vault. Here at the Re Magi I used much greater skill, gained through experience. Here I rounded the corners and flanked them with pilasters. Now I could send pairs of ribs projecting across the vault, their course uninterrupted. I made a hexagon in the central decorative panel, formed by the ribs themselves.[22] One of the parallel ribs lands on a pilaster on the opposite side of the chapel, the other ends on a vault over the window. This has been characterized as "extreme[ly] ingen[ious]" and I cannot, of course, disagree.[23]

For the side walls I used Ionic pilasters, the capitals come halfway up the galleria. I made the side chapels simple, rectangular with apsed ends, as at the chapels of the Laterano. The busts stand on plain oval cylinders of black marble, as at the tomb of Alexander III at the Laterano (but with no curved superstructure). I divided the walls by a straight entablature, this I had carried by what are properly called "severe" pilaster panels, which flank the chapels.[24] I placed the arms of Alexander VII over the altar.

Of all the vaults I made, I am most happy with the one at the Re Magi. I believe it captures the ingenuity, the flair, the geometry, and the beauty of my vaulting technique more so than any other I made.

---

[21] Blunt 185.
[22] Id.
[23] Id.
[24] Id. 185-189.

Conclusion[1]

As I reminisce over my life here in conclusion, I would like to break the discussion into several periods for you. The first, that of my youth in Lombardy, learning how to be a stonemason and stonecutter in Milan, reading voraciously everything I could about architecture.

The second, my journey to Rome when I was just under twenty, and the years I spent learning under my relative, the great Carlo Maderno, seeing and learning all that Michelangelo did in the city, and continuing to study all the work of the ancients, and amassing and reading all that had ever been written about architecture (some 123 treatises by the time I finished), maturing from a stonemason into a true architect, and eventually assuming the chief role in architecture for my aging master, who increasingly could not meet the physical demands of his role as Architect of San Pietro.

Then third, the period from my great relative's death in 1629 until 1634, a period when I had to accept that the Cavalier Bernini, and not I, would be Architect for San Pietro and for the Pope, a result I felt was unfair and humiliating, as I have told you. When I finally realized that the Cavalier would assume all credit for my work, I struck out on my own. During this period I changed my name to Borromini, for several reasons: to distinguish myself from the numerous Castelli who lived about me, and to reflect my home, where the Swiss of the Golden League of the Seven Cantons of Catholic Switzerland were called "Borromea", after Carlo Borromeo (I considered myself a "Borromea"), who founded the league. I also changed my dress to the Spanish style- black, randiglia, rosettes in my shoes, and leggings, and I wore a wig and side whiskers. I was healthy, robust, tall, and not unhandsome. I did this to be a bit standoffish to the Romans, who favored the French, whilst I favored the Spanish (who ruled Milan). Virgilio Spada was also of Spanish persuasion (he had enlisted in the Spanish army at one point!). Money was not important to me, the less I received the less I was beholden.

In the next and fourth period, from 1634 to the ascendancy of Pope Innocent X in 1644, I made my name as an architect, with the Carlino and the Oratorio. I filled my home with wax models of all my projects, and a few of clay, all by my own hand.[2] I lived frugally (my dish of tin), but happily, chaste by choice, temperate in food and drink. At times I dressed in ancient Roman fashion in finely woven stuff.[3]

---

[1] See generally, WIttkower; Studies 154-176, Appendices I-III, accompanying footnoes at 290-294. Professor Wittkower's chapter on Borromini is perhaps the best source about Borromini's character and life. The footnotes are as good as the text.
[2] Wittkower, Studies, 290 fn 7, 8, 9.
[3] Id. fn 9.
[4] Id. 291 fn 26.

The fifth period, the most glorious, was the same as the reign of the Pamphilj Pope 1644 to January 1655. Padre Vigilio Spada, my most loyal supporter, was advisor to the Pope in matters of architecture. I was commissioned for the restoration of San Giovanni, consulted in the Pope's palace, making the grand salone, engaged for Sant'Agnese, began for the Pope, made the Orologio! What a glorious time. In 1652 I was given the gold cross of the Order of Cavalier. I also received from Innocent the robe of the Knight of Christ[4] (I gave this to Cardinal Ulderico Carpegna in my will).

The sixth and final period was from the death of Pope Innocent X and the ascendancy of the Chigi Pope Alexander VII in 1655 through the end of my career in 1667. In 1657 I was dismissed from Sant'Agnese, and the congregation at the Oratorio refused to take me back there. I had to defend myself at Sant'Ivo where fissures had appeared. My work was attacked as chimeric and Gothic. This new pope, the Chigi Alexander VII, did not like me, but rather the Cavalier Bernini, who received all the commissions. The Pope was forced to engage me for the tombs at San Giovanni to maintain a consistency and honor my position as Architect there. I persevered during this period, and did fine, coherent, mature, beautiful work at the Propaganda Fide and the Re Magi Chapel, at the Palazzo Falconieri, at the dome and campanile at Andrea delle Fratte, and at the Sapienza. No one who has seen the façade at Propaganda Fide or the ceiling of the Re Magi could possibly say that my increasingly fragile mental state affected my work. There are those who point to what they would say was the exotic style of Sant'Ivo and Andrea delle Fratte and called me borderline schizophrenic.[5] Yes, during this period I was unsocial, eccentric, hypersensitive and easily excitable.[6] But my work required a lucid mind and a strong body. I controlled my inner self when I worked, and I worked steadily and fruitfully during this last period, even as I sunk into a deep melancholy and a morbid introspection.[7] The Cavalier Bernini's star continued to rise, mine I felt was falling into an abyss. At the last, I was so oppressed and distraught that I trusted no one – at one point, I even destroyed many of my plans that were unexecuted, for fear that others would use them for their own work, like the Cavalier had done to me so long before at San Pietro.[8] When my friend Fioravante Martinelli died July 27, 1667, I lapsed into a fit of hypochondria, and I was in a continuous state of frenzy.[9] Fortunately, my scalpellino Franceso Massari was still with me and attended me to the last, as did my Confessor Fra Scalpellino Orazio Callera.[10]

---

[5] Id. 154, fn 3. In the last year of his life, Borromini also did work on the Chapel of Saint Dominic at Santa Sabina (see the stucco rosettes and bands of oak leaves), more evidence he could still perform. Blunt, Baroque Guide 142. Professor Blunt believes Borromini's health at this point precluded even this work; if so query the architect here.
[6] Id.
[7] Blunt 208.
[8] Blunt 21.
[9] Morrisey 8,9.
[10] Morrisey 10.

As I leave you, I ask you not to forget my inventions as you see the architecture in your own country, which bases itself on the classical and baroque. My window at the Barberini, with its canted frame. My curved facades (especially the one at the Oratorio). My continued use of the convex and concave, juxtaposed so as to create beautiful contrast, as in the Orologio and the lantern at Carlino, and especially the lantern I designed for delle Fratte. The rectangular nave, where I eliminated the corner altogether, first at the cloister at Carlino, then at the Oratorio and Re Magi. And do not forget my invention of the ribbed vault, especially my final masterpiece at Re Magi (if I had been allowed to add the ribbed vault I planned at Giovanni, ah!). Also you must not forget the inverted volute, which I used first at the Baldacchino in San Pietro, the dolphin. The bent cornice, the best of which is in the refectory at Carlino. The giant order, in the courtyard at the Oratorio, taken from Michelangelo's Palazzo dei Conservatori. The play on perspective in the loggia at Barberini. The apses at Carlino. The colonnade at Palazzo Spada. The winged cherubs at Giovanni. The cherub herms ever present in all my work. The sinusoidal façade, at Carlino. The special fluting, as at the Sala de Recreazione at the Oratory, the Lateran and the Propaganda Fide. The stepped dome, as at Carlino and Ivo. The twin campanile framing the dome at Agnese. The uninterrupted cornice, as at Carlino. My special inverted alternated balustrade, as at the Carlino cloister. Look for evidence of all of these in your own buildings. It is my great hope that my inventions contribute to the beauty of architecture across our globe.

For those of you who aspire to architecture, a final word: follow the ancients, follow the classical, know and understand the rules embodied in that architecture. But never stop inventing. Do not be a mere copyist. That is not why you are an architect. You are an architect to create.

The Events Leading Up To My Death[1]

Yes, I know that you know that I took my own life in 1667, a result of both physical and mental fatigue. Why do people take their lives? I suppose it is most often a complete lack of hope: there is no future that can be seen.

    I have spoken briefly at several points about the desire I had to publish my plans so that my approach to architecture could be perhaps handed down to future aspiring architects. In 1647, the Padre Virgilio Spada and I decided to write a piena relazione for the Oratorio, with my role being to provide the illustrations (although I also supplied copious comments). Unfortunately, in the final Spada product only one of my drawings appears, the detailed and meticulously orthogonal façade elevation for the Oratory.[2]

    In 1650, Fra Juan de San Bonaventura, the procurator of San Carlino, and also my good supporter, began a similar relazione, this one for the Carlino. As I have told you, I resisted creating or giving a plan for Carlino (even to the Fra), and my other buildings. But in the period around 1665-1667, I did make a series of ground plans for the Carlino. These were idealized plans, smaller in size and with some modified proportions. For example, the oval does not correspond to the actual geometry I used for the dome.[3]

    Around 1650, Padre Spada wrote a treastise on the Palazzo Pamphilj. In it, with my great thanks, he showed in an abstract, diagrammatic way my novel construction features for the vault of the Salone for the Palazzo Pamphilj.[4] I also made three elevations of the Piazza Navona façade that should be seen as one reads the Padre's treastise.[5] In 1652, Padre Spada wrote a report on the Lateran Basilica restoration, and included in his Spada Codex the three presentation sheets for the elevations of the nave that were given to Innocent X for him to make a selection,[6] as well as other presentation sheets.

    Unfortunately, none of the work that Padre Spada and I did together was published during our lifetimes, perhaps because the Padre's purpose was to stress the functionality, the inexpensiveness, and the aesthetic effects of my buildings, whereas I wanted to inspire future architects with my creative inventions.[7] I must confess that I wanted to emulate Andrea Palladio, who, as you know, created a magnificent set of diagramed palaces and villas in the second book of his Quattro Libri.

---

[1] There are those who believe Borromini was murdered, for his money. See Il Giornale D'Italia, Terzapagina, Mercoledi 25 Ottobre 1995, 3. Professor Raspe's article about Borromini's suicide is as you can see from the footnotes, the source for all the information in this chapter. The Professor provides an excellent and very helpful chronology at 128-129.
[2] Raspe, Suicide 122. Professor Raspe's words.
[3] Id.
[4] Raspe, 124, quote.
[5] Raspe, illustrations 7, 127.
[6] Raspe, 123.
[7] Raspe, 125, the Professor's words.

After the death of Pope Innocent X and the ascent of Alexander VII my commissions dwindled, as the Cavalier Bernini was the Chigi favorite. I had time to work on a publication of my projects. I engaged the Frenchman Dominique Barriere to make the copper-plate engravings for the work.[8] His first engraving for me was the Oratory façade (note that it has columns instead of pilasters on the upper story).[9]

Barriere also made four plates of the Sapienza for me – the pianta giumetrale and three perspectival views. I devised these cooper-plates to my heirs, which were not published in my lifetime.[10]

In 1662, Padre Spada died. I lost a close friend and mentor, someone who had time and again come to my aid and been my guiding light, someone who supported me through my quarrels with my patrons. He was also, though, the author of my projected book.[11] Fortunately, in 1650, I had made another friend, Fioravante Martinelli, certainly no architect, but an Oratorian, a priest who was to become the scriptor hebraicus in the Vatican Library and then the scriptor latinus. He wrote the popular guidebook, Roma ricercata. In 1660, Fioravante began another guidebook Roma ornata, which was to provide detailed artistic information on the monuments of Rome.[12] I supplied many, many comments in the margins. My good friend wrote extensively about the Sapienza and its history, and I was to provide him illustrations.

In 1663, my assistant of over 20 years, Francesco Righi, died. By 1665, I had lost almost all of my important commissions, perhaps most importantly San Giovanni in Laterano and Sant'Agnese in Agone. Work on Sant'Ivo and the Sapienza and the Collegio di Propaganda Fide was nearing completion. Then in April of 1665, the Marchese Paolo del Bufalo, a good friend and patrion, died, and thus I stopped work on the presbytery of Sant'Andrea delle Fratte, which was to be his mausoleum.[13]

I renewed my efforts on my publication project, working and reworking my designs, collaborating with Messrs. Barriere and Martinelli. My project advanced to the stage of finished copperplates.[14] I made many elaborated sample drawings for these plates.

---

[8] Id. fn 36.
[9] Id. fn 39.
[10] Sebastiano Gianni included these in 1720 in the "Opera del Cavaliere Borromini". Plate X is the pianta giumetrale. Raspe, 126.
[11] Raspe, 127.
[12] Id. This book remained unpublished until 1969.
[13] Raspe, 127, 128.
[14] Raspe, 128.

In December of 1666, the unspeakable happened. My great rival the Cavalier Bernini was commissioned by Olympia Aldobrandini and Cardinal Decio Azzolini to finish my Church at Sant'Agnese. This was the first time the Cavalier had actually stolen work from me.[15] The Cavalier without hesitation, and I believe but cannot prove, with animosity, began radical changes to my façade (Carlo Rainaldi and Giovanni Maria Baratta had already mutilated it by adding a far too heavy attic).[16] The Cavalier wickedly took off all my ornamental reliefs, altered the shapes of the panels over the side doors, and then proceeded to make radical modifications to the interior decorations.[17]

In February 1667, Camillo Arcucci, then Architect of the Oratory, died, and I had hopes of being reinstated. But I was not, perhaps predictably in view of my troubled history there.

I was approaching near madness. To calm myself from the harm the Cavalier was doing to me with his work at Sant'Agnese, I left for Lombardy in the spring of 1667, thinking that a trip to my ancestral home would calm me.

On June 26, 1667, Clement IX became Pope. He too was a friend of the Cavalier. I knew I would receive no new commissions. On July 1, 1667, the commission for the tomb of Innocent X went to yes, the Cavalier Bernini! My Pope, whose portrait was in my house, who had conferred upon me the cavalierato, for whom I called myself "Architect to della Santa Innocente X". I returned to Rome, my malinconia quickly returned. I went back to my publication project in earnest. It was a partial cure. I continued to make designs, even for commissions long ago finished, or lost to other architects.[18] These included the campanile and tiburio of Sant'Andrea delle Fratte and Sant'Agnese and the Collegio Innocenziano.[19]

Then, the most devasting event of all. On July 20, 1667, Fioravante Martinelli died. My body now was in illness, I called it "indisposition" while my nephew called it "umore malinconico" and "umore ipocondrico". In the event, the news of Fioravante's death created a violent reaction in me. His so sudden demise, he my confidant and intimate colleague, created in me a deep depression. I lost not only a friend, but also the last remaining author for my book.[20] My last project, the only way left to me to publish my architectural ideas, was now finished.[21]

---

[15] Raspe, 129. The Professor's words about Bernini's theft.
[16] Id. The Professor's words here about Bernini proceeding without hesitation, mine the use of "animosity".
[17] Id.
[18] Raspe 129.
[19] Raspe 132.
[20] Raspe 130, Professor Raspe's words.
[21] Raspe 130-131.

It was at this point that I contemplated my death. I now focused on my nephew Bernardo. After the death of my brother Domenico in 1659, Bernardo had lived with me, and I did the best I could to train him as an architect, but I am compelled to relate that his skills were meager.[22] He had recently left to make his own home (he was 24).

On July 22, my illness returned as my mind focused on the loss of my friend and my project. I was now confined to my home. I called for the notario Olimpio Ricci and I consigned a sealed will to her.

On July 23, I went to the Laterano to receive the Jubilee indulgence on the accession of Clement IX. I had not entirely lost my senses. On July 29, I withdrew my will from the Notary.[23] On July 30, my condition worsened. I now knew my death was imminent. On this day, I burned all the drawings I had been preparing for engraving for my project. I did not want them to fall into the wrong hands. I now had no one whom I trusted to stay true to my methods and intentions, no one who saw things the way I saw them. The annihilation was almost complete. I spared some 700 sheets of varying purposes, but not the clean copies set aside for engraving. Any plan that could serve for the completion of any unfinished building, I destroyed. I was convinced the publication project was finished for good, and further I had no confidence that Bernardo would carry it out after my death in a satisfactory manner.[24] I also did not want my nephew to prosper where he had not labored.[25] I left Bernardo the bulk of my drawings as study material (these architectural schizzo had no market value),[26] but I destroyed anything that could be converted into cash.[27]

My nephew visited me the afternoon of August 1. That night I began to draft a new will. On August 2, at the fifth hour, my dear friend Francesco Massari, my servant (a gifted scalpellino, dean of the stonecutters' guild),[28] refused my request for a light. My nephew had instructed him to do this to ensure that I got rest. With this small and obedient act, I felt completely abandoned. Three hours of despair and impatience later, I made the final step – I threw myself on my spadino, all' hore otto e mezzo in circa (four in the morning). I leaned the hilt on the bed and put the point to my side and then pitched myself on the sword with such force that it pierced my body from one side to the other.[29] I am not sure that I really intended death, as I thrust the sword into my side, not into my

---

[22] Bernardo was at this time working with Borromini on the façade at San Carlino, which he was to continue. There are those who say he disfigured it "beyond recognition". Professor Raspe takes this from Thelen.
[23] Raspe 129. Professor Raspe notes this will "is lost". Some think Borromini withdrew the will to remove a bequest to the now deceased Martinelli. Id. at 131.
[24] Raspe 131. Filippo Neri and the Master Michaelangelo also burnt almost all their papers in their last days, the former because he truly wanted not to become a celebrity, the latter to ensure a reputation free from criticism due to any mistakes in his preparatory work and the painful effort he put into his work. Downes, Opus, 370 fn 129.
[25] Bernardo did not become a professional architect and lived a life of leisure on his inheritance from Borromini. Raspe 133.
[26] Baron Stosch bought them en masse in 1730 for a trifle. Raspe 134.
[27] Raspe 134.
[28] After Borromini's close collaborator Francesco Righi died in 1664, Francesco Massari took his position, and even served as draughtsman. Raspe 132.
[29] Quote from Borromini's account to the doctor.

stomach or heart. Francesco found me. I asked to see the notario again, and I drew a new will with my nephew as sole heir, on condition that he study architecture and marry a granddaughter of Carlo Maderno. I recounted in detail all of the events of the prior evening. I made my confession. I gave my soul to God, fortified by all the sacraments of the church.[30]

    God was so kind to me, allowing me to live for a day after I had plunged myself onto my sword in my darkest hour, permitting me and enabling me to write this for you. I was able to confess my sin, put my things in order, say my last goodbyes, and reflect on all that I have related to you above. My life ended sadly, but it was still a fruitful life, though I suffered much during it. I regret only that I was not able in my life to summon up enough strength to accept the unfairness associated with the Cavalier Bernini, to put that behind me, to humbly move forward with the commissions I did obtain. Had I been humbler, more agreeable, I would have obtained much more satisfying work. But I am still so grateful that I was able to contribute to the advance of architecture. I hope that because of my work, architecture is happier, fuller, more exciting, more beautiful, more original.

    I created five beautiful churches – Carlino, Ivo, Sette Dolori, delle Fratte and Sant'Agnese – and three beautiful chapels – the Oratorio, Re Magi, and the Landi – and I remade the first church in Rome – the Laterano, all of which have given a home to so many Christian worshippers and pilgrims. To the great glory of God, these are holy places that I believe I adorned for the greater good of God's people. I am very proud to have made my contribution to our church in this way. As you visit and pray in these places, certainly nine of the most special places for worship in the world, pray for me.

    I felt, as I passed, that I left the world a better place than when I entered it. That is all a man can do.

---

[30] Downes, Opus 309, quoting the register of Santa Maria dei Fiorentini, fn 166.

Index

A

Academia di San Luca (Palazzo Carpegna), 214
Acqua Vergine acqueduct, 189
Acquaviva, Cardinal Giulio (tomb, Laterano), 197,198
Alberti, Leon Battista, 178
Albertina drawings, 2, 40, 43, 55, 60, 67, 110, 130, 145, 154, 159, 160, 209, 226, 234, 236, 244
Albrizi, Orazio, 6
Alessandrina Library (Sant'Ivo), 168, 169
Alexander III, Pope, Rolando Bandinelli (tomb, Laterano), 192, 193, 275
Alexander VII, Pope, Fabio Chigi, 138, 140, 146, 149, 151, 155, 159, 160, 163, 165, 166, 168, 191, 192, 200, 209, 210, 260, 267, 273, 277, 280
Algardi, Alessandro, 3, 110, 173, 190
Annibaldi, Ricardo, Cardinal (tomb, Laterano), 199
Anticamera di Santo (Casa), 112
Antichita di Roma, X, 25
Antichita Romane, X
Api fountain, 11
Aqua Vergine aqueduct, 189
Archginnasio di Roma (Sant'Ivo), 137
Arcucci, Camillo, 96, 123, 282
Arigucci, Luigi, 96, 118
Arnolfo di Cambio, 199

B

Baalbek, Temple, 25, 58, 65
Baldacchino (San Pietro in Vaticano), 6, 7, 8, 9, 10, 11, 109, 121, 122, 123, 278
Baptistery, Lateran, 109, 219, 259, 260
Barberini, Francesco, Cardinal, 4, 6, 7, 8, 11, 14
Barberini, Pope Urban VIII (see Urban VIII)
Barriere, Domenico (Dominique), 144, 165, 281
Bassi, Martino, 71
Baths of Diocletian, 90

Bernini, Domenico, 141
Bernini, Gian Lorenzo, 4, 6, 7, 8, 9, 11, 14, 15, 16, 24, 74, 137, 141, 151, 190, 204, 208, 210, 264, 276, 282
Bianco, Gerardo, Cardinal (tomb, Laterano), 199, 200
Biffi, Andrea, X, XI
Bitonto, Giovanni Mariada, 226
Bonaventura, Fra Juan de, 43, 280
Boniface VIII, Pope, Benedetto Caetani (tomb, Laterano), 192, 194, 195, 196, 251, 252
Borghese, Pope Paul V (see Paul V)
Borromeo, Charles (San Carlo), XI, XII, 7, 34, 74, 184, 276
Bramante, Donato, XIII, 38, 64, 178, 226
Brumino, Giovanni Dominico Castelli, X
Bufalo, Marchese (delle Fratte), 242, 281
Buontalenti (Uffizi), 267

CHAPELS

Agnese, Sant' (San Carlino), 65
Barberini (Cardinal Francesco)(San Carlino), 63
Blessed Sacrament (San Pietro in Vaticano) (Santissimo Sacramento), 4, 5
Cappelletta (San Carlino), 66, 67, 131
Cappelletta di Santo (Casa, Oratorio), 112, 113
Cappelletta Esterna (San Filippo Neri, Chiesa Nuova), 111
Choir (San Pietro in Vaticano), 3
Coronaro (Bernini), 151
Crucifixion (San Carlino), 63
Dominic (Sabina), 277
Donati (Casa), 111
Falconieri (San Giovanni dei Fiorentini), 249-250
Filomarino (Naples), 38
Giovanni in Oleo (Porta Latina), 259-261
Landi (Santa Lucia In Selci), 9, 80, 81, 157
Madonna (San Carlino), 63, 66
Mary Magdalene (Laterano), 197
Medici (Florence), XI, 234, 236

Newman, Saint John (Propaganda Fide), 265, 266
Nicchione della Cantoria (Lodi, Santuario), 64
Orsini (Laterano), 186
Re Magi (Collegio di Propaganda Fide), 130, 132, 178, 179, 226, 263, 264, 265, 272-275, 277
San Sebastiano (San Pietro in Vaticano), 3
Sfroza (Santa Maria Maggiore), XIII, 27, 28
Spada (San Girolamo della Carita), 255-257
Ursula, Sant' (San Carlino), 65
Venanzio, San (Baptistery, tomb of Ceva), 219

CHURCHES
Agnese in Agone, 204, 207-211, 242, 277, 281, 282
Andrea della Valle, 4, 12, 13
Andrea delle Fratte, 116, 209, 241-247, 260, 277, 278, 281
Andrea in Quirinale, 167
Andrea Via Flaminia, 28
Anna dei Palafrernieri, 12, 39, 43
Carlo al Corso, 172
Carlo alle Quattro Fontane (Carlino), 9, 18, 29, 30-65, 103, 132, 150, 184, 185, 186, 243, 266, 278, 280, 283
Casa di Loreto, 34
Cecilia, 86
Chiesa Nuova, 86, 88, 97, 104, 105, 106, 111, 116
Costanza, 26, 50, 52
Duomo, Florence, XI
Duomo, Milan, XI, 28, 76, 99, 107, 108, 215
Duomo, Milan (original), 99
Fedele, Milan, 28
Gesu, 99
Giacomo degli Incurabili, 28, 39
Giovanni Battista dei Fiorentini, 2, 8, 12, 26, 249-253
Giovanni in Laterano, 74, 76, 73, 171-201, 230, 273, 277, 278, 281
Girolamo della Carita, 255-257
Giuseppe, Milan, 28
Ignazio, 4
Ivo della Sapienza, 29, 71, 76, 135-169, 219, 243, 277, 281
Lorenzo, Florence, XI
Lorenzo Maggiore, Milan, XI, 12, 71
Luca e Martina, 34, 71, 208
Lucia in Selci, 9, 79-83
Maria dei Sette Dolori, 9, 73, 127-133
Maria in Treviso, 28
Maria in Vallicella (see Chiesa Nuova)
Martina e Luca, 34, 71, 208
Martino ai Monti, 80
Maurizio, Milan, 274
Pietro in Vaticano, X, XIII, 2-12, 14, 38, 39, 43, 60, 71, 95, 109, 123, 140, 141, 149, 153, 162, 172, 208, 210, 278
Pietro in Vincoli, 60
Pietro e Marcellino, Milan, 9
Prassede, 109
Redentore, Venice, 120
Sabina, 277
Santuario dell'Incoronata, Lodi, 64
Satiro, Milan, 64
Susanna, X, XIII, 97
Teresa, Caprarola, 93

C
Callera, Fra Orazio, 277
Cancelleria, ceiling, 52
Canocchia (tomb, Capua), 25
Canopus (see Hadrian's Villa)
Cappelletta (San Carlino), 66, 67
Capitoline Palaces (see Palazzo)
Caroccioli, Cardinal Bernardo (tomb, Laterano), 199
Cartari, Carlo, 139, 141, 144, 164
Casa, San Filippo Neri, 9, 58, 76, 84-124, 150, 177
Casa Vecchia (San Filippo Neri), 86
Casino Barberini, Palestrina, 144
Casino Palazzo del Bufalo, 230
Castelli, Bernardo, 2, 35, 74, 76, 283
Castelli, Battista, X, 4
Castelli, Domenico, 283
Castelli, Padre Benedetto, 143
Ceva, Francesco Adriano, Cardinal, 219
Chaves, Cardinal (tomb, Laterano), 197, 198

Chigi (see Alexander VII)
Chimneypiece (Casa, 0ratory), 113, 114
Clement IX, Pope,Giulio Rospigliosi, 282, 283
Cloister (San Carlo alle Quattro Fontane), 36-39, 222, 270, 278
Collegio Borromeo (Pavia), 28, 37
Collegio Elvetico (Milan), 28, 71
Collegio di Propaganda Fide (see Chapel Re Magi and Propaganda Fide)
Collegio Romano, 109, 204
Colonnade, false perspective (see Palazzo Spada)
Codex Coner, 25, 109
Conocchia (Capua), 25, 242
Contraforti orbicolati (Sant' Ivo), 163
Cortona, Pietro da (see da Cortona)

D
d'Arpino, Cavalier Cesare, 82, 153
da Cortona, Pietro, 14, 15, 24, 34, 64, 71, 96, 112, 121, 123, 200, 205, 208, 250, 252, 260
da Sangallo, Antonio (Younger), 17, 71, 226, 260
da Sangallo, Antonio (Elder), 260
dal Pozzo, Cassiano, 25
de Architectura, X
de Chaves, Cardinal (tomb, Laterano), 197, 198
del Duca, Giacomo, 28
del Grande, Antonio (Sette Dolori), 128
della Porta, Giacomo, 136, 138, 144, 155, 189, 237
de Valois, Felix, 30

E
Emblemata (Junius Hadrianus), 239

F
Falconieri, Orazio, 239, 250
Farnese (see Pope Paul III)
Ferri, Ciro (San Giovanni in Fiorentini), 250, 252
Ferrari, Giovanni Battista (Flora), 63
Filarmino altar, Naples, 38
Filippo Neri, Saint (see Neri)

Fontana, Domenico
Fontana del Moro, 189
Fontana Tritone, 137
Fontana Quattro Tevere (the Four Rivers), 190, 191, 204, 208
Fulvio, Andrea, X, 25

G
Galleria (Palazzo Pamphilj), 204, 205
Garovo, Anastasia, X
Garovo, Leone, XIII, 2, 3, 7
Giannini, Sebastiano (plates), 89, 91, 92, 93, 94, 104, 117, 120, 144, 153, 157, 162, 165, 281
Giotto, 194, 195
Giussano, Cardinal Casate (tomb, Laterano), 196, 197
Golden House, Nero, 25
Golden Section, 274
Gregory XV, Pope, Alessandro Ludovisi, 6
Guarino, Camillo, 214
Guerra, Gaspare (delle Fratte), 242

H
Hadrian's Villa, 25, 26, 59, 66, 90, 131, 132, 214
Hadrianus, Junius (Emblemata), 239
Hieroglyphica (Piero Valeriano), 239

I
Iconologia (see Ripa,Cesare, Perugino)
Innocent X, Pope, Giovanni Battista Pamphilj, 122, 138, 139, 140, 155, 159, 161, 163, 172, 180, 184, 185, 204, 222, 264, 276, 277, 281, 282
Isaia da Pisa, 198

L
Lateran Baptistery, 109
Laurentian Library (Florence)(see also Ricetto), XI, 99
Lauri, Giacomo, 25
Lavamani (Casa), 117
Leoni, Leone (Milan Duomo), 215
Library (Casa), 117
Library Alessandrina (Sant' Ivo), 168, 169

Ligorio, Pirro, 25, 142
Longhi, Martino, 208
Lumaca staircase (Casa), 110

M
Maderno, Carlo, X, XIII, 2, 3, 6, 7, 8, 11, 12, 13, 14, 15, 16, 17, 20, 52, 80, 99, 141, 172, 208, 276, 284
Martinelli, Fioravante, 15, 144, 281, 282
Maruscelli, Paolo, 87, 88, 90, 97, 105, 226, 227
Mascherino, Ottaviano, 19
Massari, Francesco, 227, 283
Merlini, Clemente (tomb, Maria Maggiore), 218
Michelangelo di Ludovico Buonarroti Simoni (Michelangelo), XI, XIII, 2, 4, 6, 7, 16, 17, 18, 25, 26, 28, 34, 39, 71, 93, 99, 103, 115, 118, 123, 156, 157, 159, 167, 174, 177, 178, 210, 214, 222, 227, 234, 236, 237, 269, 271, 283
Minerva Medica, 143, 153
Montano, Giovanni Battista, X, 25, 26, 65, 70, 113
Monte di Pieta, 4, 7
Mosque of Samarra, 160

N
Neri, Saint Filippo, 36, 95, 283

O
Oddi, Muzio, XI
Olympia, Donna (see Pamphilj)
Omnia Opera, 39, 280
Oratory of San Filippo Neri, 38, 76, 86-104, 269, 271, 275, 277, 278
Orologio, Torre del (Casa) 9, 120, 121, 277, 278
Opus Architectonicum 24, 93, 94, 104, 110, 112, 119 (see also Giannini, Sebastiano)

PALAZZOS
Barberini, 8, 14-20, 34, 64, 103, 142, 177, 214, 215, 270, 271, 278
Borghese, 7
Carignano (Turin), 214
Carpegna, 213-215, 222
Conservatori (Capitolino), XI, XIII, 27, 71, 115, 119, 178
Falconieri, 230, 233-239, 245, 277
Farnese, 15, 17, 214, 222, 226, 234, 237, 267, 269
Farnese (Piacenza), 28
Giustiniani, 230
Mattei, 3, 7
Pamphilj, 203-205, 280
Porto Colleoni (Vicenza), 119
Quirinale, 19
Rospigliosi, 17
Senatori (Capitolino), 123
Spada, 86, 225-227, 278
Spagna, 120, 221, 222
Spirito Santo, 221, 222
Vaticano

P
Palladio, Andrea (Palladian) 12, 109, 119, 120, 130, 280
Pamphilj (see Pope Innocent X)
Pamphilj, Camillo Paolucci, Cardinal Francesco, 209
Pamphilj, Donna Olympia, 204, 209, 282
Pamphilj, Donna Olympia Aldobrandini, 210
Pantheon, XIII, 99, 157
Paul III, Pope, Allesandro Farnese, 6
Paul V, Pope, Camillo Borghese, 2, 6, 138
Pascali, Defindino (Casa), 123
Peretti (see Pope Sixtus V)
Peruzzi, Baldasare, 143
Petra (rock tomb), 70
Piazza Barberini
Piazza di Monte Giordano, 122, 222
Piazza Navona, 189, 203-205
Piazza Sant'Eustachio, 138, 142, 166, 167
Pieta (Michelangelo), 3
Pollio, Marcus Vitruvius, X, 12
Ponzio, Flaminio, 17, 18
Porta Pia (Michelangelo), 4, 26, 28, 99, 156, 157, 158, 162, 163, 237
Portaria (Casa), 116

Porta della Suppliche (Uffiz, Buontalenti), 267
Propaganda Fide, Collegio di, 9, 18, 76, 130, 167, 226, 252, 263-275, 277, 281

R
Radi, Agostino, 7, 11
Raggi, Antonio, 74
Rainaldi, Carlo, 96, 168, 204, 207, 208, 242, 282
Rainaldi, Girolamo, 93, 204, 207, 208
Raphael Sanzio da Urbino, 60, 100
Relazione (Fra Juan de Bonaventura), 43, 65
Repulsion of Attila (San Pietro in Vaticano), 3, 4, 110
Re Magi (see Chapel)
Ricci, Olimpio, 283
Ricchino, Francesco Maria, 28, 71
Ricetto (Laurentian Library Florence), 227, 270, 271
Righi, Francesco (Sette Dolori), 128, 281, 283
Ripa, Cesare, Perugino (Iconolgia), 162, 214, 215
Roccaburna, Tower, 39
Roma Ornata, 281
Romanello, Giovanni Francesco (Oratory), 93
Romulus, Temple of Divine, 26
Rosa, Padre Persiano, 86
Rospigliosi (see Pope Clement IX)

S
Sacristy (San Carlo alle Quattro Fontane), 36
Sala de Recreazione (Casa), 113, 114, 252, 278
Sala Rosa (Casa), 111, 219
Sachi, Andrea, 142
Saluzzi, Padre Angelo, 87, 88
Sapienza (see Church)(Sant' Ivo)
Sapolcro Dorico, 97, 100
Savelli, Camilla Virginia (Sette Dolori), 128
Scamozzi, Vicenzo, 25, 120
Scarampa, Provost (Casa), 124

Scuola di Architettura Specolativa, XI
Sepulcro Statiz Poeta (Gianicolo hill), 66
Serapeum (Hadrian's Villa), 149
Sergius IV, Pope, Pietro Martino Buccaporci (tomb, Laterano), 192, 193, 194, 246
Serlio, Sebastiano, 40, 44, 45, 46, 52
Seutonius, 25
Sixtus V, Pope, Felice Peretti, 34, 142, 242
Soldati of the Picini, 34
Sosanius, Augustan Temple of Apollo, 25, 152
Spada, Padre Virgilio, 86, 88, 97, 113, 122, 124, 141, 160, 182, 190, 191, 204, 205, 237, 256, 277, 280, 281

T
Temple of the Divine Romulus, 26, 152
Temple of Solomon, 64
Temple of Venus Genetrix, 109
Tibaldi, Pellegrini, 28, 37
Tomb of Annia Regilla, 100
Tombs, Lateran, 191-200 (see also individual tombs by name of Pope or Cardinal)
Torre dell' Orologio (see Orologio)
Tower of Babel, 159, 160
Trinitarii Scalzi, Order, 34, 39, 63, 72, 75

U
Urban VIII, Pope, Maffeo Barberini, 95, 137, 138, 139, 140, 143, 144, 159, 163, 164, 167, 222

VILLAS
Giustiniani, 184, 230
Hadrian (see Hadrian's Villa)
Ludovisi Frascati, 4
Madama, 60, 64
Pamphilj (San Pancrazio), 28, 231

V
Valeriano, Piero (Hieroglyphica), 239
Venus Genetrix (see Temple)
Vignola, Jacopo Barozzi, 28, 39, 43, 46, 267
Volterra, Francesco da, 98

Z

Ziggurats of Mesopotamia, 159, 160
Zincgref, Julius Wilhelm (Emblematum Ethico-Politicorum Centuria), 239